1. Change your default home page to one that's really useful to you.

2. Bookmark sites you might want to return to, and edit your bookmark list when it becomes unwieldy.

3. Connect to the Online Shopping Directory at www.samizdat.com/ shopping.html for hyperlinks to all the sites mentioned in this book. (That way, you won't have to type in the addresses.)

4. Sign up for rewards programs so you'll get all the benefits you can as you go from store to store.

5. When price is what matters most, use the Web's comparison sites and auctions to find the best deals.

*One luxurious
bubble bath*

*Access to most comfortable
chair and favorite TV show*

*One half-hour massage
(will need to recruit spouse, child, friend)*

*Time to recline and listen to a favorite CD
(or at least one song)*

cut

Do it

6. Print and save a copy of each order you place.

7. Don't be a loner. Dive into discussions in newsgroups, e-mail lists, forums, and chats. Share what you've learned, and learn from others.

8. Check the help files at AltaVista and the articles about using this search engine at www.samizdat.com. Learn the true power of Internet search—finding whatever you want, when you want it.

9. Play the auction game—sell what you don't need any more to help pay for what you want now.

10. Make your own Web pages, tell what rare things you're looking for, and let people who have them find you.

COUPON

COUPON

COUPON

COUPON

cut

Shop
Online

The Lazy Way™

Shop Online

Richard Seltzer

Macmillan • USA

To my family— Barbara, Tim, Mike, Heather, and Bob. Thank you for your inspiration, your help, and your patience.

Macmillan Publishing books may be purchased for business or sales promotional use. For information please write: Special Markets Department, Macmillan Publishing USA, 1633 Broadway, New York, NY 10019.

International Standard Book Number: 0-02-863173-0
Library of Congress Catalog Card Number: 99-64811

00 99   8   7   6   5   4   3   2   1

Interpretation of the printing code: the rightmost number of the first series of numbers is the year of the book's printing; the rightmost number of the second series of numbers is the number of the book's printing. For example, a printing code of 99-1 shows that the first printing occurred in 1999.

Printed in the United States of America

Book Design: Madhouse Studios

Creating/Capturing Screen Shots: Terrie Lynn Solomon

Page Creation: Heather Pope and Linda Quigley

You Don't Have to Feel Guilty Anymore!

IT'S O.K. TO DO IT *THE LAZY WAY!*

It seems every time we turn around, we're given more responsibility, more information to absorb, more places we need to go, and more numbers, dates, and names to remember. Both our bodies and our minds are already on overload. And we know what happens next—cleaning the house, balancing the checkbook, and cooking dinner get put off until "tomorrow" and eventually fall by the wayside.

So let's be frank—we're all starting to feel a bit guilty about the dirty laundry, stacks of ATM slips, and Chinese takeout. Just thinking about tackling those terrible tasks makes you exhausted, right? If only there were an easy, effortless way to get this stuff done! (And done right!)

There is—*The Lazy Way*! By providing the pain-free way to do something—including tons of shortcuts and timesaving tips, as well as lists of all the stuff you'll ever need to get it done efficiently—*The Lazy Way* series cuts through all of the time-wasting thought processes and laborious exercises. You'll discover the secrets of those who have figured out *The Lazy Way*. You'll get things done in half the time it takes the average person—and then you will sit back and smugly consider those poor suckers who haven't discovered *The Lazy Way* yet. With *The Lazy Way,* you'll learn how to put in minimal effort and get maximum results so you can devote your attention and energy to the pleasures in life!

THE LAZY WAY PROMISE

Everyone on *The Lazy Way* staff promises that, if you adopt *The Lazy Way* philosophy, you'll never break a sweat, you'll barely lift a finger, you won't put strain on your brain, and you'll have plenty of time to put up your feet. We guarantee you will find that these activities are no longer hardships, since you're doing them *The Lazy Way*. We also firmly support taking breaks and encourage rewarding yourself (we even offer our suggestions in each book!). With *The Lazy Way*, the only thing you'll be overwhelmed by is all of your newfound free time!

THE LAZY WAY SPECIAL FEATURES

Every book in our series features the following sidebars in the margins, all designed to save you time and aggravation down the road.

- **"Quick 'n' Painless"**—shortcuts that get the job done fast.
- **"You'll Thank Yourself Later"**—advice that saves time down the road.
- **"A Complete Waste of Time"**—warnings that spare countless headaches and squandered hours.
- **"If You're So Inclined"**—optional tips for moments of inspired added effort.
- **"The Lazy Way"**—rewards to make the task more pleasurable.

If you've either decided to give up altogether or have taken a strong interest in the subject, you'll find information on hiring outside help with "How to Get Someone Else to Do It" as well as further reading recommendations in "If You Really Want More, Read These." In addition, there's an only-what-you-need-to-know glossary of terms and product names ("If You Don't Know What It Means, Look Here") as well as "It's Time for Your Reward"—fun and relaxing ways to treat yourself for a job well done.

With *The Lazy Way* series, you'll find that getting the job done has never been so painless!

Series Editor
Amy Gordon

Editorial Director
Gary M. Krebs

Director of Creative Services
Michele Laseau

Cover Designer
Michael J. Freeland

Managing Editor
Robert Shuman

Development Editor
Terrie Lynn Soloman

Production Editor
Donna Wright

What's in This Book

yourself about your range of choices, narrow your search, find the right professionals to help you, or locate resources for mortgages, insurance, home inspectors, and movers.

MORE LAZY STUFF

Because the Internet is a community of people who help and share with one another, finding someone else to lend a hand is fairly easy. From user groups, to chat rooms, to forums, to personal Web sites, the Internet is based on the assumption that everyone benefits by sharing. Based on an honest, open environment, Internet users value each individual's contribution, respect each person as an individual, and encourage everyone to treat others the way that they would want to be treated. In what more fertile of a place could you look for someone else to do something for you?

If you've recently visited the computer book section of any bookstore, you know there are enough computer books to choose from to make your head spin. Here are some great recommendations to cut your book selection time in half, and get you the information you need now.

Sure, you already know that. But in case you forget the difference between a URL and an ISP, here's a list of terms to help you out.

Why Shop Online?

If you have never shopped online before, or if you have only dabbled, you're probably wondering what all the hype is about. You figure that except for those folks who live hundreds of miles from the nearest store, shopping online is a convenience, not a necessity. So how convenient could it be? What could be easier than hopping in your car and driving to the mall... and fighting for a parking space, and walking from store to store and aisle to aisle looking for the items you want, and waiting in the check-out line, and carrying those bags out to the car through a drenching rainstorm, and driving home through the traffic as the rain turns to ice beneath your wheels?

You have choices and will continue to have them. At least in your lifetime, Congress is not likely to outlaw physical stores.

But in many instances, shopping over the Internet is a quick and easy alternative. Sometimes it enables you to do things that otherwise would be impossible for you, or it can save you trouble and money—lots of it. When that isn't the case, just shop the way you always have.

You should shop on the Internet when:

- You know exactly what you want, and you want to get it over with—with a minimum of hassle and time. You don't want to spend an hour or more driving to a physical store and going through the usual routine there; if the item is out of stock at the first store you go to, you don't want to have to trek to another and another, or wait weeks for delivery.

- You know what kind of thing you want to buy, but not specifically which one (e.g., which book or CD or video). Also, you don't want to waste your money buying something you won't like and waste your time figuring out that you made a mistake.

- You know what you want to buy, but it's rare—very few stores would ever carry such a thing.

- You need to buy something that is very expensive (a car or a house). You have to comparison shop because you aren't fabulously wealthy, but you'd like to shop as quickly and effectively as possible.

- You're curious. You don't have time to indulge your curiosity in the physical world, where it takes so long and costs so much to go from one place to another. On the Internet you can go from one side of the world to another with just a click of your mouse.

- You want to buy something, but don't want to be seen buying it. Perhaps it's a gift that you want to keep secret before you give it, and being seen going into the store by family or friends would blow the surprise. Or perhaps it's something you'd be embarrassed to buy in person—cosmetics you don't want people to know that you use, or sex-related products.

- You are a bargain hunter by nature. You get a charge out of buying things at lower prices than your friends and neighbors. Saving money is nice, but not nearly as good as flexing your smart-buyer muscles.

- You can't get to the store for any number of reasons, such as illness or taking care of a sick kid or old age or bad weather or lack of transportation or lack of time or alien abduction. (Reportedly, most UFOs have Internet connections.)

Let's face it, we sleepwalk most of the time, operating on automatic pilot, doing things the way we always have, without considering alternatives. My role, and the role of this book, is to wake you up to the ease of doing your shopping a new way—*The Lazy Way*.

There are no macho techie points for doing everything online. The objective is to find and buy what you want with the greatest of ease. You are aiming for what Chinese philosophers called "wu-wei" or "perfect action nothingness." That's the effortlessness that comes from being in harmony with nature. You are learning the right way of living. You are becoming a sage. And you thought you were just shopping!

In Part 1, we cover aspects of online shopping that apply no matter what you want to buy. Chapter 1 covers the basics—how to find your way to the online stores you want by way of the paths that others have laid out for you. Chapter 2 provides the information you need to become an independent shopper, using search engines, price-comparison sites, and auctions. Chapter 3 gives you pointers on advanced techniques, which can help you become a creative shopper—sharing experiences with and getting advice from other shoppers, and becoming a full member of the online community.

In Part 2, we lead you on a series of shopping trips. In each of these cases, the opportunities differ because of the different kinds of things you are looking for:

- Chapter 4—books, music, and videotapes
- Chapter 5—computers and software
- Chapter 6—travel
- Chapter 7—food
- Chapter 8—money, including loans, insurance, and investments
- Chapter 9—cars
- Chapter 10—real estate, including houses, apartments, and roommates

You'll be amazed at the variety and wealth of what is available online in those shopping categories:

- Tools to help you decide what you really want.

- Information that can help you become a sophisticated shopper, to be able to buy, with confidence, systems and components at the lowest cost.

- Easy access to tempting choices you might never have considered and that could change your life.

- Advice, news, and tools that can help you better manage your money and to invest it for maximum benefit at minimum cost.

- Inside information and essential knowledge that can help you not only find the right car or house, but also save considerably on the cost.

Give it a try. If online shopping suits your style and your needs, perhaps you'll discover a new world and a new you.

Acknowledgments

Thanks to Andree Abecassis, my agent, for bringing this opportunity to my attention and doing everything she could to make this book a reality. Thanks to Amy Gordon, the acquisitions editor, for her vision that the time is right for just such a book, and for her flexibility in making available all the time and resources to make it the best book it could be. Thanks to Terrie Solomon, the development editor, for her keen insight, probing questions, numerous contributions, and continuing support and encouragement.

Thanks to Jim Cuthbert (Groceries To Go) for reviewing the chapter on food, and to Bill Wendell, Ron Rothenberg, and Erle Rawlins for their very helpful advice regarding real estate. Thanks to Claude Thau for his pointers to resources related to insurance and finance. Thanks to my son, Bob, for his many suggestions and for reviewing and commenting on several chapters.

Thanks to the participants in my weekly chat sessions about Business on the World Wide Web (Thursdays, noon to 1 p.m. EST, at www.web-net.org), for their insights and advice regarding the world of online shopping and the Internet business environment in general. In particular, thanks to Bob Zwick, Sudha and Shirish Jamthe, Kathleen Gilroy, Tracy Marks, Kaye Vivian, Tim Horgan, Bob Fleischer, Jeff Kane, Carol Snyder, Tom Dadakis, Todd Moyer, Reem Yared, Mike Cosgrave, Steve Woit, Terry Maugeri, Nicki Dzugan, Christian Frosch, Ed Jaros, Linda Stillborne, and Marshall Wick.

Thanks to my former colleagues at Digital Equipment, for all their many insights about the direction of computer technology and Internet business. In particular, thanks to: Berthold Langer, Tom Richardson, Bob Powell, Dan Kalikow, Danny Mayer, Jeff Black, Steve Coughlan, Ashu Bhatnagar, Dudley Howe, Kathy Greenler, Louis Monier, Sam Fuller, John Jacobs, Mark Conway, Dave Sciuto, Phil Grove, Joan Blair, Dave Cedrone, Steve Schultz, Ethel Kaiden, Roseann Giordano, Jay Owen, Tom Pisinski, Don Gaubatz, Harris Sussman, Jack Rahaim, Anne Kreidler, Jim Johnson, Steve Fink, Fred Isbell, Seth Itzkan, Phil Grove, Jonathan George, Sheila Goggin, Mike Odom, Bill Keyworth, David Marques, George Pappas, Donna Curtis, Mark Hayes, Mark Collett, Jean Bonney, Mark Fredrickson, Ann Howe, Phil Faulkner, Stan Hayami, Tom Skinner, Russ Jones, Brian Reid, Joella Paquette, Carolyn Unger, Freddy Mini, Dave Buffo, Wendy Caswell, Sharon Henderson, Jeff Harrow, Kathleen Warner, Skip Garvin, Tom Camp, Jef Gibson, Don Harbert, Kate Neson, Bob Lehmenkuler, Ray Suarez, Alfred Thompson, Kelly O'Ryan, Janice Colombi, Jeff Schriesheim, Larry Kenah, Alan Nemeth, Russ Doane, Alan Kotok, David Probert, Leszek Kotsch, Chuck Malkiel, Mark Hevesh, Deb Buckley, Win Treese, Len Segal, Mike Jamison, Ken Olsen, Gordon Bell, Larry Portner, David Stone, Win Hindle, Bob Glorioso, Cliff Clarke, Roger Heinen, B.J. Johnson, Tom Blinn, and Dallas Kirk.

Thanks to the many others who have helped me better understand the dynamics of the Internet and how it can and should be used, in particular: Larry Chase, Noreen Webber, Phil Duchastel, Diane Croft, Gordon Joly, Rik Hall, Betsey Campbell, Jeff Rayport, John Sviokla, Wes Kussmaul, Mary Cronin, and David Wheeler.

Thanks also to the folks at Acunet, where my Web site (www.samizdat.com) is hosted, in particular: George Hoff, Anthony Alvarez, and Fernando Colon Osorio.

And special thanks above all to my wife, Barbara, who provided feedback on everything and numerous suggestions, and who has put up with me for over 25 years.

Learning the New Way to Shop

Are You Too Lazy to Read "Learning the New Way to Shop?"

1 You think the automobile is a passing fad, and horse-drawn carriages go plenty fast enough. ☐ yes ☐ no

2 You'd rather drive 10 miles to the pizza shop and wait half an hour for it to be cooked than phone in your order and have it delivered to your door. ☐ yes ☐ no

3 You like to do everything on your own, alone, without asking for directions, without accepting help or advice from anyone, regardless of what they might know ☐ yes ☐ no

Chapter one

Online Shopping Basics: Shopping Along the Well-Paved Roads

The Internet is revolutionizing how we do our shopping. Thousands of companies, large and small, are racing to set up online stores. Companies that have retail outlets just down the street from where you live now offer specials and coupons online. Manufacturers that used to sell just to stores now sell directly to you online. Brand-new online-only companies operate with no physical storefronts and little or no inventory, and pass much of the savings on to you. And stores all over the world are just a click away. This new way of shopping provides you with an enormous choice of products, as well as a vast variety of detailed information to help you make the right decisions about everything from books to cars, from clothes to real estate—even money.

Also, thanks to the heated competition for your business, the situation keeps improving to your benefit. Selling online is a new experience for these companies, just as shopping online is for you. Most online stores are still learning how to attract visitors to their Web sites and how to turn those visitors into buyers. They are trying every imaginable innovation to get your attention, win your trust, earn your loyalty, and get your sales dollars. What one store sells for profit, another may sell for less than cost or even give away as an incentive for you to "join" or to buy something else. Once you learn your way around the online shopping world, you should be able to quickly find the products you want—even rare ones—and at prices that you'd probably never see in the physical world. In the process, you may also find yourself engaging in and enjoying activities you never considered before—like chat, auctions, and online trading—and making friends with other shoppers who have common interests.

As you take these first steps, expect change. In addition to describing today's shopping sites, this book will provide tips and general principles to help you find newly opened stores and services, as well as finding alternatives to some stores mentioned here that may have gone out of business by the time you read this, victims of the fierce competition.

The surviving Internet businesses will probably look different than the screen shots captured here, and they will no doubt have changed their prices and terms of sale. On the Internet, you can change your store with a few computer keystrokes—reorganizing everything,

YOU'LL THANK YOURSELF LATER

Start a shopping wish list as a document on your word processor. Add to the list as shopping-related thoughts occur to you, and keep that document open for reference as you explore and shop the Internet with your browser.

repricing everything, and adding new and improved features. The flexibility on the Internet means that online stores can rapidly and easily respond to customer complaints and requests, continually refining and improving their Web sites. To benefit, you should be flexible as well, continually learning from your online experiences.

In this chapter, we'll cover the basics of the online shopping experience and explain how to find stores by the fixed paths that merchants have laid out for you. In Chapter 2, we'll help you become more independent, introducing you to search engines, comparison shopping sites, and auctions. In Chapter 3, we'll cover advanced techniques that can help you become creative members of the online shopping community.

IT MAY NOT BE A SNAP, BUT IT'S A CLICK: MASTERING BROWSER BASICS

You can easily click on choices as they are presented to you and navigate merrily around the Internet, without caring what happens in the background, without remembering Internet addresses, without knowing any of the functions of your browser except Home and Back. This simplicity is what draws so many people to the Web—even people who never used computers before.

That works just fine for "surfing"—checking out Web sites for the fun of it. But for a more serious endeavor, like shopping, you'll want the control that comes from a

better understanding of what you can do with your browser.

Playing Favorites

When you arrive at a page that you want to be able to return to easily, click on Favorites (the Microsoft term) or Bookmarks (the Netscape term), and then click on Add. To return to that page at any time in the future, click once again on Favorites/Bookmarks, and then click on the name of that site name in your list.

For instance, when you are shopping for gifts for Christmas, birthdays, or graduation, you might browse through many stores before focusing on what kinds of things you want to buy and where you might want to buy them. You also might occasionally window-shop for things that you cannot yet afford or don't yet have a compelling need for. In either case, you should bookmark the promising sites that you find, saving yourself the trouble of duplicating that search work later. The figure on page 7 shows the National Girl Scouts Store book-marked/saved as a favorite in Internet Explorer for future visits.

No sooner do you start to enjoy the power of this feature than you find the list has grown too long to be useful. Then it's time to edit your list.

If you use a Netscape browser, click on Bookmarks, then on Edit Bookmarks. The full list includes numerous preselected sites that were built into your browser (a

With your browser (either Explorer or Navigator), you can save any site as a favorite and return to it easily whenever you are ready to place an order. This example shows the National Girl Scout Store saved as a Favorite.

form of advertising). It also includes the "personal" ones that you added in your travels. With your cursor and mouse, highlight the line or lines you want to edit, then use the commands in the pull-down File and Edit menus to copy, cut and paste, add blank separator lines, and even put groups of items into folders. By doing so, you are creating your own personal "shopping mall," with the URLs of the stores and other sites you particularly like, organized the way you want them. If you use Internet Explorer, you can also edit your Favorites list. Click on Favorites, then Organize Favorites.

Home is Where Your Default Is

If you use America Online (AOL) as your Internet Service Provider (ISP), you have the software that connects you first to their proprietary cyberworld, populated with news, stores, chat rooms, etc. From AOL, you can choose to venture forth into the Internet, with aol.com as your home base. You have no choice but to start in AOL's world.

For people who use other ISPs and have Microsoft, Netscape, or other browsers, home is whatever site the software is set to, although most people never change the default.

If your Web browser came preinstalled on your new computer, the manufacturer may have set that page. If your Web browser came from your Internet Service Provider (ISP), that ISP may have set up your browser to display the ISP's own home page as shown in the figure on page 9. In most cases, the default home is the main site of Netscape or Microsoft, which means that millions of people return again and again to those sites and depend on the navigation choices they see there. Those choices, whether for search engines or shopping sites, are paid advertising, and as such act as mini-yellow pages. Yes, the links are organized for your convenience, but they do not represent the full range of what is available or even a judicious editorial selection of sites. Even the order of the items and their position on the page sells for a price.

YOU'LL THANK YOURSELF LATER

Keep in mind that if you dial a local number to get to your Internet access provider and you have a separate phone line for your modem, you could opt for low-cost phone service for that second line, one that doesn't include long distance.

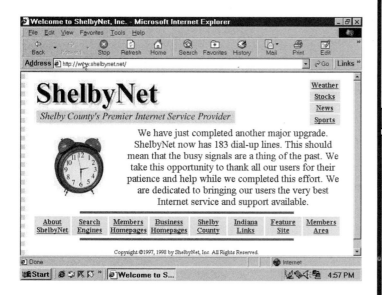

Of all your bookmarks/favorites, which is the one that you would really like to start with every time you launch your browser? You can make that page your home.

Neither Netscape nor Microsoft goes out of its way to make it easy and obvious for you to change this setting. In the past, these browsers have moved that option with each new version of their software to a location that you would least expect it. But you can track it down with Help, looking for "preferences" in Netscape and "Internet options" in Microsoft.

With Netscape's V4.5, go to the page that you want to use as your home. Click Edit, then Preferences, then in the list of categories on the left, click on Navigator. In the middle of the screen to the right, you will see the address of your current default home page. Click on Use Current Page and that address will change to the one of the page

you are now on. Click OK, and you're done. (In V3.0, click on Options, then General Preferences, then Appearance, and type in the Web address of your preferred page.)

With Microsoft's Explorer V5.0, likewise go to the page you want to be your new home. Click on Tools, then Internet Options, then the General tab. In the Home Page area, click on Use Current. Then click on OK. (In V3.0, click on View, then Options, then Navigation.)

Don't be confused by offers to "create your personal start page." For instance, in recent versions of the Netscape browser, you can click on My Netscape. That takes you to the Netscape Web site, where you see an orderly arrangement of paid-for links to news and other Internet services. You can customize your arrangement of the pieces and some of the choices, and then click to change the setting in your browser so the resulting page will be your starting point.

Remember, you can change your Home again and again, as you find new more useful Web pages that you'd like to be your regular starting point. Perhaps you might even want to change back to the original default, if that suits your tastes. But you should know that you have a choice.

Two Browsers Are Better Than One

As you go from store to store on the Internet, you'll find that some sites have been "optimized" to work with either Netscape or Microsoft browsers. Whichever browser you use, there will be some things on some sites that you won't be able to access.

In their competition with one another, these two companies each added proprietary enhancements to their software, and then encouraged Web sites to design features that work only with their proprietary enhancements. Reportedly, they now both have promised to abide by a single set of standards, and over time this problem may go away. But for now, if you have the necessary disk space available, you should install both browsers on your computer. Use your favorite one most of the time, and switch when you encounter a Web site that requires the other browser.

Both browsers are free, and each can be downloaded from their sites—Microsoft is at www.microsoft.com, and Netscape is at www.netscape.com. At either site, you'll find detailed downloading instructions. But be forewarned—the latest versions of these files are large, each taking up over 50 megbytes of your hard drive and taking a long while to download, even with a relatively fast modem. Much of the bulk consists of features you will probably never use. If you have limited disk space, you might want to get an earlier version (V3.0 and above have all the important capabilities you'll need for shopping) and select the "minimum." That way, you'll only have to download five to six megabytes of data.

At the time this book was written, Microsoft's site for downloading Internet Explorer was set up very simply. Just click on Download in the top bar, then in the left column click on Alphabetically, then scroll down to Internet Explorer, and pick the version that matches your operating system and your needs. At Netscape, click on Download in

QUICK PAINLESS

With today's fast and powerful computer systems, you can launch two or more copies of the same browser or even run two or more different browsers simultaneously. They all share the same phone or cable line on the Internet. This capability comes in handy for comparison shopping, letting you see two or more competing stores side by side in small windows, or in rapid alternation.

the top line, then Netscape Browsers. The Navigator series is the browser only. The Communicator series has numerous other features as well and is far larger.

Keep in mind that there are a few banks and other financial sites in the United States that require you to use "strong encryption" to access your account information. Unless you want to do business with one of those institutions, the security features in a standard browser are probably sufficient for everything you would want to do. The United States has restrictions that prohibit export of "strong" or 128-bit code. That is why Netscape and Microsoft both have to offer this as an option rather than including it in every browser, and why they make you fill out detailed legalistic forms before you can download it. If you need this option, at Microsoft, select Extra Security 128-Bit Browser; at Netscape, select 128-Bit Strong Encryption.

If you have difficulty downloading or installing your browser, or if you need some extra assistance in getting started with your browser's basic operation, check out another book in this series, *Surf the Net the Lazy Way*, by Shelley O'Hara. That book offers step-by-step instructions for Internet beginners.

What to Do If Your Browser "Breaks"

Sometimes your browser will stall or crash. Don't panic. Here are a few suggestions:

- Often Web sites that want to make a sale go overboard trying to impress you with their fancy design effects. Their technical gymnastics sometimes make their pages very demanding for ordinary PCs connected to the Internet with ordinary modems. And the designers don't always do a very good job of making sure that what they have created will work with all popular browsers. If your screen freezes or it seems to take forever for a page to load, close your browser, then relaunch it and go to other sites. If all goes well at the other sites, then the problem was theirs, not yours.

If, on the other hand, other pages load sluggishly or your browser crashes again soon, the cause is probably that the "cache"—the memory and/or disk space allotted to saving pages that you look at—is full, and the automatic function that should periodically clear that didn't work. (Browsers save page content in order to give you faster results. When you return to the same page over and over again, you see that page very quickly because you are seeing what is stored in your computer, rather than fetching the same thing time and again over the Internet.) To try to fix your problem, relaunch your browser and make a minor adjustment. In Microsoft, click View, then Options, then Advanced, then Settings. If you have lots of disk space to spare, adjust the "Disk Space to Use" upward. Then click Empty Folder. In Netscape, click Edit, then Preferences. In the left column, click on the + sign beside Advanced. Then click Cache (that means a temporary storage area). Click Clear Memory Cache and Clear Disk Cache; if you have memory or disk space to spare, adjust those numbers upward.

YOU'LL THANK YOURSELF LATER

If you have call waiting on the same phone line you use for your modem, then every time someone dials your number, your Internet connection will get cut off. That can be very annoying when you are putting the finishing touches on an order. To disable call waiting, precede the number you dial for your Internet provider with 1170 or *70.

The Lazy Way

- Sometimes you'll click on a link, then find that you can't use your Back button to return to the page where you were before. This may happen when using a Netscape browser to access pages optimized for Microsoft. It may also happen because a clever Webmaster has done something deliberate in the page design to make it likely you'll stay longer at his site and view more ads. To break free, in Microsoft, you can view your list of recently visited Web sites by clicking on File or History; in Netscape, select Go. Then click on the one that you want to go back to.

By the way, if you'd prefer that other folks who use this same machine not know every place you have been, periodically clear your History file. In Internet Explorer V5, click on Go, then Open History folder. (If you have Explorer V4, click History on the toolbar or select View from the Explorer bar, and then select History.) In Netscape Communicator, click on Communicate, then Tools, then History. (If your particular browser version is laid out differently, check Help.) Once there, highlight the items you want to eliminate from the list, then click Edit, and Delete.

- Sometimes, a Web site will cause your computer to launch a second copy of your browser, and when you try to go back to the page where you were before, an advertising page will launch and possibly another and another. This effect is typical of temporary sites designed to promote adult entertainment sites. Their advertisers pay based on the numbers of people who see the ads. Hence, the creators of the site have good motivation to use every trick at their disposal to put more ads in front of you. You will know that this has happened when you see multiple copies of the icon for your browser at the bottom of your screen. To get out of this mess, close each and every instance of your browser, then launch your browser again fresh. If you keep clicking on Back, in extreme instances, your browser may launch enough times to eat up all your computer's resources and cause it to crash. If that happens, just turn the machine off and then on again, and avoid that site in the future.

- Most pages will print with just the print command from your browser. But some sites use fancy features that make printing difficult or impossible. If a page doesn't print on the first try, click on a link for another page at that same site, then hit your back button, and try to print again. That will work sometimes, but not always. Netscape offers a nifty Print Preview option that lets you see what will be printed before you put it on paper. This additional option also helps if you want to pick out selected areas of a page for a partial printout.

- Sometimes a fancy animated graphic will hang your browser up interminably. If you suspect that is the case, and you have a recent Netscape browser, click on View and then Stop Animations. The rest of the page should load immediately.

LEARNING HOW TO STEER

When you launch your Web browser, you immediately connect to an Internet site that can serve as a launch point for all of your Internet travels—either the one that came preset with your software, or the one you selected yourself as described above. From that point, all you need to do is click on highlighted words (called hyperlinks or links) and a new Web page will appear on your computer screen in a matter of seconds. The new page you see may be at the site you were on before, or it might be at another company's site on the other side of the world. You can return to your starting point at any time by clicking on Home in your browser's navigation bar.

When you click on a link, whether it is just a highlighted word or a flashing graphic banner ad, the browser software automatically inserts the associated Web address, or URL. When you place your cursor over the link, the URL appears on the bottom of your screen. The address where you currently are appears in a space on your navigation tool bar at the top of the page. These addresses are typically in the form "http://www.someplace.com." Sometimes an address can include many subdirectories (separated by a slash, "/"), and perhaps an immense string of characters at the end. If there's a page with a long address, don't try to write it down or remember it. Rather, you should make it a favorite/bookmark, or use your history log (mentioned above) to go back to it later.

QUICK ⬬ PAINLESS

Look before you click. The text and look of an ad may be catchy, but the site may be one you've been to before and would prefer never to return to. When you place your cursor over a hyperlink, the full address of the page that you would connect to appears, typically at the bottom of your screen. The domain name (e.g., amazon.com) is often the same as the company name.

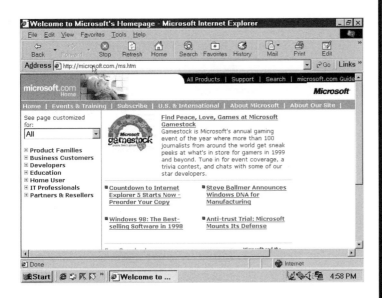

Type a valid address into the navigation bar and travel to that site without delay.

If the address is short enough that you can remember—perhaps one that a friend told you about or you saw in a TV commercial— you can type it in where the current address appears; then hit Enter, and you are off to the new location (presuming you didn't make a typo). The figure above shows Internet Explorer's navigation bar, where you can directly type in addresses to different Web sites. (With recent browsers, you don't need to type "http://.")

Let's take a quick look at how these address are constructed.

- Many, but not all, Web addresses begin with the letters "www," which stands for World Wide Web. The Web is the technology that allows for this global point-and-click, interlinked environment.

- If the Web site is in the U.S., the three-letter extension at the end or before the first slash will indicate what kind of entity it is. An extension of ".com" means commercial; ".org" means a non-profit organization; ".gov" means government; ".edu" means education; and ".net" usually stands for an Internet service provider or related business. Two-character suffixes indicate countries outside the U.S.: ".ca" for Canada, ".uk" for United Kingdom, ".jp" for Japan, ".de" for Germany (Deutschland), etc.

- The element in combination with the .com (etc.) is known as the "domain name." A domain name consists of a single word or series of words connected with punctuation (other than a period or slash) and combined with its extension (such as .com). (One company could have fast.com as its domain name, and another could have fast.net.) Companies zealously guard their domain names like trademarks, and try hard to buy the rights to domain names that are the same as or similar to the name of the company and its major products. In the background, that name gets translated to a number code that is the true address. A site owner could set up any number of domain names that he owns to serve as "aliases" (alternative names) for the same number address.

- In front of the domain name, you might see a subdomain—a term separated from the domain name by a period and designating a distinct piece of a large site. Hence, you will see such addresses as www.yahoo.com, quote.yahoo.com, shopping.yahoo.com, etc. Subdomain addresses often do not include www.

- A word to the right of a slash that does not end with a period stands for a directory. Web sites can have any number of directories and subdirectories, just like you can on your computer.

- If the address ends with .com (etc.), a country extension, index.html, or home.htm, then it stands for the "home page" or preferred starting point of a Web site—the front door that has been set up for you.

- If the address ends in .html, .htm, or .shtml, but isn't index or home, then it stands for one of many documents at a site.

- If the address ends in another three- or four-letter extension (like .asp), chances are that the site is set up to automatically create pages from a database. If you remember such an address and type it in later or bookmark such a page and click later to return to it, you will probably end up at the home page of that site, not the particular Web page you wanted.

- If the address ends in an extremely long series of numbers and letters, perhaps too large to view all at once in the address window, the site probably uses special software to either give you a unique personal view of their content based on information you have given them about you, or based on a tracking system known as "cookies." We'll explain cookies later in this chapter.

QUICK ••• PAINLESS

Often companies that started on the Web, such as Amazon.com, deliberately select a company name that also serves as their Web domain name. That makes it easy to remember their Web address.

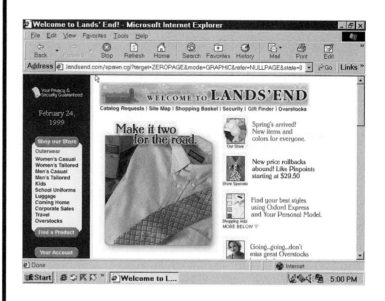

Most prominent retailers' Web sites can be located by simply entering their company name as their URL. For example, the clothing catalog company Land's End may be located by entering www.landsend.com in your browser's address locator.

Most major corporations have gone to great lengths to obtain the rights to all the imaginable variants of addresses that include their company names and their major brand names. Hence, you will often be able to go straight to the site of a well-known retail store by just typing in the likely address. For instance, www.gap.com stands for the Gap and www.landsend.com stands for Land's End, as shown in the figure above.

DO IT "THEIR" WAY: WELCOME TO PORTALS, DIRECTORIES, AND MALLS

A handful of companies compete with Netscape, AOL, and Microsoft trying to be your starting point on the

Web—to be a page to which you return often (though not necessarily every time you turn on your machine) and from which you can follow well-organized links to get to many other Web sites, including shopping sites. These "portal" sites generate revenue from banner advertising, and also from charging for the inclusion of links and the placement of links on their main pages. The more traffic they get, the more advertising revenue they receive. They advertise themselves both online and offline to induce you to click to or type in their address. They hope that what you see when you arrive will be so compelling that you will bookmark their site or make it your home. The figure below shows the home page of Yahoo! (www.yahoo.com), one of the largest Internet portals.

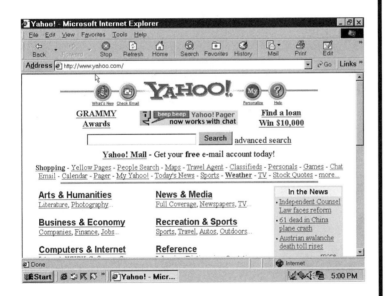

Portal sites like Yahoo! provide an enormous variety of services, including links to numerous Web destinations, organized in ways that are easy to understand. They try to cater to the needs of millions of people.

Start a list of the gifts you give to relatives and friends. Keep it as a document on your PC and add to it as you buy gifts from the list or think of new items to add. Maintaining this list will make shopping a lot easier next Christmas, birthday, or anniversary.

Every time you click to see another page on a portal's site, one or more graphic strips known as "banners ads" will appear. These ads entice you to click on their images and words and go off to the site of an advertiser. The folks in the ad business count how many times people like you see those ads, how many times they "click through," and how many times they then buy. The ad sales companies use those statistics to determine the price of advertising.

Just remember, when shopping on the Internet, you are king. Without consumers like you, the whole online shopping movement collapses. Thousands of very creative people are striving to serve you. So don't be surprised if these "portals" make your shopping experience easy and comfortable.

Some major portals, like Yahoo!, LookSmart (www.looksmart.com), and Magellan (www.mckinley.com) began as directories—carefully edited, categorized lists, somewhat like a yellow pages or a printout of a library catalog, but organized as a cascade of menus. Click on a category and see the subcategories, until you eventually get to the link that you want. Magellan, shown in the figure on page 23, not only lists but also reviews and rates tens of thousands of Web sites. To become "portals," these sites have added other useful services to attract and hold you, such as e-mail, weather, news, stock quotes, chat, maps, Internet search, white pages (search for people), and yellow pages (search for businesses).

Magellan lists, reviews, and rates tens of thousands of Web sites.

Other popular portals—such as AltaVista (www.altavista.com), Hotbot (www.hotbot.com), Excite (www.excite.com), Lycos (www.lycos.com), and InfoSeek (www.infoseek.com)—began as search engines. Directories collect information about hundreds or thousands of sites by hand—either hiring people to look at sites for possible inclusion, or accepting submissions of brief descriptions from Web site owners. Search engines collect their information about the Internet by sending out robot programs, known as "Web crawlers," to find all the pages that they can and add the full content of those pages (not just brief descriptions of entire sites) to their indices. The largest of the search engines, AltaVista, shown in the figure on page 24, currently includes over

140 million Web pages. No one sorts through this information to categorize it. Rather the user enters "queries"—formatted search commands—then gets back a hyperlinked list of pages that contain the words and phrases in the query.

We'll talk about how to use search engines in Chapter 2. For now, what matters is that these sites have added many of the same kinds of features as Netscape, Microsoft, and Yahoo! You can use the various services and links, just as you can with those of other "portals," to help guide you on your way to the major shopping sites, without ever dealing with the search engines that are at their core.

Another set of popular portals began by offering everyone the ability to create and post their own Web

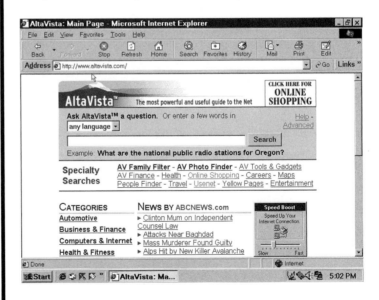

AltaVista has the full text of over 140 million Web pages in its index.

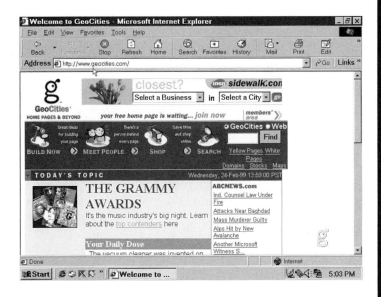

Geocities (www.geocities.com) offers everyone the ability to create their own Web pages and post them at no cost.

pages at no cost. Geocities (www.geocities.com) as shown in the figure above, Xoom (www.xoom.com), and Tripod (www.tripod.com) now each have millions of members and offer additional free services. They also have large directories of Web sites, including online stores.

A wide variety of other sites that began by providing popular services of various kinds now have millions of users and generate major advertising dollars. These sites keep adding portal-like features to give you more reasons to come back and to compete for your continuing loyalty. These sites include Mapquest (www.mapquest.com), which provides free customized maps and travel directions, and ICQ (www.icq.com), which provides "instant messaging," an alternative to e-mail and chat

for connecting with your friends and colleagues online. Expect to see similar features at major news sites like ESPN, CNN, and USAToday, and at sites that began as telephone number search sites (white pages and yellow pages), like AnyWho from AT&T (www.anywho.com), Switchboard (www.switchboard.com), Infospace (www. infospace.com), and BigYellow (www.bigyellow.com).

Basically, any site that draws millions of users will probably head in the same direction, trying to get the media attention, advertising revenue, and stock-price boost that come with recognition as an Internet portal. The opening pages of all these sites—whether they started as directories or search engines or other services—tend to look remarkably similar. All of them will provide you with organized lists of shopping choices and other useful links.

Newspapers such as the *Boston Globe* (www. boston.com) and the *Washington Post* (www. washingtonpost.com) often provide such services on a local scale. Their directories list local businesses. Microsoft is also competing in this arena with a series of local "sidewalk" sites for major cities, like (www. boston.sidewalk.com), shown in the figure on page 27/, which serves the Boston area.

You'll also find hundreds of online "malls." These sites focus specifically on the needs of shoppers. Some consist of just linked, categorized lists of stores. In other cases, the stores are all hosted at the same site and share some common features, such as a way for you to search through them all or to use a single shopping cart and buy

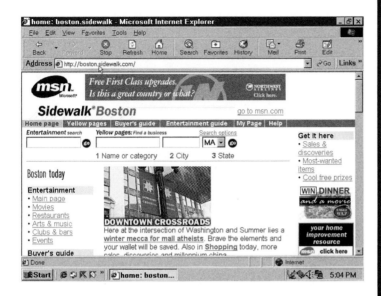

This site (www.boston.sidewalk.com) is an online directory of local businesses in Boston, maintained by Microsoft.

from them all with a single credit card transaction. General-purpose online malls (ones that include a wide variety of products) include

- Access Market Square (www.icw.com/ams.html)
- The All-Internet Shopping Directory (www.all-internet.com)
- Beyond.com (www.beyond.com)
- Bottomdollar.com (www.bottomdollar.com)
- BuyItOnline (www.buyitonline.com)
- CyberShop (www.cybershop.com)
- The Globe.com Marketplace (www.shoptheglobe.com)

- Internet Mall (www.shopnow.com)
- Internet Shopper (www.internetshopper.com)
- Internet Shopping Network (www.internet.net)
- iVillage.com, the Women's Network (www.ivillage.com)
- NetMarket (www.netmarket.com)
- ShopperConnection.com (www.shopperconnection.com)
- Shopping.com (www.shopping.com/store)
- Shopping 2000 (www.shopping2000.com)
- Snap (www.snap.com)
- Value America (www.valueamerica.com)

Many other malls focus on a single class of products, like computers. We'll deal with those as we come to them in our "shopping tour" chapters.

The Buyer's Index (www.buyersindex.com), shown in the figure on page 29, extends the online mall concept to the physical world as well. They have a searchable directory of over 10,000 Web shopping sites and North American mail order catalogs, with over 66 million products for businesses and individuals.

Check out these sites, and see if one or more of them has an organization and range of choices that suits your tastes. In that case, "their way" is "your way," and there's no point in making things complicated for yourself. Just bookmark your favorites, or even make one your home/startup page.

IF YOU'RE SO
INCLINED

To save a snippet of text from a Web page—perhaps a product description or a price list you'd like to save for reference—click the left button on your mouse, hold it down, and drag it as you move the cursor over the text you want, highlighting it. Then click Edit in the navigation bar, and then Copy. Open a document in your PC word processing software and paste the text there.

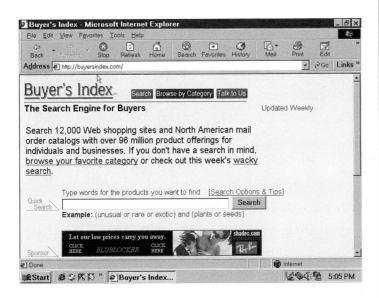

Buyer's Index (www.buyersindex.com) offers over 10,000
Web shopping sites.

DEALING WITH ELECTRONIC SHOPPING CARTS, SHIPPING, AND CUSTOMS

When you arrive at an Internet store or multi-store mall, as you see items that you might want to buy, you can place them in your electronic shopping cart, a temporary online storage space assigned to you for this visit. When you are ready to make final buying decisions, you'll typically leave the main shopping area and click through to a "secure" area, where you can take another look at the choices in your shopping cart, their prices, and the total, and can change the quantities. (Usually, you can eliminate an item that you no longer want to buy at that stage by entering a quantity of "0," which the shopping

Don't make decisions based on discounts alone. Be sure to add shipping charges when making price comparisons. For low-priced items, the shipping might be greater than the discount, and (if price is all that matters to you) you might be better off buying locally.

cart interprets as an order of that item of zero.) When you've made your decision, enter your name, address, and credit card information; or, if you've been there before, enter a username and password. The figure below shows the online Godiva Boutique (www.godiva.com), featuring their world famous chocolates.

Usually, one of your choices will be the shipment method, which typically ranges from overnight delivery to regular mail. Internet shopping has led to an enormous boom in the shipping business. Yes, you can download information and software over the Internet. But most of what you buy needs to be physically moved from one place to another, which takes time and costs money—your money.

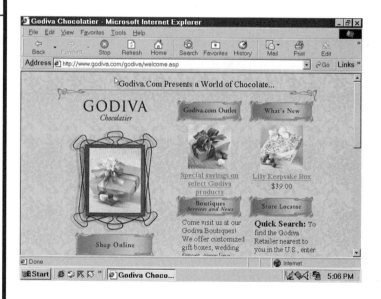

After you have selected some Godiva chocolates, you proceed to the Godiva Boutique checkout area.

Before paying a premium for fast shipping, be sure to check the vendor's promises for how promptly they'll assemble your order. The shipping clock doesn't start ticking until the product goes out the door, and some companies may take a week or two to do that.

Also, remember that while the Internet is global and you can theoretically buy from online stores all over the world, if you are ordering a physical object (not just a computer code or information that you can download), you are going to face the usual physical world hassles. Products going across international borders are subject to customs duties and delays (even when dealing with Canada, despite NAFTA). In addition, the shipping charges are likely to be high.

In any case, be sure to print and/or save the final page, with your choices and the prices, before leaving the site. That will be your reference point if you have any questions about delivery or credit card payment or the product itself once it arrives. Many retail stores also put a confirmation of your purchase into your e-mail box that you can print out to keep for your records.

ARE YOU AT RISK USING CREDIT CARDS ONLINE?

Do you remember the first time you got cash from an ATM machine? The first time you gave your credit card information to an 800-number service? The first time you used a credit card at all?

We all went through those scary experiences not knowing whether this new-fangled technology would shortchange us.

QUICK ⬤ PAINLESS

Some online stores, like Amazon.com, ask at check-out if the purchase is a gift and offer to gift-wrap it, enclose a personal message, and send the item straight to the recipient.

Look over your credit card agreements, and you'll see that the terms and the limits on liability are no different online than they are in the physical world. Also, the guarantees are just as good. If a credit card company guarantees your purchases, that applies online as well. And just as in the physical world, if a charge shows up on your bill that shouldn't be there, you can go to your credit card company rather than having to go back to the vendor. The credit card company then acts as your proxy, challenging the charge and insisting that the vendor provide proof. The online vendor, just like one that you deal with over the phone or in person, has lots of motivation to deliver the goods promised and to make sure you are satisfied because:

- Billing queries are time-consuming and costly.
- The charge may be reversed and they'll end up stuck with penalty fees in addition to losing the purchase.
- If they don't satisfy the demands of the credit card company and its requirements for reliability, they could lose their right to take credit card orders.

In other words, dealing with an online store that accepts credit cards gives you leverage that you wouldn't have if you simply mailed in a check.

So what happens when you give your credit card information to an online store? Policies and procedures differ from one store to another, and it's always a good idea to check a store's "help" or "frequently asked questions" (FAQ) files to find out just what they do. But standard practice involves the use of "encryption" capa-

YOU'LL THANK YOURSELF LATER

Many online stores save details from your first order and expedite your future purchases at the "checkout counter," recognizing you by your registration (with username and password). This saves you the trouble of retyping things like name and address and even credit card number, if those are the same.

bilities that are built into your Web browser. Think of Cold War spies sending one another coded messages. Your credit card info passes over the Internet in a form that nobody but the vendor or the credit card company or a gifted counterspy can understand.

I mention counterspy because no security is perfect. The amount of effort and money you are willing to spend to protect information or property should be consistent with the value involved. If you are guarding the Hope Diamond or are sending the breakthrough formula for cold fusion, you will take far more extreme measures than if you are buying a music CD. Using a store's standard procedures is rather like protecting your house with ordinary door locks—quite sufficient under ordinary circumstances.

YOU'LL THANK YOURSELF LATER

Plan ahead and order early. Then you won't have to pay extra charges for quick delivery.

Visit a mall-style area known as "Excite Shopping" (www.excite.com/shopping), and you can buy from several different stores but enter your credit card information only once.

Now some major Web sites are beginning to act as a middleman between you and the credit card companies, to make it easier for online stores to gain your trust and to collect money. For example, when you go to the mall-style area known as "Excite Shopping" (www.excite.com/shopping), as shown in the figure on page 33, you can buy from several different stores but only have to enter your credit card information once. Other companies are starting programs to "certify" the trustworthiness and reliability of online merchants, thereby reducing your anxiety when dealing with a store you have never heard of before and that you can't physically enter.

A variety of other efforts are under way to establish online equivalents of the Better Business Bureau. For instance, Public Eye (www.thepubliceye.com), as shown

The Public Eye (www.thepubliceye.com) helped organize an "Alliance of Certified Safe Shopping Sites."

in the figure on page 34, helped to organize an "Alliance of Certified Safe Shopping Sites," and has also launched a project to raise safety standards for transactions conducted through online auctions and classifieds.

Basically, wherever there is an area of online shopping that people are reluctant to dive into because of a lack of trust, companies will do whatever it takes to gain your confidence by emphasizing their trustworthiness. New businesses have been built around ways to give other companies the scrutiny and certification needed to allay customer fears.

In any case, the record for online purchases by credit card is remarkably good. In fact, buying online is probably much safer than handing your credit card over to a waiter or giving the information to an operator at an 800-number service.

By the way, if you run into a problem at any stage in your shopping experience or you believe a Web site needs improvement, tell the folks who maintain that site. Many Web sites have a built-in mechanism for sending e-mail back to them. Look for a link that says "contact us" or "help" or "customer service." When you click on the appropriate spot, a pop-up e-mail form appears. The figure on page 36, shows the e-mail option for contacting the decision makers who maintain Yahoo! Enter your comments, criticisms, or questions, and most likely, your message will be read and considered.

If you don't see an e-mail address anywhere that's obvious, then try sending e-mail to the Webmaster or support at their domain name; for instance:

Webmaster@store.com or support@store.com

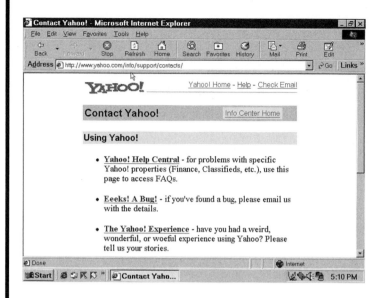

You can send e-mail to the folks at Yahoo! (www.yahoo.com) with your comments, criticisms, or suggestions.

If that, too, doesn't work, and you really want to get in touch with this store, go to www.networksolutions.com/internic/internic.html. That is an online "clearing house" that keeps track of Internet site ownership information. Enter the domain name (the address after www and before the /). You'll see street address, contact name, e-mail address, and phone number.

If the site doesn't have its own domain name, but rather sits in the subdirectory of another company's domain (perhaps hosted for free at a site like Tripod or Xoom), then you might have considerable difficulty trying to locate the responsible people.

WHAT PRICE PRIVACY?

Based on your visits to Web sites and your online transactions there, companies can gather information about
your buying habits and preferences. In fact, that's an
important incentive for them to sell online. Many companies hope to do "datamining"—using sophisticated
software tools to dig through immense quantities of
information about you and millions of other shoppers.
From that data, they want to learn

- What products and services they should sell

- How they should modify their current offerings

- What marketing messages and techniques work best

- How they should modify the look and feel of their
  Web site to maximize sales

When an Internet store
gets so big that it carries
virtually every item in its
chosen realm, you can
benefit from using its
searchable catalog as a
research tool, even when
you don't intend to buy.
For instance, a search at
Amazon.com covers not
only every book in print,
but also more than a mil-
lion titles that are only
available secondhand.

Ideally, they'd like to get to "one-to-one marketing,"
where the messages and the choices you see are tailored
for you.

Is that bad? Maybe, and maybe not. It all depends on
your personality and sensitivities. On the one hand, these
sites may provide you with a "personalized" experience,
which makes your shopping easier and more effective,
saving you time and bringing to your attention bargains,
special offers, and coupons that you might otherwise
miss. On the other hand, some of this data gathering is
involuntary. They may do it without your informed con-
sent, which may make you uncomfortable on principle,
regardless of the practical benefits.

Let's consider what the online vendor can find out
about you and how.

THE ONLINE COOKIE MONSTER—
FRIEND OR FOE?

If your browser supports "cookies" (and all the more recent browsers do), then there's a file stored on your computer that can automatically relay to sites that you visit information about your recent Web surfing experiences—for instance, what page you saw just before coming to their site.

The site you are visiting will know your "domain" (the part of an e-mail address to the right of the @ sign), but won't know your username and hence your complete e-mail address, unless you provide that information (for instance, by filling out a registration form). Once they have that information, they can correlate it with "cookie" information, to learn more about your experiences and preferences at their site.

Your browser will come with the default setting of accepting cookies. You can change that. In recent versions of the Netscape browser, click on Edit, then Preferences, then Advanced. You can choose to disable cookies, which will prevent you from entering many of the shopping sites that you want to visit. Or you can have your browser warn you whenever a Web page wants to get to your cookie file. But the warnings become a major nuisance. Each page might have as many as half a dozen cookies associated with it, meaning you'd have to click separately to accept each of them before you could view the page.

As an alternative, you could sign up at The Anonymizer (www.anonymizer.com), as shown in the

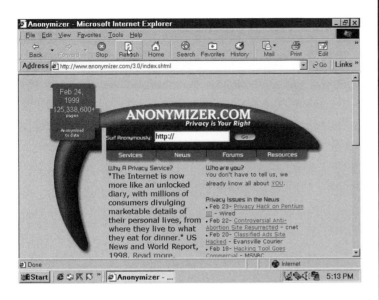

If you sign up with The Anonymizer (www.anonymizer. com), you can surf the Internet without anyone knowing your true identity, even if you accept all cookies.

figure above, for identity-free surfing even with your cookies turned on. But when you want to make a purchase, you'll still have to positively identify yourself.

Basically, the effort you put into fighting cookies might be better spent in other ways.

Besides, since vendors want to get as much information as they can about the people who buy their products and services, you can expect that new, more sophisticated techniques will soon be developed to help them gather it. For instance, when Intel announced their Pentium III chip in January 1999, one of the main features touted was that it would automatically signal to online stores even more—and more accurate—

information about you and your Web travels than cookies do. The uproar from the consumer public was so enormous that within two days, Intel turned around and promised that it would ship Pentium III with the identity code turned off and would give users the option of turning it on.

If you think about this issue from a pragmatic point of view rather than as a matter of principle, you'll probably end up volunteering far more information than automated techniques could gather.

Think of online registration forms as you do the mail-in warranty cards that come with electronics products you purchase. On such a card, you might tell the manufacturer your age, location, salary range, line of business, and job title, as well as when and where you bought the product. In return, it is easier for you to receive service or replacements if something goes wrong. The manufacturer will also send you information about bug fixes and other improvements to the product, news of related products, and quick notification in case of a product recall.

Depending on the application, Web sites require varying levels of assurance that you are who you say you are. For instance, banks and airlines with frequent flier accounts will require a password for access and probably have cookies to keep track of your path through account information. That way they can confidently present you with the information you want, without your having to reenter your password with each new request for data.

Magazine and newspaper sites that provide information for a fee on a subscription basis typically use your cookie file to automatically recognize you and let you in without your having to remember and enter your username and password. Grocery stores might, on the basis of your cookie file, give you easy access to lists of your previous purchases to help guide you in compiling this week's order. And an online mall might let you enter your personal and credit card information just once to make purchases at half a dozen member stores, based once again on your cookie file. In other words, registration plus cookies, and perhaps also the use of passwords, can make your shopping experience far simpler and more rewarding.

This surrender of private information in exchange for some retail-related benefit is similar to supermarket bonus cards. The store offers you discounts on certain items if you use your card, and the card lets the store keep careful track of everything you buy. Some people refuse to use such cards. But many are willing to give up some degree of privacy in exchange for a benefit. Expect online vendors to come up with a wide range of incentives to encourage you to provide more and more information about your buying preferences.

In fact, some sites use special software ("collaborative filtering") that lets you tell more and more about your preferences. For instance, you might rate the books or music or movies that you are familiar with, and that information will be correlated with the tastes of tens of thousands or even millions of others. Then, instead of depending on the opinions of professional reviewers, you can get lists of suggestions based on the ratings of

QUICK ⬭ PAINLESS

When you visit Amazon. com after you've made your first purchase there, you'll be greeted with a personalized message, addressing you by name and offering you a selected list of book recommendations based on your past purchases and the preferences you and others with tastes similar to yours have indicated (see the figure below). Technology based on "cookies" and "collaborative filtering" makes this seeming magic possible.

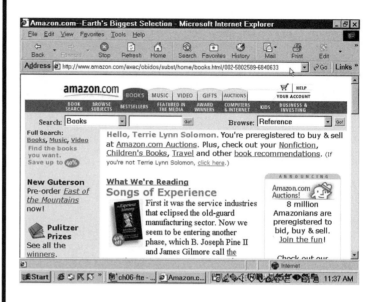

Amazon.com's home page greets its returning visitor, Terrie Solomon, developmental editor of this book, with a personal suggested list of books.

people whose tastes are similar to yours—not just people with the same age, race, income, or education, but people who like what you like. Amazon.com offers suggested purchases to repeat customers as shown in the figure above.

THE CURSE OF "SPAM" AND THE BLESSING OF "OPT-IN E-MAIL"

You may not mind a vendor collecting information about you when that information is used for your direct benefit. But what if the vendor sells your e-mail address to others? Then we venture into territory that is still largely unexplored, where laws and rights have not been sufficiently tested and defined. The practical effect is that if you indiscriminently provide your e-mail address to many commercial sites, it's likely that your address will soon be on many distribution lists and your inbox will be swamped with unsolicited e-mail known as "spam." These messages will offer you instant wealth, fabulous sex, and perhaps even eternal life.

Ironically, true "spam" is the opposite of one-to-one marketing. In this case, vendors often don't know anything more about you than your e-mail address. Their intent is to take advantage of the fact that there is no charge for sending e-mail over the Internet. With the right list and the right software, they can quickly send their message to tens of millions of people at a time, at near zero cost. That means a very low rate of return can still be profitable. In the early days of the Internet, such behavior was immediately punished vigilante style, by bombarding the e-mail account of the sender with numerous nasty replies. Now the spammers have grown more sophisticated, so the return e-mail address may be phony, and the call to action is to check a Web site. Hence, some states have adopted anti-spamming laws to reduce the level of this nuisance mail and its drain on overall Internet resources. But the Internet is a global phenomenon and matters of jurisdiction can be very fuzzy, with spamming services operating from little island countries where laws let them do what they please. Don't expect this problem to be resolved any time soon. Just learn to live with it.

Not all ads by e-mail are bad. In fact, the latest online marketing craze is "opt-in e-mail." You would welcome certain kinds of commercial announcements that tell you about offers you are interested in. You might even ask to receive particular kinds of messages from particular sites. For instance, you might want an e-mail from Amazon.com telling you that one of your favorite authors just came out with a new book or that an out-of-print book you had been looking for is now available. Or you might want to sign up at Continental Airlines (www.flycontinental.com), as shown in the figure below, for their "Cool Travel" e-mail alerts about last-minute bargain airfares. Responsible companies promise to use your e-mail address information only for the purpose for which you intended, and do not sell or give your address to other companies without your explicit permission.

Sign up at Continental Airlines (www.flycontinental.com) for their "Cool Travel" e-mail alerts about last-minute bargain airfares.

YOU'LL THANK YOURSELF LATER

If blatant spam says, "Reply to this address if you don't want to receive messages like this in the future," don't. Often this is just a trick to have you confirm your e-mail address.

Sign up for BonusMail (www.bonusmail.com) and receive rewards for receiving and reacting to online ads.

Then, too, you might want to sign up at Bonus Mail (www.bonusmail.com), as shown in the figure above, or My Points (www.mypoints.com), both of which are run by the same company, Intellipost. These services, which already have over two million members, reward you for receiving and reacting to e-mail ads. When you sign up, you volunteer information about yourself and your interests. You receive their e-mail in a Web-based format, with images and links. You get rewards for clicking in response to the message. These rewards might be frequent flier miles on your favorite airline or points toward products or services of interest to you. In addition, the messages are often about special shopping offers and limited-time bargains of the very kind you are interested in. Reportedly, the members' number one complaint is, "Send me more e-mail. I'm not getting enough."

Window-shop online. Go through all the steps of finding and selecting something you really want but can't afford yet. Bookmark the page, or add it to your "favorites." Then relax, knowing that when you're ready, you can consummate the purchase with the greatest of ease.

Getting Time On Your Side

	The Old Way	The Lazy Way
Getting where you want to be	5 minutes, clicking through the ad-filled pages (your "home" is what you got stuck with by default)	1 second, when you launch your browser to go straight to the page you use the most
Finding a site that you can't remember the address of	30 minutes	1 second (it's in your bookmarks)
Time spent panicking because your browser is is going so slow, it must be "broken"	30 minutes	30 seconds, clearing your cache (files automatically saved by your browser)
Going back and forth between two Web sites, when you can't decide which item to buy	30 minutes	5 minutes (you keep two browser windows open)
Trying to decide which book, CD, or video to buy next	1 hour	5 minutes (after you've entered your preferences, the store can provide helpful suggestions whenever you return)

two

Search, Compare, and Bid: Finding What You Want on Your Own

You can save time, hassle, and money by shopping for brand-name consumer products at the brand-name online stores prominently positioned on Internet portal sites. It's only natural that that's how you begin your online shopping experience.

Since the online world is new and strange, you are most likely to turn to the names that you trust. Confidence in dealing with other stores will come from isolated experiences, chance encounters, recommendations, and from interacting with other online shoppers.

Eventually, your curiosity will grow, and you'll crave more exotic shopping experiences. You will sense that you have just barely touched the surface and wonder: What's really out there? How do you find truly unique items? How do you find the amazing bargains? Where is the revolutionary experience?

In this chapter, we'll introduce you to some basic tools that can help you take advantage of the unexpected opportunities lurking in the chaotic immensity of the Internet: search engines, comparison shopping sites, and the places where ordinary people like us can both buy and sell from one another without stores—classified ads, newsgroups, and auctions.

DIRECTORIES AND SEARCH ENGINES—WHEN TO USE WHAT

At the large Web sites that call themselves "portals," you will probably have a choice of searching or browsing through the content of their site and/or of the Web at large. You search when you know exactly or fairly close to what you want. You enter the appropriate word or words in the syntax required by that search engine and ideally you go to a hyperlinked (or "linked") list of pages that probably contain the information you want. If you don't find what you want on the first try, that's either because the information isn't available, or because you need to improve your "query"—that is, make your search terms more precise and make sure you are using proper syntax. Syntax is the structure for the query that this particular search engine requires—for instance, the use of punctuation. (There are no standards. They all do it their own way.)

When you are uncertain—maybe you know the category, but are looking for suggestions or ideas—you should browse or surf through directory listings. In this case, you look at organized lists of choices, perhaps with descriptions attached and probably with hyperlinks to more detailed choices. This is like walking into a book or music store, going to your favorite section, and scanning the shelves to see what's new and what might catch your interest.

Most people favor one style more than the other—it's a matter of personality. Beginners strongly favor directories because they feel familiar—like yellow pages listings. Sometimes you think in categories and sometimes in specifics. If I want to find a college in Southern California, I'll go through a directory, checking under colleges, then United States, then California, then Southern California, scan the list, and pick the ones I want to check out. If I want to find driver software for my BJ200 Canon printer so I can run it with the new operating system I just installed on my computer, I'll use a search engine and go straight to the Web site I want. Everybody will probably use both these modes of operation at one time or another.

With a directory, you depend on the judgment and hard work of others to sort out what information is important and how pieces of information relate to one another. Using such a service exclusively would be like having someone else arrange your house, categorize your e-mail into folders, arrange your books, and organize your CD collection or your videotapes. Most people prefer to define "order" based on how their own mind works and makes associations, rather than on the tastes of someone else. At first someone else's order might seem convenient, but as you become more familiar with

QUICK ⬤ PAINLESS

Want to go to a physical store to see, touch, and maybe buy something you found online? Go to the Web site Mapquest (www.mapquest.com) to request map and driving instructions for free to a local store that is associated with the online store.

the Internet and what's really possible, these structures begin to get in your way.

With a search engine, if you go through the trouble of learning the commands, you can pluck whatever you want from the massive disorder of the Internet whenever you want, and quickly. And you aren't limited by the decisions of others. The search engines send out robots on expeditions of exploration and discovery, so you don't have to. But they don't make judgments of relevance or worth—that's your role, and that way the one item that is most important to you doesn't get filtered out before you learn that it exists.

PLAYING THE PORTAL GAME

There are fewer search engines and directories than you probably thought. The major players keep buying up related and competing services, and they also use one another's services.

Excite, a search engine shown in the figure on page 51 which was bought by the Internet cable service @Home, owns Webcrawler (search engine), Magellan (directory), and Classifieds2000 (massive classified ad site). Lycos (search engine) owns HotBot (search engine) and Tripod (massive Web-hosting site).

In the Internet world of search engines and directories, much change is rapidly occurring, and many such services are connected in some business sense. For example, AOL Netfind uses Excite in the United States and Lycos in Europe. Netscape Search uses Excite. LookSmart (directory) uses AltaVista (search engine) for the search

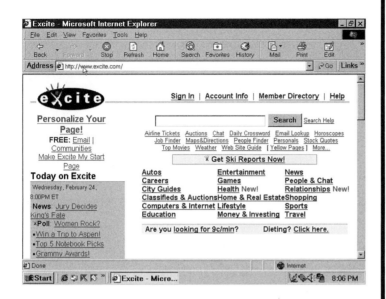

Excite (www.excite.com) is a search engine that was recently purchased by the cable television company @Home.

part of its service, and AltaVista and HotBot use LookSmart for the directory part of their service. Magellan (directory) uses Webcrawler (search engine). Search.com uses InfoSeek (search engine). InfoSeek partnered with Disney to create the GO Network (www.go.com), shown in the figure at the top of page 52, which includes ESPN.com, Disney.com, ABCnews.com, ABC.com, and Mr. ShowBiz. Inktomi (search engine) powers HotBot, NBC's Snap, Yahoo!, and iAtlas. And Microsoft's MSN just announced that it is switching from Inktomi to AltaVista for search. By the time you read this paragraph, these relationships and many others will most certainly have changed yet again.

Despite appearances, you really only have a choice of about eight major search engines (AltaVista, Inktomi,

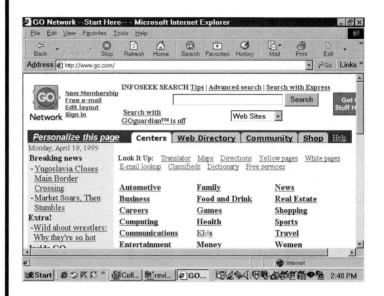

InfoSeek partnered with Disney to create the GO Network (www.go.com).

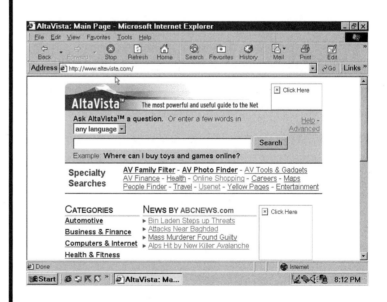

AltaVista (www.altavista.com) is the largest Internet search engine and covers over 140 million Web page documents.

Northern Light, Excite, InfoSeek, Lycos, Webcrawler, and a newcomer named Google).

How big are these search engines? WebCrawler covers about 2 million Web pages (documents), which by physical standards sounds immense, but by Internet standards is tiny. AltaVista weighs in at 140 million Web page documents (see the figure at the bottom of page 52), while Inktomi has 110 million, Northern Light 80 million, Excite 55 million, InfoSeek 30 million, and Lycos 30 million.

WHEN TO USE WHICH SEARCH SITE

When you want quick and simple results, without having to learn anything about search engine syntax or commands, try Excite (www.excite.com), Lycos (www.lycos.com) or InfoSeek (www.infoseek.go.com), as shown in the figure on page 54. Just enter a word or two or three, and you'll get your results "directory-style"— with a handful of "recommended" sites at the top of the list, followed by results from a directory, then followed by general Web index results. The emphasis is on ease of use rather than precision or power.

By the way, don't be fooled at Lycos. Their search form is at the top of the page and looks likes it's part of a banner ad. You could easily miss it and think that all this search engine offered was its directory choices.

The Excite site adds an interesting twist known as "intelligent search." In addition to looking for occurrences of the exact words in your query, it also matches synonyms, and not just from a thesaurus but based on

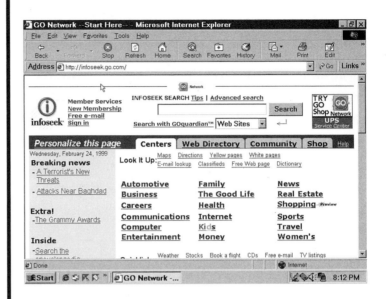

InfoSeek (www.infoseek.com) will give you "directory-style" search results, which are easy for beginning shoppers to use.

what it has learned about related concepts from the documents in its index. Excite gives the example that a search for "elderly people financial concerns" would find both sites mentioning the economic status of retired people and the financial concerns of senior citizens. To use this feature, click on Results for Other Possible Interpretations under the query box. This type of search for heart disease is shown in the figure on page 55. (N.B.—The need to "understand" the meaning of the content limits this approach to English language Web pages.)

Newcomer Google (www.google.com) ranks the results based on the number of links to a particular site. It uses that as a measure of popularity, even though it is probably more a measure of how long the site has been active. It takes time for people to recognize how good a site is and to create links to it, and then it takes many months before those sites get indexed again by Google. As with Excite, InfoSeek, and Lycos, here you are basically limited to typing in a few words. Google does, however, have one very helpful unique feature. Your results list shows the piece of text where your query words appear, so you can see the context and judge if that's what you really want.

AltaVista, Inktomi, and Northern Light (www. northernlight.com) give you far greater power over the results you get.

In the HotBot (www.hotbot.com) version of Inktomi, you can click on More Search Options and use preset

IF YOU'RE SO
INCLINED

If a page is temporarily unavailable due to system or network problems, or if the page no longer exists on the Web, Google will provide it for you. The service saves all the pages that it indexes, and can serve them up on request.

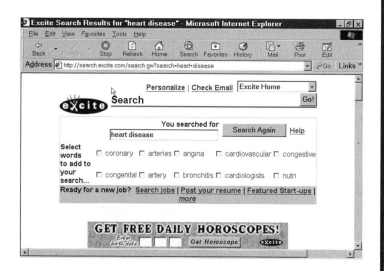

If you use Excite's "intelligent search" and enter the query "heart disease," Excite presents a set of related words to help you refine your query, like "arteries," "congenital," "coronary," and "stroke," as well as several others.

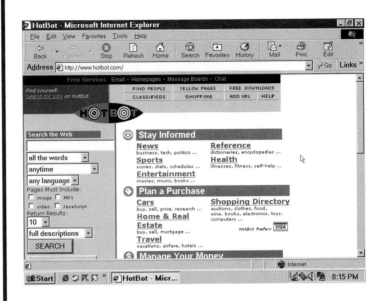

The HotBot search engine (www.hotbot.com) was created by the publishers of Wired Magazine *and maintains that magazine's flashy look and feel.*

forms to indicate your choices. (HotBot was created by the publishers of *Wired Magazine* and retains the magazine's flashy graphic look and feel, which is shown in the figure above).

To control your query at Northern Light, click on Power Search. There you'll find preset forms similar to those at HotBot; however, you can search not only through Web pages, but also through over 5,000 full-text documents in the "Special Collection." These documents aren't available on the Web because the people/companies who created them want to be paid for them. The cost for an article is usually in the range of $2.

You'll find Northern Light particularly valuable when you are looking for current news. News sites typically keep their stories in databases, which search engine robots can't normally access. And news changes far faster than the typical search engine updates its index. This special service at Northern Light allows you to search through 33 online news sources with a single query, rather than having to go to their separate sites. (See the figure below.)

At AltaVista, you have three different ways to search. Simple Search is what you see first. There, just like at Excite or InfoSeek, you can type a few words and get results quickly. And once you get your results, you can choose to refine your search, providing you with automatically generated categories associated with your category words, and even a graphical view of your choices to help step you through constructing a more complex query that includes some terms and excludes others. If

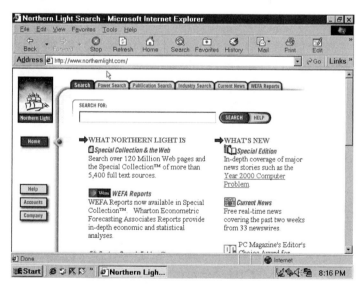

The Northern Light (www.northernlight.com) search engine features a special service to search 33 online news sources with a single query.

you click on Advanced Search, you arrive at a realm where you can use a series of commands to very precisely define what you want.

For example, go to AltaVista to access the Advanced Search option, as shown in the figure below. Click on Advanced. In the top (ranking) box, describe with a series of words what you want to buy. In the bottom (query) box, type the words "for sale" (including quotation marks). Then click Search, and you'll see a hyperlinked list of Web pages that match what you're looking for. You can refine your search by entering dates to get only the most recent information. When two or more words must appear in a certain order, enclose them in quotations marks so they will be treated as a phrase.

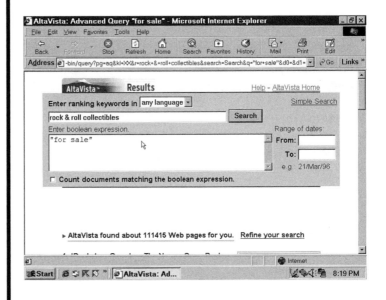

Altavista's Advanced Search (www.altavista.com) operates with a series of query commands that define with great precision the information you are requesting.

The commands that you use in the bottom (query) box are

- AND—means that the term before and the term after must both be on a Web page for it to be a match (e.g., house AND Boston)

- OR—means that if either the term before or the term after are on the Web page, then it's a match (e.g., outdoor OR indoor)

- AND NOT—means that the next term cannot be on a page for it to be a match (e.g., Washington AND NOT D.C.)

- NEAR—means that the term before and the term after must both appear on a page within 10 words of one another, in any order (e.g., Richard NEAR Seltzer would match with Richard Seltzer or Seltzer, Richard or Richard W. Seltzer)

Help files provide a bare-bones description of these commands and other unique elements of the AltaVista search syntax. If you'd like more detail, check the free tutorial and related articles at my Web site, www.samizdat.com/#altavista, as shown in the figure on page 60.

AltaVista also allows you to search not just the Web, but the Internet wildlands known as "newsgroups." To get to that area, click on Usenet under Specialty Searches. ("Usenet" is a term left over from the old pre-Web pioneering days of the Internet.) We'll give some examples of what you can do with Advanced Search later in the chapter when we talk about newsgroups.

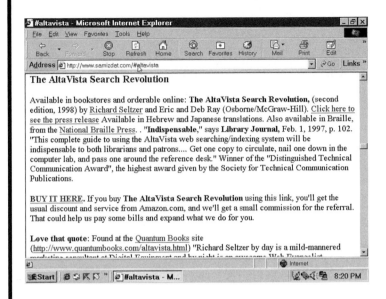

For a free tutorial and related articles on how to perform effective searches at the AltaVista search site (www.altavista.com), visit my Web site at www. samizdat.com/#altavista.

THE NEXT GENERATION: AUTOMATIC DIRECTORIES

In January 1999, iAtlas (www.iatlas.com), a brand-new company, announced that it has software and services that can bridge the gap from indexes to directories (see the figure on page 61). By matching the information it has about Web sites (what companies own them, what industries those companies are in, their location, etc.) with the information about the content of specific Web pages (as contained in the vast unstructured index of an Internet search engine), iAtlas can generate orderly categorized directories. By so doing, it eliminates (or speeds up) the tedious, costly, and slow process of building

Internet-related directories (à la Yahoo! and LookSmart). It also produces more inclusive and more pinpoint directories (city, industry, zip code, etc.)

For its initial demo, iAtlas is partnering with Inktomi. You can do a search at the iAtlas site and filter your results by industry or by city. It can also enable searches by zip code and site popularity, iAtlas claims. This approach should make it possible to create directories (for instance, of a city) automatically, rather than by hand. By the time you read this book, dozens of popular Web sites will probably have adopted this approach, broadening the range of how you can find what you want when you want it.

In January 1999, iAtlas (www.iatlas.com), a brand-new company, announced that it has software and services that can bridge the gap from indexes to directories.

COMPARISON SHOPPING, THE LAZY WAY

In your first online shopping excursions, you will probably focus on shopping at a few stores that you know through real-world equivalents, or that you may have heard about through advertising or from friends. You may also first rely on stores that you find easily and quickly by way of a major portal site.

As you become aware of the Internet's wide range of choices, you'll gain greater confidence about shopping at online stores you might never have heard of before. As you increase your number of preferred shopping sites, you will want to compare prices. You will especially want to compare prices for brand-name, mass-manufactured merchandise—items that should be identical in quality regardless of the retailer. The major portal sites are either adding software or linking to other sites that make price comparison extremely easy. There is no need to go to a dozen or more separate stores and take notes on the prices offered for the goods you want. Rather, you can go to a single comparison site that covers that class of goods, enter a specific query—the kind of product, the brand, the specific model or size, even major options—and learn which stores carry it and what they charge for it.

If you know exactly what you want—a brand-name, mass-manufactured item—and all that matters to you is price, then try one of the following sites. The look and feel of these sites are likely to be very similar since many use the same software, which typically sends out a robot program or Web crawler (like a search engine gathering information for its index). The difference lies in what kind of stores, how many stores, and which stores they include in their results, all of which change very rapidly.

- AltaVista Shopping Guide (shopping.altavista.com)
- BottomDollar (www.bottomdollar.com) (See the figure below)
- Excite Product Finder (www.jango.com)
- Hotbot Shopping Bot (shop.hotbot.com)
- Junglee Shopping Guide by Compaq (compaq.junglee.com)
- Yahoo! Shopping (shopguide.yahoo.com)
- WebMarket (www.webmarket.com)
- Yahoo! Travel (travel.yahoo.com)

When you want to shop for brand-name, mass-merchandised items, try the BottomDollar (www.bottomdollar.com) Web site.

Unfortunately, the promise of comparison shopping is much greater than the reality. Wouldn't it be great to compare prices on one item at thousands of online stores in a single search? But today, these sites typically only sample a handful of vendors in any particular shopping category. In some instances, the shopping service may have only a single vendor for a particular type of product, so your search provides no real comparison. If every search produces results from only one store and the same store every time, you'd be better off going directly to that store, or better still, to a competing comparison site that has some real content. However, you can expect that over the next year, these sites will vastly increase the number of stores they include in their price comparisons.

Note also that sites offering price comparison searches typically provide hyperlinked "buy" buttons next to every item in the results list they display. But, in most cases, clicking that button does not add your choice to a common mall-like shopping cart. Rather it takes you to the actual vendor's page, the one who is offering that quoted price, and you have to make all your purchases separately. In all probability, common shopping carts should be introduced soon.

APPLES TO APPLES, ORANGES TO ORANGES, AND DUST TO DUST

The farther you venture from the major portals and the sites that they point to by advertising or in select directories (of the "best" or "top" sites), the more you are going to want consumer-oriented guidance that helps

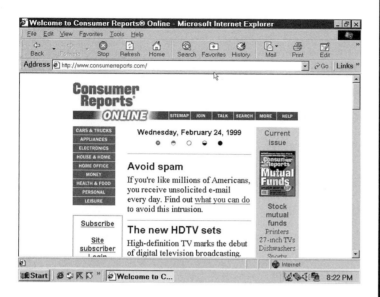

For general consumer advice, check out the online version of Consumer Reports (www.consumerreports.com).

you compare the quality of products and also the quality of online stores.

For quality comparisons, seek sites that focus on a single category of product (like all the sites that sell books), and sites that provide easy access to information (usually more than just price) from many vendors. Some of these might use multi-stage search technology that lets you specify all the key parameters necessary to configure a complex product like a computer. The site then would provide you with a list of vendors who can deliver such a product in your price range. We'll introduce you to some sites like that in our shopping tours, which span Chapters 4 through 10.

You can also check the online version of Consumer Reports (www.consumerreports.com), which is shown in

QUICK ●■● PAINLESS

the figure on page 65. Casual visitors get general consumer advice. For a paid subscription fee (currently $2.95 per month or $24 per year), you get access to product and service comparisons, ratings, and recommendations.

Consider also

- Compare.net (www.compare.net): This site offers "complete and unbiased product information" on a wide range of consumer products. (But, unlike Consumer Reports, this site accepts advertising from the companies whose products it compares.)

- Consumers Digest (www.consumersdigest.com): This site is the online version of the print publication, with product reviews and articles covering household goods, electronics, travel, food, and cars.

- eSmarts (www.esmarts.com): This site reviews and rates shopping Web sites, focusing review information on stores rather than products. eSmarts does not sell anything directly, and it reportedly does not receive any commissions on sales.

- Microsoft's Sidewalk sites (like boston.sidewalk.com): Microsoft's Sidewalk sites that reportedly are going through a transformation which will make them consumer report-type sites, each with a local twist.

MAKING ONLINE SHOPPING AUTOMATIC

In the fast-paced, ever-evolving Internet world, you should expect innovations in both technology and business practice to make shopping increasingly easier. In the not-too-distant future, keep an eye out for "bots," "robots," "agents," "spiders," or "crawlers." These different names all refer to the same kind of technology: a program that can travel throughout the Web and automatically do all the things that a human Web surfer can do. Search engines already use programs like these to fetch the information they store in their indices, and shopping comparison sites use them to quickly check current prices on the same item at many stores.

To get a sense of what the current generation of bots can do, check BotSpot (www.botspot.com). In particular, test drive the applications highlighted in their "Best of the Bots" section, as shown in the figure below, as well as the shopbots list at www.botspot.com/search/ s-shop.htm.

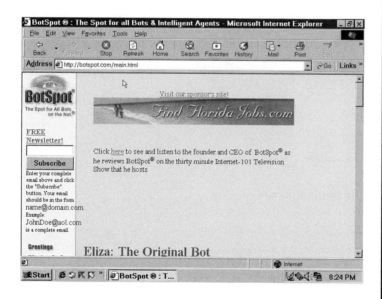

Check out the "Best of the Bots," as featured by BotSpot (www.botspot.com).

Today, the most common bots just investigate multiple search engines for you. If you have only a vague idea of what you want and can enter only a word or two as your search query, using a bot could be a useful alternative. If you find yourself in this situation, try InferenceFind (www.infind.com), as shown in the figure below, and you may be able to locate the item you need.

With the bot method of searching, however, you lose your ability to take advantage of the unique and powerful search commands featured at sites like AltaVista, HotBot, and Northern Light. If you have a clear idea of what you are looking for, you are better off mastering the capabilities of a single search engine, rather than

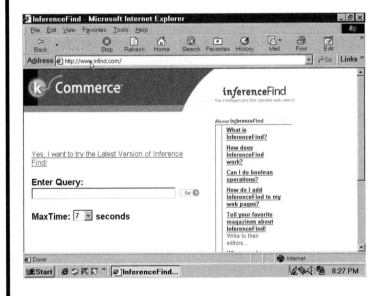

If you can only describe in a word or two the item for which you are searching, try InferenceFind (www.infind.com) for some assistance.

SHOP ONLINE The Lazy Way

using a bot with a single command to submit a poorly constructed query to dozens of separate search engines.

In the future, bots might serve as your own personal shoppers. Securely supplied with your passwords and credit card information, a properly engineered bot could perform a wide variety of tasks for you, including not only finding goods and information at the prices you want, but actually making the purchases for you. Imagine telling a bot to keep an eye on the price of certain stocks, and giving it the authority to buy and sell for you as soon as those stocks hit certain price points. Or, imagine using a bot to continuously scan through auction and classified ad sites for hard-to-find items you desperately want, and then to buy or bid for it at a price within your guidelines.

Recently, the increased use of a new standard known as "XML" has simplified the work performed by bots and shopping-oriented search engines. Many commercial sites will include special coding in their Web documents to identify that they have products for sale, the types of products, and at what prices. That coding will make it much easier for a bot to fetch and compare information of this kind.

In other words, these Web documents will "describe themselves" in a way that makes it possible for the entire Web to operate like a single unified database. When this standard is in widespread use, you should be able to ask detailed, structured questions, and search the catalogs of hundreds of thousands or even millions of stores with a single click.

BARGAIN HUNTING IN CLASSIFIEDS AND NEWSGROUPS

The Web has its equivalent of the classified ads you see in your local newspaper. In fact, most online newspapers have classified sections, which often mirror the listings they offer in their traditional printed paper versions, with the added benefit that the online ads are easier to search through than ones that are printed on paper. Other online classified sites specialize in the sale of specific items, like real estate or automobiles. The Internet also features a handful of classified ad sites, like Yahoo! Classifieds (classifieds.yahoo.com), Classifieds2000 (www. classifieds2000.com, as shown in the figure below), and Classified Warehouse (www.classifiedwarehouse.com).

Classifieds2000 (www.classifieds2000.com) is a classified ad site that covers the entire world.

These sites list classified ads from all of the United States or the entire world. As you shop these classified ads, keep in mind that distance adds shipping costs and makes buying an item a bit more complex. If you are buying something through a classified ad and at a long distance, you can't inspect the goods before completing the deal, and, in general, you will probably find it more difficult to fully trust the seller.

For the online equivalent of yard sales, you might want to venture into newsgroups. In Chapter 3, we'll talk about how to use newsgroups and other forms of online discussion to get help and advice from other shoppers. If your main intent is to buy through newsgroups, your best starting point is AltaVista. From the area called Specialty Searches, click on Usenet, as shown in the figure on page 72.

Once you are in the Specialty Search area, AltaVista will then display a query box. Enter the phrase

+ newsgroups: forsale +whateveryouwant

and replace "whateveryouwant" with the type of item for which you are looking. If you are entering a phrase rather than a single word, put the phrase in quotation marks and put a + sign in front of the first quotation mark. When you get your list of results, to read an entry, just click on its name. If you want to get in touch with the person who posted the information and is selling the item, click on the associated e-mail address. Keep in mind that while you will see many tempting offers in newsgroups, be cautious. No one but the seller is providing

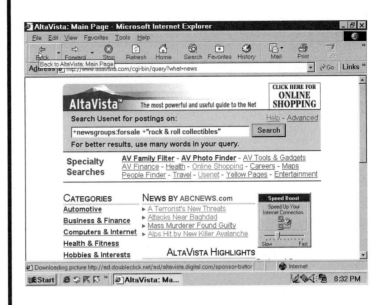

If you want to investigate buying items through newsgroups, try starting at AltaVista (www.altavista.com) in an area called Specialty Searches.

you with any assurances about your would-be purchase. Responding to these ads is like responding to notes posted on a bulletin board at your local grocery store, except the seller probably doesn't live in your neighborhood or even your city—he or she might even be in another country.

If you want to post your own ad in a newsgroup and have never used newsgroups before, your best place to start is at Dejanews (www.dejanews.com). Be sure to read the general information at Dejanews that explains what newsgroups are, how they work, and the proper way to use them. Follow the instructions there for finding the right newsgroup(s) to post your item in, and how to do the posting from the Dejanews site.

ONLINE AUCTIONS—WHERE BUYING MEANS "WINNING"

Online auctions combine characteristics of bargain hunting through classified ads and competing with other buyers in live, face-to-face auctions. When you bid at an online auction, you'll probably feel like you would gambling with slot machines, and you'll probably feel the rushing excitement similar to the final minute of a close-scoring football game. As with classifieds ads, you can search these sites for categories that interest you, and you can scan the auction's listings for items you find interesting.

Similar to face-to-face auctions, you are bidding against other people who want the same goods and are looking for a great bargain or trying to get hold of something that is very hard to find. But unlike a live auction, you don't have to be on hand at a certain time, and you don't have to wait while the auctioneer sells all the other goods which you have no interest in bidding. With an online auction, you bid on any item—or items—you like, however often you like. Each item being auctioned has a certain time frame during which it will be offered for sale. As each offered item's auction deadline approaches, the online action intensifies. The name of the game is to just barely outbid the next highest bidder, as near to the deadline as possible. Then you "win," and have the honor of paying for and receiving the merchandise. At the auction's close, you—the buyer—deal directly with the item's seller to arrange payment, shipping the purchased item, and any remaining details.

At some auction sites, you buy directly from the manufacturer or from a store rather than individuals, and the merchandise for sale is new or refurbished. These sites, designed to quickly turn overstocked inventory into cash, often go out of their way to heighten the excitement and draw buyers back. Some hold "flash auctions"—auctions which begin and end in a very short time period, rather than lasting for days or weeks, which is common at sites where individuals sell to one another. For instance, at First Auction (www.firstauction.com) you will find numerous auctions that last just 30 minutes, and where the first bid—even on merchandise worth hundreds of dollars—is always just $1. Such a setup can easily create a bidding frenzy.

Like a competitive contest, participating in online auctions can become very exciting. Especially at a flash auction, you might get caught up in the competitive thrill of the moment. If you are not cautious, you could wind up buying things you don't want or need. As with gambling, you could become addicted. But if you can manage to maintain some self-control, you can find bargains and hard-to-find collectibles, along with enjoying the exhilarating experience. One additional sideline benefit is that you'll meet lots of people online who have similar interests to yours. Here is a listing of a few sites to get you started in the thrilling world of online auction activity:

- eBay (www.ebay.com): This site is one of the largest auction sites, boasting that it currently has nearly two million items for sale in over fifteen hundred

A COMPLETE WASTE OF TIME

The 3 Worst Things to Do at an Auction:

1. Offer something for sale, then withdraw it.

2. Find the item of your dreams, right after bidding has closed.

3. Bid against yourself.

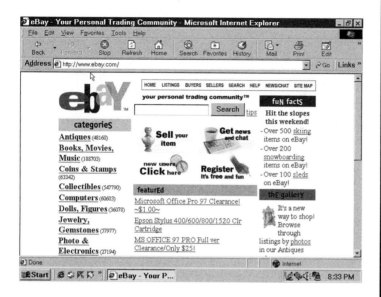

eBay (www.ebay.com) is a great place to check out your first online auction.

categories. (See the figure above.) This site receives over 140 million hits per week. With so much to offer, eBay is a great place to check out as your first online auction site. But before you begin bidding, first read the tutorial and frequently asked questions to learn the rules of how eBay conducts its business and charges fees for participation.

- Amazon.com (www.amazon.com) The Internet book-selling giant entered the auction business in April 1999, with many of the features and much of the look and feel of Ebay.

- The Internet Auction List (www.internetauctionlist. com): This site is actually a list of over 1,400 different auction sites, and lets you search for specific types of auctions in a variety of ways, including by

IF YOU'RE SO
INCLINED

Clear out your attic and basement of old books and knickknacks, things that you once collected and now no longer care about. Go to eBay (www.ebay.com) and put them up for sale. You'll get cash you can use on your next shopping trip, and you'll free up space to accommodate the new stuff you pick up.

geography. Depending on what you want to buy or sell, you may prefer an auction site in your state, or at least in the same country, to reduce shipping and customs costs, delays, and hassles.

- BidFind (www.bidfind.com): This site is a searchable index of items for sale in ongoing auctions at numerous sites (including eBay).

- OnSale (www.onsale.com): This site holds auctions for manufacturers and resellers that are trying to reduce excess inventory. So while you'll see lots of used and collectible merchandise at eBay, here you can look for bargain prices on new goods in the categories of computer products, sports and fitness, home and office, and travel.

If you decide to venture into the world of online auctions, make sure you have a fast and reliable connection to the Internet. Auctions are time-constrained. The delays you might put up with when you are doing ordinary shopping might prove extremely annoying or even disastrous if you are trying to buy something you "absolutely need" and the bidding goes down to the last second. You don't want to be waiting for a page to load while your competitor places the winning bid, just one cent more than yours, in the last second of the event.

Getting Time On Your Side

	The Old Way	The Lazy Way
Finding the store you want on the Web, and getting to the place that has what you want	30 minutes (going from one menu to another at a directory site, and then clicking through store pages)	3 minutes (using a search engine like AltaVista, and taking the time to learn how to use it)
Checking online stores for the best price on a brand-name product	2 hours	2 minutes (using a price-comparison site)
Agonizing over which product is best in quality	2 hours	10 minutes (checking the write-ups at product quality sites)
Looking for a rare item to add to your collection	Years (if you ever find it)	Hours (checking online classifieds, newsgroups, and auction sites)
Looking for the rock-bottom price on a new computer	Days, checking hundreds of stores	30 minutes at a flash auction

Advanced Techniques: Becoming a Creative Online Shopper

Congratulations. Having mastered the navigation techniques discussed in Chapters 1 and 2, you are now ready to become a fully functioning participant in the Internet online shopping community. Once you become part of this special group of people, then you'll begin to realize the true benefits of the Internet. By sharing information and experiences openly with other shoppers you encounter on the Internet, you will gain access to the wisdom, experience, insights, and fellowship of tens of thousands of other online shoppers who have interests similar to yours.

Just tens of thousands of people? Not millions? No—only a small percentage of those who shop online actively participate in the online community. Most online shoppers just pass through their shopping experience, buying one thing here and another there. But I hope that you'll aspire to more than that, wanting to achieve the truly active effortlessness that comes when you make online shopping an integral part of your life and identity. You'll live it, you'll breathe it, you'll love it. What the heck, it's fun.

What do we mean by the online shopping community? The Internet offers a variety of ways by which you can and should interact with other shoppers, and not just with shopping carts and credit card transaction processing programs. Here is a brief summary:

- Chat is "real-time" dialogue that occurs on the Internet between several people who are online simultaneously in the same chat area. In that chat area, you will be able to see what other participants type and they see what you type—live, as it's happening in real time.

- Forums are like bulletin boards. You post a message. Somebody comes by later and posts a response. Somebody else responds to that response. Over the course of days, weeks, months, years, threads of discussion grow.

- With e-mail distribution lists, you "subscribe" to receive and send e-mail messages in a given subject area. These e-mail distribution lists are sent by and to other online participants who also subscribe.

- With newsgroups (also known as "Usenet newsgroups"), you can post and read messages in a given subject area without having "subscribed," simply by going to the right place within the newsgroup to read.

Using one or more of these mechanisms, you can help and be helped by others like yourself, getting recommendations and giving advice that you will gain from your own Internet experiences.

WHAT IT MEANS TO BE A "FULL PLAYER"

When you first ventured online, you probably had some misgivings about all these stores run by unknown people. After all, how can you know where these stores are, who the people are who run them, and whether they'll actually produce the goods they promise. But you aren't alone in your online shopping experience out there in Cyberland. Rather than "buyer beware," it's the vendors who should be wary—regardless of how big or small the store, or how well-known or obscure the company happens to be. You see, the online vendors are at the mercy of active and involved customers like you, who openly share information about their shopping experiences. If the online vendor messes up, word spreads fast among the online shopping community, and that vendor's business dries up.

Once you know how this online community stuff works, you should also consider becoming a full player:

- With your own Web pages, you can publish recipes, tips, experiences, ideas, and advice of all kinds, as well as lists of collectibles for which you are looking. Invite the entire world to take a look at your Web pages. The figure on page 82 shows the Web page of K&K Antique Tractors

QUICK ⬤ PAINLESS
See something you want to share with a friend? With Netscape, click on File, then Mail Document. Fill in your friend's e-mail address and add a message, if you like.

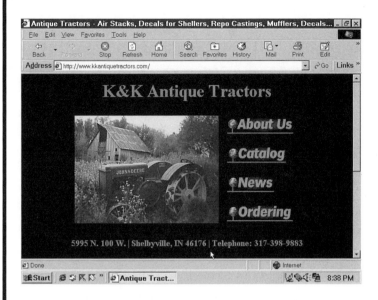

Even small companies like K&K Antique Tractors of Shelbyville, Ind., can increase their business and advertise worldwide with a Web site on the Internet.

(www.kkantiquetractors.com), a small antique tractor restoration business located in Shelbyville, Ind.

For about $100 per month, rather than depending on auctions and classifieds, you could use the lessons you've learned as an online shopper to open your own online store to sell your mother's jewelry or your wife's herbal tea. That's the base price that Yahoo! Store (store.yahoo.com) charges today to let you sell up to 50 different products in their storefront area. Or course, that doesn't include the time you might put in or other related costs (like getting a merchant credit card account). But they are aiming to make building and running an online store as simple as possible for beginners.

A WORD OF CAUTION BEFORE YOU DIVE IN

The Internet is about connecting people to people. It also happens to allow you to make purchases and to access enormous quantities of information, but connecting people to people is the heart of the matter.

As you meet new people in newsgroups, forums, and chat sessions, you can benefit from their advice and suggestions, and you can help others as well. Just remember that people are people even in cyberspace, with all their good and bad traits. You should proceed with caution, listening more often than talking, until you've had enough online experience to develop cyber-street smarts.

You have learned to proceed cautiously when approached by a street hawker or a door-to-door salesperson or when you get an unsolicited phone call from a stranger. You need to get used to the Internet equivalent of these encounters, to sense when you should hold back and when you should be open and sharing.

CHAT IN A HAT—FOR IMMEDIACY

As you pass through portals and browse through shopping malls, lingering at large and interesting stores, you will repeatedly see a hyperlinked phrase including the word "chat." Click on it to enter the local chat room and join in the live discussions happening there. Often these rooms are wide open 24 hours a day with people randomly dropping in and talking about whatever's on their mind. But some have scheduled events, with a host to

IF YOU'RE SO INCLINED

If you can't find a store's e-mail address (unfortunately, a common occurrence these days), try the following method. If the Web address is www.greatstore.com, then send e-mail to "webmaster@greatstore.com" or "support@greatstore.com." If that doesn't work and the message bounces back as "undeliverable," then look them up at one of the online yellow pages sites, such as AnyWho (www.anywho.com), Switchboard (www.switchboard.com), or Big Yellow (www.bigyellow.com).

keep the discussion moving in helpful directions and appearances by experts or celebrities. For example, Yahoo!'s forthcoming chat events include talks about fitness, heart disease, and celebrity chats with soap opera stars, as shown in the figure below.

In most cases, you first will arrive at a registration page where you apply for a password, or you can just sign in, then click to enter and immediately join in the discussion. Sometimes your browser software will suffice for you to participate in the chat room's activity. Other times, you will be given instructions on how to download special chat software. Unfortunately, there are dozens of different chat programs, and different sites use different ones. Don't sweat it. Follow the instructions you find at each chat room. Just dive in—read and react. It won't

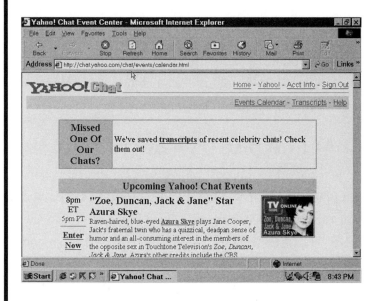

Yahoo!'s forthcoming chat events include talks about fitness, heart disease, and celebrity chats with soap opera stars.

take long for you to get the drift of how it works, and when you come to the same chat room for the second time, it will be even easier to join in.

In most cases, you type your messages in a form, and in a viewing area you see what you and others have been saying. You'll also see hyperlink buttons to click on to submit what you've typed or to change the look and feel of the page for your convenience. If you are confused, check the chat room's help files. Better yet, speak up. Type what you are thinking. Ask your questions and let the folks like you who are connected help you. Once you start participating in the chat, just go with the flow of activities. You'll be surprised how soon this seemingly stilted and awkward communication mechanism becomes second nature to you. You'll almost start "hearing" it. (Imagine telegraph operators in the days when Edison was young, who heard words when the uninitiated just heard clicks.)

This medium is great when you need suggestions for a gift, or advice on what is the best of this or that, or tips on the best place to get what you need. When you have a question and need an immediate answer, or just need to vent to and relate with people in the same kind of circumstances, give chat rooms a try.

If by chance the first chat room you enter is empty or the people rub you wrong, try another. If you are really unlucky that day, and the second try flops, too, then come join in my chat program about business on the World Wide Web, as shown in the figure on page 86. Check www.samizdat.com/chat.html for details. We'll

QUICK ⚡ PAINLESS

For links to scheduled chat programs with experts and celebrities, check Yahoo! Net Events (events. yahoo.com), On Now (www.onnow.com), Yack! (www.yack.com), and TalkCity (www.talkcity. com). To talk anytime about anything with anyone, go to Excite People and Chat (talk.excite. com), ICQ (www.icq.com), Yahoo! Chat (chat.yahoo. com), Tripod (www.tripod. com), or Xoom (www. xoom.com).

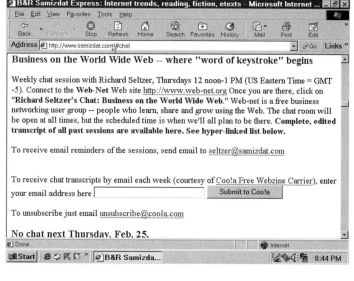

My weekly chat session discussing commerce on the Web meets every Thursday from noon to 1 p.m. EST at www.web-net.org.

help get you started with chat and answer other questions you might have about online shopping.

FORUMS—FOR THOUGHTFUL REASONED DIALOGUE

Forums let you carry on discussions across barriers of time as well as space. Your crazy schedule and time zone differences needn't get in the way of your discussing recipes or disk drives with an online friend in Thailand. Because you aren't faced with the urgency of everyone being connected to the Internet at once (like you are with chat rooms), you can pause and reflect and even edit your question or answer or comment before posting it to the forum. Days, weeks, maybe even months later, you'll be

IF YOU'RE SO
INCLINED

If you really get into the mode of relating to other people in chat, go to Xoom (www.xoom.com) and start your own free chat room. Tell your online friends about it, and gather there at pre-set times to talk about whatever interests you.

able to go back and see what you said, and what was said in response, as well as whether the conversation went any further from there. You might even tell your friends about this discussion and ask them to take a look and add their thoughts.

Where do you find forums? You'll see links to some of them at portals and malls and major shopping sites. Or you can go to Forum One (www.forumone.com), which has a searchable directory of over 225,000 Web-based forum discussions. (See the figure below.) They also list several hundred recommended forums, organized by categories.

To participate in a forum, you don't need any plug-ins or different software. All you need is a Web browser.

YOU'LL THANK YOURSELF LATER

If you love the forum style of discussion, consider creating your own forum for free at Delphi (www.delphi.com).

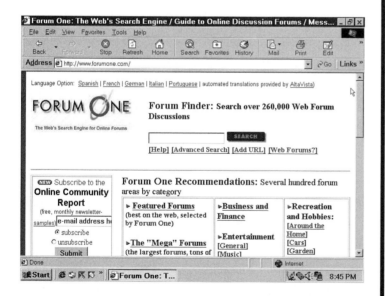

Forum One (www.forumone.com) has a searchable directory of over 225,000 Web-based forum discussions.

Ever want to talk to a friend while in the middle of an online shopping excursion? Go to Mirabilis (www.mirabilis. com) and read how their ICQ "instant messaging" software works. Download and install it. Then get your friends to do the same.

E-MAIL VIA DISTRIBUTION LISTS: WHEN YOU KNOW THE SUBJECT— NOT THE PEOPLE

Imagine sending a letter not specifically to "James and Joyce," but rather to "everybody who is really interested in antiques." That's what happens with public e-mail distribution lists.

Many of these e-mail distribution lists use automated software, so you sign on and off with a standard message to a particular address. The smaller distribution lists have posting addresses, and everything sent there by a subscriber gets automatically forwarded to the entire subscriber list. The larger distribution lists have one or more moderators who filter the mail and perhaps put the best postings together into "digest" messages.

A public e-mail distribution list's audience is typically a few hundred people and sometimes as large as a few thousand. The larger the subscriber group, the more likely the list will have a moderator; otherwise, you could get so many e-mails from the group that they become a nuisance rather than a help.

How do you find these public e-mail distribution lists? Go to "Liszt, the mailing list directory" at www.liszt.com, as shown in the figure on page 89. (That's not a typo; this site spells its name like that of the Hungarian composer.) The searchable directory includes over 90,000 public e-mail lists that you can join. This Web site also provides a recommended subset, organized by category.

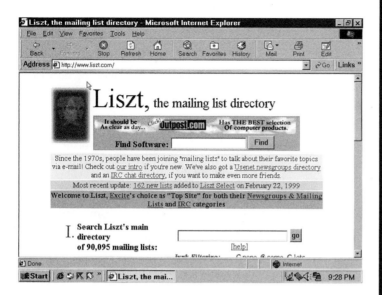

Liszt (www.liszt.com) is a good place to find public e-mail distribution lists.

Search Liszt for "antiques," and you'll find four matches. Click on the category "business," then "shopping," and you'll find

- Gift giving: help for the gift giving challenged (e.g., helping men find gift ideas for women)

- The Internet Cheapskate Newsletter: information on free and cheap Internet services

- McDonaldSv: surplus items for office, home, or work, at low prices

- RummageFun: for selling anything and everything, like a big yard or rummage sale

- Shopping: weekly updates of online shopping opportunities

YOU'LL THANK YOURSELF LATER

Concerned about the volume of e-mail you might get from distribution lists? Sign up for free e-mail accounts at places like www. hotmail.com, www. yahoo.com, and www.excite.com. You can use a different account to subscribe to each list. You can then pick up messages from a particular distribution list by going to the e-mail account that you used when you signed up for that particular list.

NEWSGROUPS: REACH OUT TO AN EVEN BROADER COMMUNITY

With newsgroups (known to pre-Web Internet veterans as "Usenet newsgroups"), you post a message to a group using one of the following three items: special newsgroup software, e-mail, or a Web-based service. The audience for a particular group might be tens of thousands, or maybe even hundreds of thousands of readers, but most of the postings are likely to come from the same handful of outspoken and prolific writers. The messages are stored on numerous "news servers." These news servers are dedicated computers around the world that have been set up on a volunteer basis specifically to act as newsgroup hardware hosts. Postings are typically available for about four to eight weeks, depending on the policies and whims of the folks who run the servers. The discussions are usually "threaded," similar to forums, where the newsgroup's subject line makes clear one message is in response to another one, and so on. The most useful messages often get posted to multiple newsgroups, forwarded over e-mail distribution lists, and eventually posted on the Web by fans, sometimes at multiple Web sites.

Liszt also has a newsgroup directory, and AltaVista lets you search through newsgroup postings. But the most comprehensive source of information about newsgroups is Dejanews (www.dejanews.com), as shown in the figure on page 91. On peak days, this Web site processes over a million postings from hundreds of thousands of people to over 50,000 different newsgroups.

A COMPLETE WASTE OF TIME

The 3 Worst Things to Do in Newsgroups:

1. Post the same message to many different groups.

2. Post messages that don't relate to the topic of the group.

3. Type in all caps. (In Internet-speak, that's shouting.)

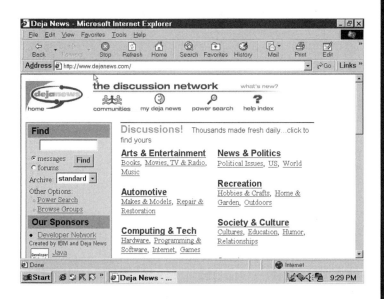

Dejanews is the most comprehensive source of information about newsgroups.

Click on "New Users" at the bottom of Dejanews' first page for information on how to get the most out of its free service. This Web site makes it easy for you to find and read the items you want and also to post items to any of these groups. Some examples of advice or information you can post requested responses for are as varied as looking for a rare collectible or seeking advice on what DVD system to buy.

WEB PAGES: MAKE YOUR OWN AND LET PEOPLE FIND YOU

Millions of people like you have created their own Web sites, using free space provided by their Internet service providers or by portal sites like Geocities (www. geocities.com), Tripod (www.tripod.com), and Xoom.com

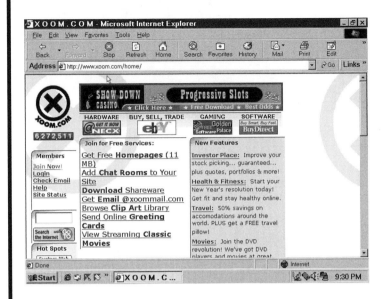

Sites like Xoom.com (www.xoom.com) provide free space for people to create their own Web pages.

(www.xoom.com), as shown in the figure above. The service that gives you the free Web space will also provide you with basic tools and advice for creating and posting your Web pages.

I've created my own Web site; over the last three and a half years, I've built my site to include over 900 documents, some of which are entire books. The figure on page 93 shows my Web site's home page. In any typical week, about 4,000 people visit my site, most of whom found their way to my site by using search engines. Often, they are looking for advice about doing business on the Internet or using the AltaVista search engine, or they have read a book or author that I've read or mentioned. Some also come looking for my online shopping directory (www.samizdat.com/shopping.html), which has links to all the sites mentioned in this book.

But why would you want to create and maintain your own Web site? Here are some great reasons:

- Post lists of what you want to buy so sellers can find you.

- Share with others hyperlinked lists of sites that you want to recommend (perhaps with your personal reviews).

- Post useful content related to areas of particular interest to you, so others with similar interests will find your pages and then contact you.

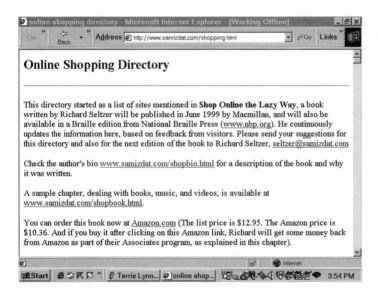

My Web site, www.samizdat.com, receives about 4,000 visitors in an average week. ("Samizdat" is Russian for "self-published," and implies "underground publishing," as in the days of Soviet Russia).

Take advantage of affiliates and associates programs offered by stores where you buy frequently, so you can get discounts on what you buy and also get referral fees (cash or merchandise credit) when people click from one of your pages to that store and then buy something.

By the way, if you are curious about affiliate/associates programs and how they work, check at Amazon.com. They have hundreds of thousands of associates—mostly people like you who have their own Web pages and mention books and music that they like, with links to Amazon.com for the convenience of others who might want to buy. If those visitors do buy, the referral fee ranges from 5–15 percent, depending on how much of a discount the customer is getting. For

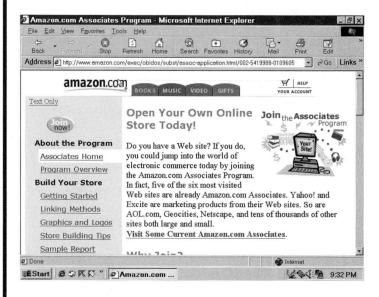

For details on how Amazon.com operates its associates program, visit the Web page www.amazon.com/associates.

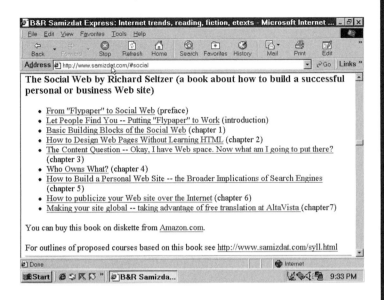

The Social Web by Richard Seltzer (a book about how to build a successful personal or business Web site)

- From "Flypaper" to Social Web (preface)
- Let People Find You -- Putting "Flypaper" to Work (introduction)
- Basic Building Blocks of the Social Web (chapter 1)
- How to Design Web Pages Without Learning HTML (chapter 2)
- The Content Question -- Okay, I have Web space. Now what am I going to put there? (chapter 3)
- Who Owns What? (chapter 4)
- How to Build a Personal Web Site -- the Broader Implications of Search Engines (chapter 5)
- How to publicize your Web site over the Internet (chapter 6)
- Making your site global -- taking advantage of free translation at AltaVista (chapter7)

You can buy this book on diskette from Amazon.com.

For outlines of proposed courses based on this book see http://www.samizdat.com/syll.html

For insight and assistance in creating and advertising your own Web site, download a free electronic copy of my book, The Social Web, from my Web site at www. samizdat.com/#social, or order a copy on diskette from Amazon.com.

details, check the Web site www.amazon.com/associates, as shown in the figure on page 94. Also check Chapter 4 of this book, where we discuss in detail shopping for books, music, and videos.

For ideas on what to include in your Web site and why, how to design your pages, and how to publicize your site for free over the Internet, check my book, The Social Web, which is available for free at www. samizdat.com/#social. (See the figure above.) For now, my book is only available in electronic form. You can read it at my Web site and save and print it, just like you would any other Web page. You can also buy it on diskette from Amazon.com.

OPENING YOUR OWN ONLINE STORE

Having experienced online shopping as a consumer, and having created your own Web pages, you might be tempted to open your own little online store, especially considering that the cost of starting a small online store is very little. For instance, at Yahoo! Store (store.yahoo.com), running a store selling up to 50 items currently costs only about $100 a month. (See the figure below.) Additionally, Yahoo! Store charges no start-up fee and no per-transaction fees, and you do not have to make any minimum time commitment.

While you can expect other companies to make similar offers, Yahoo! Store is leading the way in making it easy for ordinary people to open and run small online stores. Yahoo! Store already has over 280,000 products listed, and this mall-style collection of stores gets millions

With Yahoo! Store (store.yahoo.com), you can run a small online store for about $100 a month.

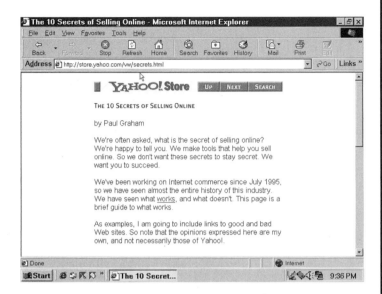

The 10 Secrets of Selling Online - Microsoft Internet Explorer

File Edit View Favorites Tools Help

Back | Forward | Stop | Refresh | Home | Search | Favorites | History | Mail | Print | Edit

Address http://store.yahoo.com/vw/secrets.html

YAHOO! Store | UP | NEXT | SEARCH

THE 10 SECRETS OF SELLING ONLINE

by Paul Graham

We're often asked, what is the secret of selling online? We're happy to tell you. We make tools that help you sell online. So we don't want these secrets to stay secret. We want you to succeed.

We've been working on Internet commerce since July 1995, so we have seen almost the entire history of this industry. We have seen what works, and what doesn't. This page is a brief guide to what works.

As examples, I am going to include links to good and bad Web sites. So note that the opinions expressed here are my own, and not necessarily those of Yahoo!.

Done | Internet

Start | The 10 Secret... | 9:36 PM

You can read Paul Graham's excellent article, The 10 Secrets of Selling Online, at store.yahoo.com/vw/secrets.html.

of page views per month. Shoppers can do a single search across all the stores. A single "shopping basket" keeps track of your choices, as you move from store to store within the site. And Yahoo! Store enables secure credit card transactions. As one of their storekeepers, you need no special software—just your browser. The folks at Yahoo! claim you can build a store and start taking orders in minutes.

But please don't underestimate the time and effort required to successfully run an online store. If you want to try running an online store because you love what you'll sell, go for it. If you want to get rich quick, go to Las Vegas instead—your odds will probably be better there. Before deciding, read the excellent article, *The 10 Secrets of Selling Online,* by Paul Graham at store.yahoo. com/vw/secrets.html. (See the figure above.)

Okay. You've become a shopping guru. Why not use the money you've saved to throw a party for the friends you've met online? If you live in far-flung locations, arrange to "rendez-vous" at a vacation spot. To work out your travel plans, maybe hold a weekly chat or carry on your discussion in a forum. To get the best travel deals, check the sites discussed in our travel shopping tour found in Chapter 6. And when you get back from your great vacation, post pictures and notes at your own Web site.

The Lazy Way

Getting Time On Your Side

	The Old Way	The Lazy Way
Looking for someone who used this product before and can tell you about it	3 days	3 minutes (searching through newsgroups at AltaVista or Dejanews)
Getting shopping advice from an expert	Next to impossible	1 hour (participating in a scheduled chat session with the expert)
Sharing tips and inspirations with people of common interest	Years finding the right people	1 month, trying out related newsgroups and e-mail distribution lists
Trying to find people willing to sell rare items you want	Years	Months (creating Web pages listing, describing what you want, and entering them in search engine indexes)

Part 2

Your Personal Shopping Tours

Are You Too Lazy to Read "Your Personal Shopping Tours"?

1 You are frightened by choice and would rather go to a store that had only half a dozen CDs and books, rather than one that had millions. ☐ yes ☐ no

2 You'd rather buy a car that's sitting on the dealer's lot or a preconfig-ured computer system sitting on the store shelf than learn something about what you're buying and get a better one at much less cost. ☐ yes ☐ no

3 You're proud that you have so much money that you can pay 10 times as much for your airline seat as the person next to you, and the differ-ence doesn't bother you a bit. ☐ yes ☐ no

Getting "Booked" for a Shopping Tour: Buying Books, Music, and Videos

Books, music, and videos are relatively simple consumer items. You can hold one in your hands, read the label, and know pretty much what you'd get if you bought it. But there are so many different books, music CDs and cassette tapes, and videos that no store could ever possibly stock them all.

Books, for example, have been traditionally sold through physical stores that have limited shelf space. Publishers battle for this shelf space, and only the best-selling books are stocked. Thousands of other books don't make it, and even the ones that do soon get pushed aside by new titles. The losers are shipped back to the publishers as "returns," with the store receiving full credit for the unsold books. The returned books eventually show up as "remainders," and are liquidated at enormous discounts.

Compare this traditional book sale model with today's online bookstore—a "virtual" store with no such physical constraints. The Internet version of the bookstore can include millions of different items, storing the information in a database so that you can find what you want quickly, searching by author, subject, or title.

CHOICE: HOW MANY MILLION IS ENOUGH?

The super-size online bookstores typically boast that they have a million or more titles. You've probably heard the Amazon.com (www.amazon.com) ads, with workers looking for a place that's big enough to store all the books they have for sale. Their joke underlines the fact that online stores don't need warehouse space, or don't need anywhere near as much of it as a comparable physical store would. The fact that you find a title listed at the Amazon online store just means that if you want it, they can deliver it. In most cases, they don't own or physically have on hand the book they are selling you, but they can get that book to you in a matter of a couple of days.

So with an Internet-based bookstore, where do all the books come from? Typically, the basic listings come from *Books in Print* (http://bowker.com/bip/home/index.html, a site that requires an annual subscription). *Books in Print* is a publication of R.R. Bowker (http://bowker.com), which attempts to catalog all books published in the U.S. This company's Internet edition includes more than 900,000 titles published since 1979. A would-be superstore sets up a searchable database starting with that information and makes business partnerships with one or more distributors.

Some online superstores, like Barnes and Noble (www.barnesandnoble.com), shown in the figure below, are connected with preexisting physical stores or chains of stores. Others, like Amazon.com, are new to this business and will probably never go to the expense of building brick-and-mortar stores. The typical superstore will have some best-selling books in stock for very quick turnaround. They'll forward other orders to their distributors for shipment in a few days. And others they'll special order from the publisher for delivery in a few weeks. If you need a book quickly, you might want to shop around

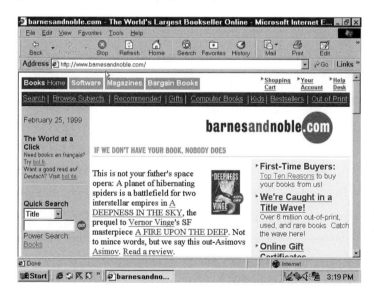

The well-known superstore Barnes and Noble offers its online version at www.barnesandnoble.com.

the various superstores to see which one guarantees fastest delivery for that particular title.

The highly publicized success of Amazon.com has attracted lots of competitors. Here's a list of the best-known online book retailers today, but expect plenty more to join the fray.

- A1Books (www.a1books.com)
- alt.bookstore (www.altbookstore.com)
- Amazon.com (www.amazon.com)
- Barnes and Noble (www.barnesandnoble.com)
- Book Stacks Unlimited (www.books.com)
- Books-a-Million (www.booksamillion.com)
- Books Now (www.booksnow.com)
- Borders (www.borders.com)
- Buy.com (www.buy.com)
- King Books (www.kingbooks.com)
- Powells (www.powells.com)
- Shopping.com (www.shopping.com/ibuy/books)
- Wordsworth (www.wordsworth.com)

Keep in mind that all these stores are not equal, even though they may boast similar numbers of titles. Those that base their database entirely on *Books in Print* will have out-of-date information, depending on updates from R.R. Bowker, which come at fixed intervals rather than in real time. That means that you might search for a book and find the old edition, but not the new one. Others, like Amazon.com, get information straight from publishers as soon as it's available, even prepublication information. Competition between booksellers should push the surviving online stores in that direction.

How do some of these stores offer numbers of titles far greater than those found in *Books in Print*? Some, like Amazon.com and Barnes and Noble, bolster the number of items they have for sale by including out-of-print books (for which they have finder services.) Amazon also has a program, Advantage, for small presses. This program accepts books on consignment. Those efforts make available to the general public literary and other rare works that otherwise would be almost impossible to find and difficult to purchase.

SPECIALTY BOOKSTORES— SURVIVING GODZILLA'S ATTACK

So why would you ever go to a small online bookstore? If the "Godzilla" stores like Amazon.com have everything and make it easy to find anything you want, why go anywhere else?

I have to admit that I'm an Amazon addict. I spend an average of $100–$200 a month there, and a lot more at Christmas when I buy gifts. But I also regularly buy books at Daedalus and Schoenhofs.

Daedalus (www.daedalus-books.com), shown in the figure on page 106, regularly sends me a printed catalog which has thoughtful, well-written mini-reviews of books I would otherwise probably never have heard of and that I very often find delightful. For the most part, these are low-priced remainders—hardcovers now going

QUICK ☜☞ PAINLESS

Looking for a specialty store—for instance, a Jewish bookstore or a jazz music store? Just go to AltaVista (www. altavista.com) and enter exactly those words as your query. You might get back millions of matches, but the ones at the top of the list will be pages that include every word of your query and are just what you are looking for.

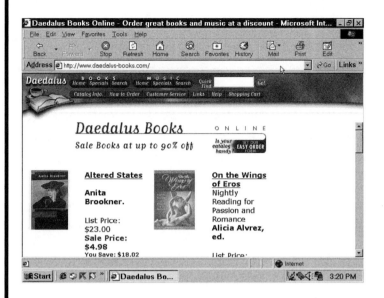

Daedalus (www.daedalus-books.com) has an extremely well-done printed catalog as well as a Web-based store from which you can make great book selections.

into paperback or gems that for one reason or other didn't make it in the bookstores.

I shop at Schoenhof's (www.schoenhofs.com), as shown in the figure on page 107, for their enormous selection of foreign language books—French, German, and Russian. But while I'll check their Web site, I'm probably more likely to phone them because their knowledgeable sales staff can let me know about alternative editions and related titles.

Whatever your tastes, there are probably niche stores on the Internet that can make it easy for you to decide what to buy, learn about new books in your field, or find a particular book when you don't know the title or the author.

Here's a sampling of the Internet's niche bookstores. You will find many others by links from related Web pages and also by using the major search engines and directories (discussed in Chapter 2).

- African American Literature Bookclub (www.aalbc.com): This site offers specialty books with the African American focus.

- Bibliofind (www.bibliofind.com): This site lists over nine million old, used, and rare books offered for sale by thousands of booksellers around the world.

- Cherry Valley Books (www.cherryvalleybooks.com): This site tends to specialize in children's, young adult, and parenting titles.

Schoenhof's (www.schoenhofs.com) specializes in foreign language books and has a knowledgeable sales staff to assist customers on the phone.

Looking for a really great buy in books? Want to sell your books for instant cash? Half Price Books (www.halfpricebooks. com) is the site for this rapidly growing chain of bookstores. They don't yet sell online, but they list contact information for individual stores so you can check out a book's availability or for information on selling or exchanging your used books. This retailer also sponsors a number of Half-Pint Libraries, children's reading areas set up in community centers and hospitals.

- Cody's Books (www.codysbooks.com): Cody's Books is the online service of a well-known bookstore in Berkeley, Calif.

- FatBrain.com (www.fatbrain.com): FatBrain lists all those computer books you need to master software and hardware.

- Future Fantasy Bookstore (www.futfan.com): This site is an online science fiction bookstore.

- Quantum Books (www.quantumbooks.com): This site is a technical and scientific bookstore, with its physical store's location near MIT.

- Politics and Prose Bookstore and Coffeehouse (www.politics-prose.com): This Washington, D.C., site includes only books personally selected by its owners.

- Schoenhoff's (www.schoenhofs.com): This site specializes in foreign language (French, German, Russian) texts.

- Sky Publishing (http://store.skypub.com/): Sky Publishing's online store features astronomy books, as well as other star-gazing paraphanalia.

- Tattered Cover Internet Store (www.tatteredcover. com): The Tattered Cover is an online service of several physical stores in Colorado.

- Victor Kamkin (www.kamkin.com): This site specializes in Russian language books and magazines.

THE RISE OF PSEUDO-STORES ONLINE

As you search for online bookstores that cater to your individual tastes—books on sailing or gardening or Jewish culture—you will often find that the store is an "affiliate" or "associate" of one of the superstores. Basically, many online superstores have programs that let members who have their own Web sites link to the superstore for book purchases. The resulting "pseudo-stores" (as I call them) carry no inventory and don't have to worry about collecting money or filling orders. All they do is provide links, and for that they get paid a referral fee when visitors buy. If you find yourself buying at stores of that kind often, you might want to consider opening one of your own. It's simple, quick, and costs nothing.

I operate a pseudo-store at my Web site at www.samizdat.com/#readers, as shown in the figure on page 110. There I have a list of every book I've read for the last 41 years (so I'm a bit obsessive), plus lists of my favorites and reviews. Because those pages of mine are indexed at the major search engines (and especially at AltaVista), I get lots of e-mail from other readers who have enjoyed the same books as I did. That e-mail is my best source of recommendations for what to read next. It's also a lot of fun getting in touch with people of similar interests and sharing ideas with them.

Since I'm an Amazon.com associate, I get the 5–15 percent referral fee on my own purchases, in addition to what visitors to my site might chance to buy. I have links from the books I mention at my site to the particular

IF YOU'RE SO INCLINED

Looking for a poetry reading or book signing in Washington, D.C.? Go to the Washington Post (www.washingtonpost.com), and click on Books. In other cities, check the site of your local newspaper.

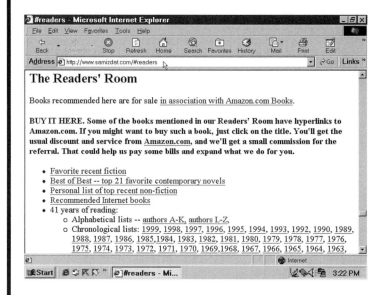

The Readers' Room

Books recommended here are for sale in association with Amazon.com Books.

BUY IT HERE. Some of the books mentioned in our Readers' Room have hyperlinks to Amazon.com. If you might want to buy such a book, just click on the title. You'll get the usual discount and service from Amazon.com, and we'll get a small commission for the referral. That could help us pay some bills and expand what we do for you.

- Favorite recent fiction
- Best of Best -- top 21 favorite contemporary novels
- Personal list of top recent non-fiction
- Recommended Internet books
- 41 years of reading:
    - Alphabetical lists -- authors A-K, authors L-Z,
    - Chronological lists: 1999, 1998, 1997, 1996, 1995, 1994, 1993, 1992, 1990, 1989, 1988, 1987, 1986, 1985,1984, 1983, 1982, 1981, 1980, 1979, 1978, 1977, 1976, 1975, 1974, 1973, 1972, 1971, 1970, 1969,1968, 1967, 1966, 1965, 1964, 1963,

I run my own pseudo-store at my Web site, www.samizdat. com/#readers, where you can buy from my list of all-time favorite books.

page at Amazon.com where that book is on sale. And whenever I want to buy a new batch of books, I add those titles with Amazon.com links to my "/readnext.html" Web page and click from there to Amazon.com to make my purchases.

You can do the same. It's relatively simple, and here are the steps:

1. Post one or more Web pages at a free Web-hosting site like Xoom (www.xoom.com), Tripod (www. tripod.com), or Geocities (www.geocities.com), as described in Chapter 3.

2. Sign up for an affiliate/associate program at one of the book superstores. Signing up typically costs

nothing and takes about a day for verification that you do have a Web site and that you don't seem to be doing anything illegal there.

3. Make a list of books that you love and would like to recommend, preferably around a common theme, so your "store" will have an identifiable niche.

4. Following the instructions from the superstore, make hyperlinks from your pages to the pages at the superstore where those particular books are offered for sale.

5. Add additional content, such as reviews, to let visitors know more about the books you have chosen and to encourage them to click on the hyperlinks.

6. Anyone who clicks gets connected to the superstore, where they get more information and where they can place orders online.

7. The superstore collects the money and fills the order, periodically sending you reports about activity from your site. The store also sends you a check with a finder's fee that typically amounts to 5–15 percent of what the customers paid for the books they bought.

If you are considering creating a pseudo-store, don't get inflated expectations. You aren't likely to get rich this way. But if you love books and like to share your enthusiasm, this is a way to pick up a little "found money."

The difficult part is getting enough traffic to your little Web site to generate sales of this kind. For tips on building traffic to your Web site, you can check my book, *The Social Web*, which you can read online at www.samizdat.com/#social.

WHAT PRICE GLORY?

Why do I buy so many books online? Is it price? No. If that were the case I would hop from store to store chasing the best price for each item. But, for me, that would be a waste of time. I'm happy if the standard discount (plus my referral fee, as noted above) offsets the shipping charges. And when I buy many books at the same time, making the per-book shipping charge relatively low, I'm inclined to spend my savings by ordering some recently released hardcovers instead of waiting until those titles come out in paperback. But I'm very skeptical about advertised single-title bargains.

Yes, an online store may try to lure you in with ads about special prices on particular books, but so do physical stores, which heavily discount the best-sellers and hope you'll buy more books once you're in the store. But shopping online, you'll be hit with shipping charges, which decline the more you buy. If you only want that one item, the shipping will bring the real cost up close to list, or certainly no better than you could do at the physical store around the corner. You only get the benefit of the advertised cost savings on the one title by buying several or even half a dozen other books at the same time; however, those additional titles probably don't have the same high discount.

If you do insist on buying one book here and another there, while the nominal cost for each item might be less, the total cost, including shipping, will be much higher than if you bought them all at the same superstore.

By the way, you can't use a search engine like AltaVista and Hotbot to find out which online stores have the book or music or video you want. That's because the stores keep their catalog information in databases, and public search engines today cannot access databases. You can, however, use a comparison site like PriceScan (www.pricescan.com), shown in the figure below, or Acses (www.acses.com) to check the availability and price of a particular title across a dozen or so online stores.

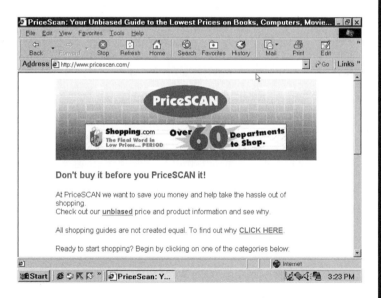

PriceScan (www.pricescan.com) can check the availability of a particular book from about a dozen online superstores.

Logically, you might expect to get the best deal by eliminating the middleman and going straight to the publisher's site. In fact, you could use the search capability at an online superstore to find out who the publisher is and then go to the publisher's site to make the purchase. But the industry doesn't work that way.

Major publishers typically give bookstores and distributors a discount in the range of 40–55 percent, depending on the size of their orders. But, believe it or not, they are not set up to handle individual orders themselves and can't do so economically, even though they'd get the full undiscounted price.

For instance, at Macmillan's site (www.mcp.com), you can search and browse their complete catalog (more than 2,000 new titles published each year), and see a description, the table of contents, and a sample chapter of each. But you can't buy the book online there. Rather, they expect you to make the purchase at retail bookstores. Smaller publishers, whose books are carried by a limited number of stores, will probably include a list of those stores at their site. Only the very tiniest publishers, who sell primarily by direct mail and whose titles may not appear in stores at all, are likely to sell directly over the Internet.

That means that a superstore like Amazon.com is not in competition with the publishers, but rather works in partnership with them. In fact, Amazon.com welcomes all the information and excerpts and pictures that the publishers are willing to provide. Hence, the Amazon.com site becomes the simplest way for a publisher to sell single copies, without all the logistical headaches and cost of trying to deal directly with hundreds of thousands or even millions of individual customers.

If you know of a publisher that specializes in books in your field, you may want to check the publisher's Web site for its latest catalog and browse to see what's new. Then you can go to an online superstore to make your purchase.

IT'S ALL A MATTER OF TASTE

You buy a car maybe once every three years. As for books, music, and videos, you can consume dozens of these in a month, all different, and you have literally millions of different items to choose from. So how do you decide what you want? And how do you avoid wasting your time and money on ones that you don't like?

To help us make these decisions, we traditionally rely on best-seller lists, awards, reviews, and the opinions of friends. We also sample the goods—flipping through books in a physical store, or hearing music on the radio or TV or seeing previews of videos. Online superstores typically give you easy access to best-seller lists, award lists, reviews by professionals, and also reviews by people like yourself. (For instance, at Amazon.com you can post your own reviews of the books you've read.) And, thanks to their partnerships with publishers, they sometimes provide detailed descriptions, tables of contents, and even sample chapters.

That's enough shopping for today. Take a break and read a book instead of buying another one. Or, better still, go chat with an author at Barnes and Noble (www.barnesandnoble. com) in their "Authors Online" area.

The Lazy Way

If you are a glutton for reviews, check AcqWeb's Directory of Book Reviews on the Web at www.library.vanderbilt.edu/law/acqs/bookrev.html, as shown in the figure below.

This site will link you to all the major traditional sources of reviews, including *Library Journal*, *Booklist*, the *New York Review of Books*, the *New York Times*, *Salon Magazine*, the *Los Angeles Times*, and the *Atlantic Monthly*. It also includes links to publications that review scholarly and interdisciplinary books, children's books, and computing and Internet books.

You also could and should spend some time checking the book-related newsgroups, including the monstrously

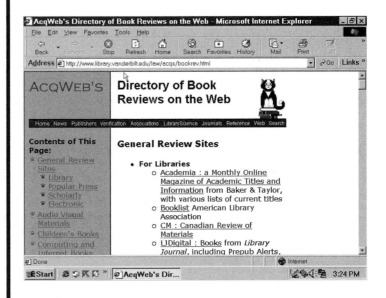

The AcqWeb's Directory of Book Reviews on the Web (www.library.vanderbilt.edu/law/acqs/bookrev.html) features the most comprehensive listing of book reviews available online.

large and very active rec.arts.books, and its offshoots (rec.arts.books.childrens, rec.arts.books.hist-fiction, rec.arts.books.marketplace, and rec.arts.books.tolkien). And science fiction lovers should consider rec.arts.sf.fandom, rec.arts.sf.marketplace, rec.arts.sf.misc, rec.arts.sf.science, rec.arts.sf.starwars, rec.arts.sf.superman, and rec.arts.sf.written. If you don't have access to a news server by way of your Internet service provider, you can search through and read and post to all of these at Dejanews (www.dejanews.com).

In any case, avid readers should definitely check Evelyn C. Leeper's home page at www.geocities.com/athens/4824/, shown in the figure on page 118. Evelyn has been a regular and prolific contributor to book-related newsgroups for many years. At her personal Web site, she has posted her numerous insightful reviews, along with the "frequently asked questions" (FAQ) documents from rec.arts.books and rec.arts.sf.written, which may well answer some of your own questions. You will also find there a very complete list of physical bookstores worldwide, generated and updated by the collaborative efforts of newsgroup participants over many years.

But for buying books and music and videos, the online shopping experience is truly unique, and not just a matter of easy access to enormous quantities of information. The superstores can actually help me to better understand my own tastes and then to find the works that match. That's basically why I do nearly all my shopping for this class of goods online today, and why the

QUICK ☞ PAINLESS

Want suggestions on what books to buy/read next? Check my Web site at www.samizdat.com/#readers for a list of every book I've read in the last 40 years, plus lists of favorites, reviews, etc.

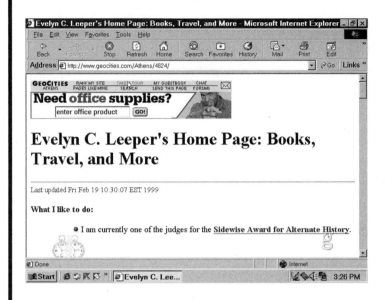

Evelyn Leeper's personal Web site (www.geocities.com/ athens/4824/) features insightful reviews, a complete list of physical bookstores worldwide, and many other bits of useful information for serious book lovers.

unplanned, impulse purchases I make there are very often winners.

The simplest form of online personal recommendations matches you with others who have purchased an item in which you are interested. For instance, at Amazon.com, when I read the details about a particular book or music CD, I immediately see a list of the top three items that purchasers of this item also bought.

A class of software known as "collaborative filtering" takes this a giant step forward. Based on your previous purchases and on any information you provide regarding your tastes (for instance, rating titles that you are familiar with), the system learns your preferences. At the same time, it is learning the preferences of tens of thousands or hundreds of thousands of other consumers of books, music, and/or videos. It builds a profile of your preferences and matches you with others who have similar tastes. Then your list of personal recommendations (which you can access at the store's Web site or get periodically by e-mail) includes those items that your cybersoul mates have given high ratings to and that you have not yet rated. The more people who provide details on their preferences, the more effective the system is in predicting everyone's likes and dislikes; so when you take the time to give your input, you not only help yourself, but also the community of others like you. You learn what others like you enjoy, rather than what professional reviewers prefer. And the recommendations are truly tailored to you as an individual, rather than to some fictitious notion of you based on statistical averages.

This approach is very different from the demographic data used to target advertising and programming to mass audiences. Demographics are static categories of people based on factors such as age, sex, race, education, and income. Advertisers try to find correlations between those factors and what people watch and what they buy. But individuality gets lost in averages. The "average man" is a statistical fiction. Such data helps advertisers define their target audience, determine what they are likely to watch, and craft messages that are likely to appeal to many of them. But they are useless for helping you determine what book or record or video is most likely to please you.

YOU'LL THANK YOURSELF LATER

Go to Amazon.com (www.amazon.com). Click on Recommendation Center, then on BookMatcher. Rate dozens or even hundreds of titles. The more effort you invest now, the better the recommendations you'll get in the future.

By the way, these online preference services provide a strong incentive to return over and over again to the same superstore. For instance, once you've taken the time at Amazon.com to rate dozens or even hundreds of books or music CDs or videos, you can count on getting useful recommendations there. And as you buy more there and rate more there, the recommendations keep improving.

INTERNET: VIAGRA FOR THE BOOK INDUSTRY

Before the advent of personal computers, book publishing was a moribund business. Pundits lamented that due to television and movies, fewer and fewer people read books, and book sales remained stagnant while the population continued to rise. You might have expected that computers and the Internet would further erode demand for books. But, on the contrary, we are seeing a resurgence, with particular demand for books about the Internet. (A search at Amazon.com yields nearly 5,000 books with "Internet," "online," or "Web" in the title.) And bookselling is the hottest segment of online shopping today.

Basically, online book shopping changes not just how you buy, but the whole economics of the publishing industry. You have far greater choice today, and even greater choice in the future, as publishers choose to keep their books in print longer because now they have an outlet that isn't limited by shelf space. They also could publish more books because they no longer depend on large print runs and traditional distribution methods. They might, for instance, take advantage of print-on-demand technology that allows them to print a few copies or even a single copy economically, as orders come in. At the same time, very small and do-it-yourself publishers that have no hope of making it into physical stores can sell their books through the same online superstores that the major publishers do, giving you even greater choice.

ELECTRONIC BOOKS: BOOKS THAT SELL WITHOUT EVER BEING "IN PRINT"

In the near future, you will also be able to download many popular books in electronic form. This innovation will mean:

- No manufacturing and warehousing cost and no waste from returns, hence lower prices.
- Immediate online delivery, with no shipping costs or delays.

We can see the beginnings of electronic books today. Consider, for example, the sample chapters provided by many publishers at their own Web sites and also at online superstores.

Also, a few innovative publishers, like Macmillan (www.mcp.com/personal/), also make the complete text of selected books available to be viewed for free over the Web. Meanwhile, hundreds of volunteers are making the full text of thousands of public domain classics available

for free in electronic form—for the good of all—through projects like Gutenberg (www.promo.net/pg), as shown in the figure below.

With computer displays the way they are today, very few people would be inclined to read an entire book online, and printing out an entire book on your personal printer is far more expensive than buying a book. So publishers who put the full text of books up on the Web are basically giving you an unlimited set of samples to consider—just like you could at a physical book store. Reportedly, the publishers who offer full texts of books free for viewing at their Web sites typically see a 20–30 percent increase in print sales for those same books.

The Gutenberg project's volunteers make classic works available to download for free in electronic form (www.promo.net/pg).

The exception is the blind, who, thanks to computer-based text-to-voice converters, can and do read electronic books that are made available in plain text form (without fancy formatting and graphics).

We are just now beginning to see in the public marketplace inexpensive computer-like devices devoted to displaying electronic books. As such gadgets catch on, and as the displays for ordinary PCs improve, the market for books sold, delivered, and read in electronic form should soar, changing the standard practices of publishers and the buying and reading habits of people like you.

MUSIC: A SOUND INVESTMENT

Shopping for music online is very much like shopping for books. The selection is enormous, and so is the amount of related information. Many of the same superstores that sell books also sell music. And some of them offer useful personal recommendations, like those for books. Here are some of today's largest online music stores:

- alt.bookstore (www.altbookstore.com)
- Amazon.com (www.amazon.com)
- Barnes and Noble (www.barnesandnoble.com)
- Best Buy (www.bestbuy.com)
- BlockBuster Video (www.blockbuster.com)
- Borders (www.borders.com)
- Buy.com (www.buy.com)
- CDNow (www.cdnow.com)

QUICK 🖱 *PAINLESS*

Interested in free electronic copies of works by authors like Jack London, or Charles Dickens? Check the On-Line Books Page (www.cs.cmu.edu/books.html) for searchable listings and links to over 8,000 free books online.

If you sign up with ClickRewards (www.clickrewards.com), you can get some great offers via e-mail. One such offer I recently received was for $10 off my first CD purchase with Music Boulevard. After my initial purchase with my $10 off offer, I got a new Aerosmith CD for about $7, and I got ClickRewards for my purchase. Now that I've made my first purchase from Music Boulevard, I've gotten two additional offers for 3 CDs for $30—that's a tremendous savings from what I can get off-line!

- CD Universe (www.cduniverse.com)

- Columbia House (www.columbiahouse.com)

- Compact Disc Connection (www.cdconnection.com)

- The Intelligent Tunes Music Network (www.tunes.com)

- K-Tel (www.ktel.com) With this site, you can build your own custom music CD.

- Music Boulevard (www.musicblvd.com)

- Music Favorites (Kmart) (www.musicfavorites.com)

- MyLaunch (www.mylaunch.com) This music community uses special software to help match people of similar tastes and to provide recommendations based on what people similar to you like.

- Spree (www.spree.com)

- TotalE (www.totale.com)

- Tower Records (www.towerrecords.com)

- Wherehouse (www.wherehouse.com)

Once again, this is a very competitive market. Expect lots of newcomers to join battle, with interesting new offers and features to tempt you. For example, one interesting twist offered by K-Tel (www.ktel.com) is the capability for you to build your own custom music CD. (See figure on page 125.) At this site, you can sample hits from the 1950s, '60s, '70s, and '80s to build your own music mix online. K-Tel then ships you your customized CD. This type of customization will become more commonplace as the features battle between music store Web sites continues.

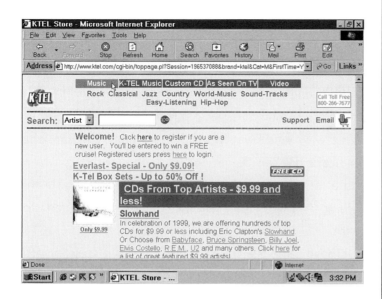

At K-Tel's music Web site (www.ktel.com), you can build your own custom music CD.

Also, thanks to affiliate/associate programs, expect to see lots of little pseudo-stores that sell music. These pseudo-sites will also provide information and recommendations about particular kinds of music and then provide links to superstores for particular titles, in return for referral fees or credit on future purchases. As in the case of books, if you are a serious music lover as well as buyer, you may want to consider becoming an affiliate/associate yourself and setting up your own Web pages, as described in an earlier section of this chapter. Hundreds of thousands of people like you have done so already.

When shopping for music, the online search capabilities at the superstores are particularly useful here.

Categories of music tend to be very subjective and idio-syncratic (is that pop or folk or rock?). While one physical store might shelve a particular CD in one category, another might put it in a different category. And if you are trying to buy music as a gift—shopping for kinds of music with which you are not personally familiar—the physical store can be very intimidating, and it can take you a long time to find what you want unless you are able to find a helpful salesperson with a moment to spare.

Those same search capabilities make it easy for you to find and learn about independent labels and artists, whose music is now for sale online, but who couldn't get shelf space for their CDs and cassette tapes in physical stores.

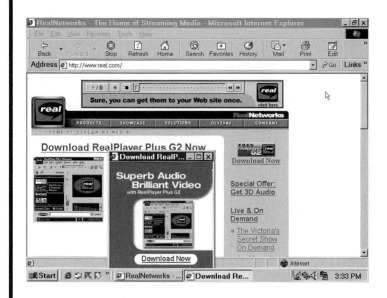

You can download a plug-in from RealNetworks at www.real.com, which most music sites use for playing their audio samples.

For you to be able to hear music samples to help you make your online music-shopping decisions, your PC needs an audio card and related software, and you also need to fetch the appropriate plug-in software for your browser. (Most music sites use plug-ins from RealNetworks, which you can download from its Web site at www.real.com, as shown in the figure on page 126.) For the best sound, you may want to get quality speakers. Then you'll be able to get the most out of the music sampling capabilities at online stores.

As with books, the trend is first to provide excerpts/samples online, and later to sell the product in electronic form so you can download it directly to your PC, rather than waiting for delivery of a physical CD or tape. You'll find the beginnings of electronic delivery today at a handful of sites, such as Music Boulevard.

At Music Boulevard, click on Download Music to see the selections. A single song might cost about a dollar and take about half an hour to download. But first you'll have to download and install a free e-mod music player, which will take you another five minutes.

If you are going to buy music in electronic form, you will want a portable way of saving it. Otherwise your hard drive will get filled quickly, and you will be frustrated when you want to play the music on a device other than your PC. You might consider adding one of the new CD drives that lets you write as well as read CDs.

For music, radio stations provide samples all day; you pick a station that suits your tastes, hear some tunes that you like, and buy them. But the stations only play a small

IF YOU'RE SO
INCLINED

Also, keep in mind that if you have a CD-ROM drive, you can listen to your music CDs on your PC (while shopping). So, adding good speakers to your PC configuration might be well worth the money.

percentage of what's available. What about the rest? In the past, those options were dead; an artist or group either "made" it or didn't. Now those unknowns can sell their CDs and tapes through online music superstores. But how do you find out that the "unknown" exists? (Yes, you can search for an "unknown" by name, but you already have to know their name to search for them.)

Emerging artists now have the opportunity to take matters into their own hands and offer samples of their music or complete works online at their own Web sites. We discussed in Chapter 3 how ordinary people like us can create our own Web pages at sites like Geocities, Xoom, and Tripod that offer free space and the tools you need for ordinary pages consisting of text and graphics. If you love music or have your own music group and are ambitious, you can take this approach a step further and build a site with audio content, as well as text and graphics, at very little cost.

Audio files are much larger than text files: a single song might take up 10 times as much space as an entire book (5 MB vs. 500 KB). So you wouldn't want to do much, if any, audio if you were limited to just 5 or 10 MBs of space (which is typical with free Web-hosting accounts). But TierraNet (www.tierra.net), as shown in the figure on page 129, currently offers unlimited Web space for as little as $15 per month. TierraNet is also set up to handle "streaming audio," where the listener hears the sounds as they arrive, rather than having to download an entire file and then play it back. With free software from RealNetworks (www.real.com), you can

QUICK ⬤ PAINLESS

Looking for secondhand cassette tapes and music CDs? Check Second Spin (www.secondspin.com).

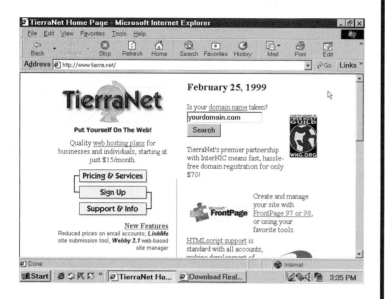

TierraNet allows you to host your Web site without any size limitations and provides you the ability to deliver sound as well as text and graphics starting at only $15 a month.

turn your sound files into the format needed for "streaming audio" and post them on your site at TierraNet.

If you are really ambitious, you could create many such personal files—voice as well as music—and run your offerings regularly, operating your own Internet-based radio station at very low cost and without needing FCC approval. (Keep in mind that $15 a month is the base price. The more you do, the more it costs, but you'll be amazed at what is possible on a shoestring.)

To see how online radio stations work, check the RealGuide at RealNetworks (www.real.com/realguide/index.html), as shown in the figure on page 130. Some of the sites linked to from there feature music from artists

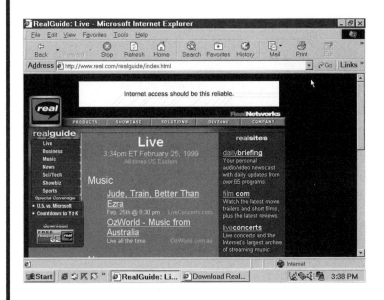

To see how online radio stations work, check the RealGuide at RealNetworks (www.real.com/realguide/index.html).

who have not yet hit the mainstream. You might also want to check Musicnet's HotPicks (w w w . m u s i c n e t . c o m / h o t p i c k s / index.html), which offers over 2,000 music clips.

You can also learn about new music artists through newsgroups which you can search for at Dejanews (www.dejanews.com), and through e-mail discussion lists, which you can search for at Liszt (www.liszt.com).

VIDEO: SEEING IS BELIEVING (ESPECIALLY AT HIGH BANDWIDTH)

Delivering video over the Internet depends largely on connection speed. At typical modem speeds, the best video you can see are tiny pictures that move jerkily— worse than the old-time silent movies. But if your

Internet connection is a fast one, perhaps cable based or DSL, then the video you can see on the Internet becomes the same video you see everywhere. When these faster Internet transmission speeds are common, you will be able to receive full-screen television quality over the Internet. With ever-increasing Internet data transmission speeds, ever-more efficient compression technology (fitting more content into smaller files), and ever-greater disk space on new PCs, you will also be able to download entire movies in the not-too-distant future.

For now, though, the Internet is limited pretty much to buying or renting a video or DVD, and this process online is very much like buying a book. Nearly all the online superstores that sell both books and music (listed in this chapter) also sell movies, and provide the same

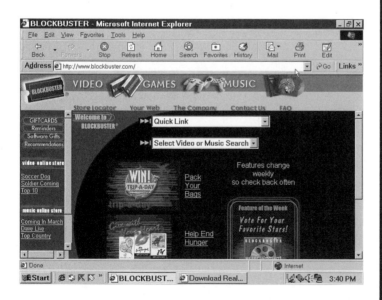

Blockbuster (www.blockbuster.com) still has a long way to go to catch up with the well-done sites, like Amazon.com.

IF YOU'RE SO INCLINED

If you recently bought a DVD player for your PC, you may be able to test out a new hybrid way of getting full-screen, full-motion video, known as "Web DVD." The sample disk that came with the system may provide you with the username and password you need to get into www.driveon.com, a Warner Brothers site that interacts with the content on that sample DVD to deliver unique entertainment experiences.

kinds of capabilities to help you make your video choices. You will also find some new players online that just specialize in movies, like Blockbuster Video (www. blockbuster.com), as shown in the figure on page 131, and Reel (www.reel.com).

Compared with sophisticated sites like Amazon.com, the Blockbuster site looks like it's still in its infancy. But Reel has an enormous selection of new and used videotapes to buy, DVD movies to buy, and videotapes to rent. With over 35,000 movies for rent, the Reel Web site is where you get hard-to-find films (foreign, cult, rare, classic, offbeat) and independent movies, as well as all of the mainstream ones.

Keep in mind that "finding" is not necessarily the same as "receiving." Online vendors typically work through distributors, and some are better than others at providing realistic estimates of how long it will be before the item ships. The fact that a video appears in an online catalog is no guarantee that you'll receive the goods in reasonable time. Over time and forced by competition, service should improve.

If you are addicted to movies, Reel has an affiliate program (similar to those discussed above for books and music), which will let you "build your own video store."

If you need more info to make your choices, check the Internet Movie Database (www.us.imdb.com), which is owned by Amazon.com. This database is purportedly "the ultimate movie reference source and covers everything you could possibly want to know about movies." Continuously updated, it also has hyperlinks to thousands of related external Web pages. It currently covers

IF YOU'RE SO
INCLINED

Would you like a personal guide to help you find Internet riches? Check The Mining Company. They have hundreds of volunteers who scan the Web for material in their specialty, provide links, and write articles for people like you. The section dealing with books, music and movies is at home. miningco.com/arts.

over 170,000 titles.

If you are interested in recent releases, check at the search sites like AltaVista—these days nearly every major new motion picture has its own Web site, packed with graphics, multimedia effects, and info for fans.

If you are really into movies and might even consider writing one yourself, be sure to visit these Web site locations:

- Drew's Scripts-O-Rama (www.script-o-rama.com): This site boasts links to over 600 complete scripts, including scripts of major feature films like *Star Wars* (in some cases, with several different drafts), as well as scripts by independents (like me) that have not yet been produced.

- The Screenwriter's Utopia (www.screenwritersutopia. com): The Utopian Home Page has information geared for the needs of screen writers, including space for hopefuls to share tips and insights.

- Scripts Now (www.scriptsnow.com): This site showcases new scripts and writers looking for producers.

- American Zoetrope (www.zoetrope.com): This site is the home page for Francis Ford Coppola's production company. One part of the site now accepts submissions of feature-length screenplays over the Internet, as shown in the figure on page 134. The site managers ask, "For each screenplay that you submit we ask that you read and review four screenplays submitted by other screenwriters. The screenplays you submit will in turn be read and reviewed

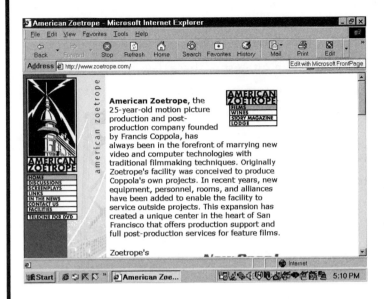

Francis Ford Coppola's Web site, American Zoetrope (www.zoetrope.com) offers a site section that accepts submissions of feature-length screenplays over the Internet.

by others. American Zoetrope staff, who are always looking for good new screenplays to produce, will read the best-received screenplays."

For information on all aspects of the movie business, as well as fan reactions to your favorite movies, check the movie-related newsgroups, such as:

- rec.arts.movies.current-films (This newsgroup now has over 8,000 articles posted at this location.)
- rec.arts.movies.international
- rec.arts.movies.erotica
- rec.arts.movies.lists
- rec.arts.movies.misc (misc = miscellaneous)
- rec.arts.movies.movie-going

- rec.arts.movies.past-films
- rec.arts.movies.people
- rec.arts.movies.production
- rec.arts.movies.reviews
- rec.arts.movies.tech

In addition, of course, you can search across all the newsgroups at Dejanews (www.dejanews.com) and AltaVista (www.altavista.com).

Finally, for a personal view of video and movies that are worth watching, check the Web site of Mark R. Leeper (husband of Evelyn Leeper, mentioned earlier in this chapter) at www.geocities.com/hollywood/6960. Mark has been a longtime active participant in movie-related newsgroups, and he posts at his site helpful and informative reviews of the many movies that he sees.

A COMPLETE WASTE OF TIME

The 3 Worst Things to Do When Shopping for Books, Music, or Videos:

1. Sign up for more than three book or music or video mailing lists. (You'll get inundated with e-mail and have no time to read the postings).

2. Get caught up in a "flame war" at a newsgroup like rec.arts.books. (A "flame war" is a heated argument with other posters about a matter of taste.)

3. Buy more than you have time to enjoy. (Thanks to the Internet, you'll be able to find and buy that CD or book later. You don't have to pluck it up now for fear you'll never see it again.)

Getting Time on Your Side

	The Old Way	The Lazy Way
Driving to and from the mall	30 minutes	Not needed at all by doing it *The Lazy Way!*
Trying to find one particular book	15 minutes	15 seconds
Trying to decide what other books to buy	1 hour	5 minutes
Looking for the music CD your daughter asked for	2 hours (3 stores)	15 seconds
Looking for videotape of Eisenstein's Alexander Nevsky	Forever (without ever finding it)	15 seconds
Waiting in the checkout line	10 minutes	2 minutes (posting order)

Chapter five

Surfing Online for Computers and Software

At first, I was reluctant to buy computer products completely online. Many of the online computer stores used to sell exclusively through printed catalogs, addressing the needs of the technically astute. I found those printed catalogs intimidating and confusing, and preferred to go to a physical store, where knowledgeable sales people could guide me through the maze of choices, explaining the benefits and risks and costs.

When Egghead, the prominent software retailer, closed its physical stores and decided to operate solely on the Internet, I was shocked and disappointed. I had shopped regularly at the local Egghead store and depended on explanations and advice from their salespeople whenever I needed either hardware or software.

Also, I greatly valued the fact that when I bought new add-ons or upgrades for my PC, I could pay to have them installed on the spot.

When I didn't have a store like that anymore in my neighborhood, I had to go online, which meant I could no longer rely on someone else's expertise and judgment. I was forced to learn more about computers than I ever wanted or expected to learn. As it turns out, that's probably a good thing, both for my budget and myself.

Basically, when it comes to computers, you should learn before you shop, especially before you shop online. The products are complex assemblies of standard commodity parts made by multiple manufacturers. The more you understand about your choices and their implications, the better you'll be able to take advantage of the opportunities available on the Internet.

Today, the computer industry is a commodity, standards-driven marketplace. Computer "manufacturers" are really just assemblers. They buy processors from one source; software, disks, memory, etc., from other sources; and assemble them into systems. The competition is fierce and the profit margins are slim. In terms of the basic specs—speed, memory, and storage—what we now define as a "complete system" for home use would have made a wealthy technical guru tremble with envy 10 years ago. This dream system now sells for about what it would cost to buy a wooden table for your kitchen. Does this make sense?

And this dream system has barely enough capacity to perform what we now perceive as basic tasks because the latest versions of the software we depend on, and even the games we play, require the latest and greatest of hardware to run properly. Does this make sense?

Did you ever hear of "built-in obsolescence?" We are seeing the computer equivalent in action.

Fifteen years ago, it seemed inconceivable that an ordinary individual would ever want or need a 100 MHz machine with one gigabyte of disk storage space. Yes, we could forecast that such machines would be available and at reasonable cost because of predictable improvements in technology. As a rule of thumb (known as "Moore's Law"), the speed of commercially available processors doubles about every 18 months. Typically, the new model sells for about what the old one did, and the value of the old one drops in half. While, at some point, technology must meet barriers that will slow the pace of change, the computer industry has been adapting at this incredibly rapid rate for more than two decades now, with great regularity. And the software industry has been keeping in lockstep with these hardware developments by making each new version of the common applications that people depend upon more and more complex and bulky, requiring the full capacity of the latest and greatest hardware. I don't believe this software inflation results from a conscious conspiracy. Rather, we're seeing the consequences of human nature—software expands to fill the capacity available for it.

That means that even if you don't want to do any more with your system in the future than you do right now, to stay compatible with other people with whom you have to share files, sooner or later you will have to upgrade your software. And the new versions of software will make your equipment seem painfully slow in two years, and obsolete in four.

A COMPLETE WASTE OF TIME

The 3 Worst Things to Do with a Computer

1. Stare at the screen-saver.

2. Use your modem to dial a friend's phone number and listen while your friend tries to talk back to your computer.

3. Use the CD-ROM drive as a coffee-cup holder. (People have actually done that.)

IF YOU'RE SO
INCLINED

You can also learn about the latest and greatest computer products at trade shows. If you might be interested in checking out a local one or taking a vacation computer-shopping trip, check Trade Show Central (www.tscentral. com). Nearly all the major shows are listed there.

In other words, in defiance of all logic, even though your computer could probably function well for another 10–15 years and could do everything you really need to do with it, you will find yourself compelled to make major upgrades or buy a complete new system every two to three years.

Considering the enormous resources available today, I'm amazed at what we were able to do back in 1983–84. Back then, my Atari 800 with no hard drive and 48 KB of memory seemed lightning fast and capable of miracles. Today, my year-old 266 MHz laptop with two gigabytes of storage and 96 MB of memory (2,000 times more than that old Atari) feels sluggish and limited.

Basically, "Moore's Law" plus software inflation means that the computer system you buy today, no matter how well chosen, will not last. You'll be back shopping for add-ons and upgrades and new systems again and again. In other words, you should invest some time learning about these gadgets and the commodity upgrades you can buy for them, so you can make full use of the shopping resources on the Internet and save again and again.

READ WHAT'S PUBLISHED, OR PERISH

You can only take advantage of the best deals if you understand your choices—why you might want to buy what, the key criteria, what works well with what, how to use what you have, how to cope with problems. Without that knowledge, you depend on brand names (at premium prices) and complete packaged systems (where you pay for pieces you'll never use).

You don't need to learn to program. You don't need to learn the skills of a technician. But you should familiarize yourself with each of the major commodity pieces that can go into a system and which you can later add or upgrade. You should understand the terminology and the measures of speed and capacity, and how they relate to your needs. And you need to keep up-to-date on major new options as they become available.

Impossible task? Hardly. There are thousands of people making a living providing information like that for people like you in the form of articles, magazines, books, and courses. This information is available in traditional form and/or over the Internet. Here's a sampling of the resources available to you:

- CNET: The Computer Network (www.cnet.com) provides articles intended to help you make decisions about buying computer products. The Hardware section (www.computers.com), as shown in the figure on top of page 142, helps you determine what is available in various product categories, at what price, and where you can find it. The Computer Network lets you filter your searches by price, processor, RAM, hard disk, screen size, etc. Its Shopper.com (www.shopper.com), as shown in the figure on the bottom of page 142, provides a similar service. If you want to purchase, you are connected to the vendor. The software download section is quite large.

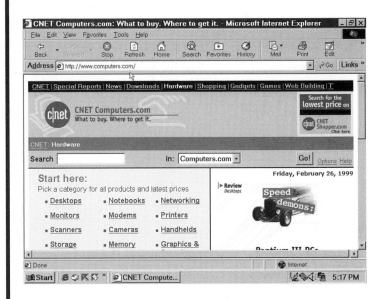

The Computer Network's hardware section (www.computers.com) helps you determine what computer system items are available and at what price.

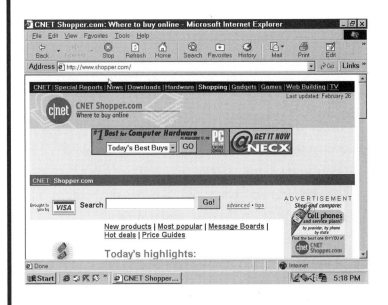

The Computer Network also has a section called Shopper.com (www.shopper.com) that automatically links you to a large number of online software vendors.

■ The Ziff-Davis Network (www.zdnet.com), as shown in the figure below, offers a complete line of magazines that includes

1. *Family PC* (wwww.familypc/) provides advice on buying hardware and software for use in the home. It is written for a general (rather than a techie) audience.

2. *PC Magazine* (www.pcmag.com) tests equipment and software and publishes the results as PC Labs Reviews. The download section includes free software, shareware (which you can download for free, but are expected to pay for if you decide to use it), software reviews, and articles.

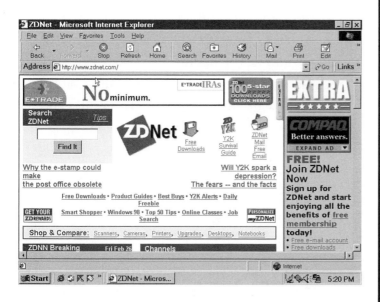

The Ziff-Davis Network (www.zdnet.com) offers a complete line of magazines that offer extensive information on how to select both hardware and software.

3. *PC Computing* (www.zdnet.com/pccomp) provides "best of the best" picks in all major product categories, plus "tips and tricks," product reviews, and software downloads.

4. *PC Week* (www.zdnet.com/pcweek) emphasizes the latest product and business news, rather than in-depth or how-to articles.

5. *MacWEEK* (www.macweek.com) and *Macworld* (macworld.zdnet.com) offer news and reviews of Apple products, plus downloads of software.

In addition, Ziff-Davis University (www.zdu.com), as shown in the figure on the top of page 145, offers online courses in many computer-related topics. Currently, for a subscription fee of $7.95 per month, you can take as many of these courses as you like. The experience includes reading texts assigned by the instructor (you have to buy the books), and interacting with the instructor and other students in forums and sometimes in chats as well, for the duration of the class (typically about five weeks). Topics include: Building Your Own PC, Maintaining Your Own PC, Troubleshooting Your Own PC, and Upgrading Your Own PC.

PC World (www.pcworld.com) provides helpful articles, product reviews and software downloads, and its picks of the top 400 products in each of the major PC categories. (See the figure on the bottom of page 145.) *ComputerWorld* (www.computerworld.com)

YOU'LL THANK YOURSELF LATER

For Windows 95 tips and training and Web wisdom of all kinds, check Tracy Marks' Windweaver site (www. windweaver.com).

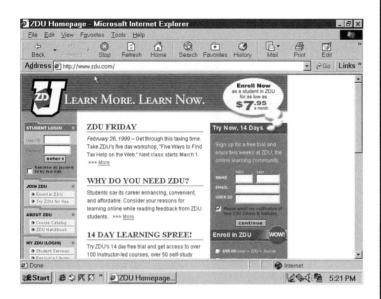

From the Ziff-Davis University (www.zdu.com), you can take any one of several PC courses offered for a subscription fee of only $7.95 per month.

PC World Online (www.pcworld.com) features a list of the top 400 products in each of the major PC categories.

provides news on computer products, companies, and trends.

- McGraw-Hill publishes *Maven, Business Week's Computer Buying Guide* (www.maven.businessweek.com), which includes product reviews and comparative ratings. Their "picking a system" explains the key factors and helps you "uncrack" the code of "computerese." The same company also owns Osborne Books (www.osborne.com) and McGraw-Hill Online (www.mhonlinelearning.com), which offers online technical, computer-related courses, typically for about $300–$400 each. (See the figure below.)

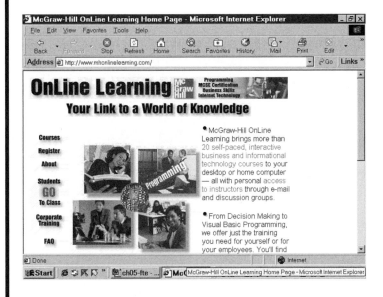

McGraw-Hill Online (www.mhonlinelearning.com) offers online technical, computer-related courses ranging in price from $300–$400 each.

Macmillan Computer Publishing maintains its supersite at www.mcp.com.

- Macmillan (www.mcp.com), publisher of *The Lazy Way* series, also offers a wide range of other books intended to help you better understand computers and related technology. (See figure above.) In particular, their Que imprint (www.mcp.com/publishers/que) includes such titles as "How Computers Work" and "Upgrading and Repairing PCs," as well as the Complete Idiot's Guides (www.mcp.com/publishers/que/series/complete_idiots_guides). These guides are "designed for anyone not familiar with a topic or technology. Rather than covering every way to accomplish each task, these books focus on doing things 'the simplest, most straightforward way.'"

- O'Reilly Associates focuses mainly on highly technical books aimed at programmers, Webmasters, and Web page designers. But their "In a Nutshell…" series of computer software tutorials (nutshell.oreilly.com) addresses the needs of a more general audience.

- The online version of *Wired Magazine* (www.hotwired.com), as shown in the figure below, discusses high tech entertainment and communication products in an entertaining and futuristic vein. Wired puts technological trends into a social and economic context. They seem to find a new revolution to announce almost every month. It's fun. And here is the place where you might first see mentioned a product or class of products that you will eventually want to shop for. They also offer a few free online tutorials on such subjects as Web design, animation, and Java.

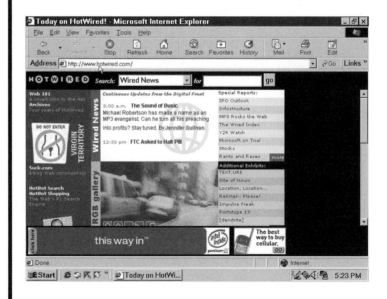

Wired Magazine's online version (www.hotwired.com) puts technological trends into a social and economic context.

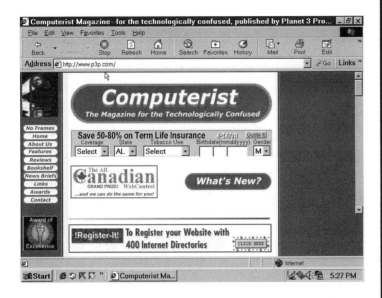

Computerist (www.p3p.com) calls itself a magazine for the technologically confused.

- Computerist (www.p3p.com), as shown in the figure above, calls itself "a magazine for the technologically confused." Far smaller than the productions of the major computer publishers, it does offer news, independent reviews, information and opinions on computing and technology, all written in ordinary, non-technical language.

WHAT'S IN STORE FOR YOU?

The computer hardware and software marketplace changes at a dizzying pace. You buy a great computer today, and tomorrow you see another even better one advertised at a lower price. That means that you should always delay buying computer gear until you actually need it—until the last moment. Except under rare circumstances (such as the shortage of a key part like a popular processor or memory chip, or a highly publicized launch of a radically new product), computer equipment is not in short supply. When you are ready to buy, you'll find numerous vendors anxious to sell you functionally similar products. Use the extra time to learn more.

Also, with your inevitable need for upgrades, you should think of your computing capability not as a fixed asset, but rather as a regularly recurring expense for a consumable. You will periodically refill your system box, rather like refilling the oil tank for your furnace. Hence you should seriously consider creative financing arrangements, such as leasing and/or guaranteed future trade-in agreements.

When considering leasing, the length of the lease is critical. If, for your use, the system is likely to become obsolete in two years, you don't want to be saddled with it (and its payments) for three or four years.

When considering a prearranged trade-in/upgrade agreement (such as that now being offered by Gateway), remember that while you will be able to get back some of the value of the system you buy today, you are at the same time locking yourself into a particular vendor. In this volatile industry, by the time you need to upgrade, there may well be better choices elsewhere—including free PCs.

Also, look for and invest in extended warranties and service contracts. Sooner or later you will need help, either to pick the right product or to install it or fix problems later on. So make sure that as part of your purchase,

IF YOU'RE SO INCLINED

Some Internet businesses are giving away PCs to customers who make long-term commitments to their company, for example, if you sign a long-term agreement with an ISP. Keep an eye out. Oppor-tunities of this kind are likely to multiply.

you are going to have access to experts who can help you either online or by phone. If it is by phone, the company should provide a toll-free number and assurances that you won't be stuck on hold for endless hours, if you are lucky enough for your call to ever get through.

You also should look for online stores that offer not just the ability to search for the best price and performance on all the different pieces that can go into a computer or an upgrade, but also tools designed to help you "configure" your system. In other words, you want to make sure that pieces made by different manufacturers or by the same manufacturer at different times will really work well together, and make sense. (What's the point of a part that's 10 times faster than the rest of the system can handle?) Only if you have that kind of information can you really take advantage of commodity prices and price comparison tools and even auctions. And you want this online decision-support program to be organized and worded in ways that make sense for your level of knowledge—not just for the 8-year-old computer guru who lives next door.

The creative financing, warranty, service contracts, and online configuration tools can come from either the manufacturer/assembler or an independent store (which may also assemble a system to your custom requirements). The cross-company search capabilities at various online superstores might help you determine which make and model you want. Then you might go to the manufacturer's site to use the configuration tool there as a check against the store's recommendation and price;

and you might also want to see if the manufacturer is offering better deals on financing and service.

Price Comparison

If you know what you want, need no further help, and price is your main selection criterion, you want to start at a price-comparison site. Even if you don't know exactly what you want, you might want to do some trial searches for products in the general category you are interested in, to see which online stores consistently offer the best prices.

At Pricescan (www.pricescan.com), as shown in the figure below, you can search for the hardware, software, and computer supplies you need across dozens of online stores. You enter the features, parameters, and price

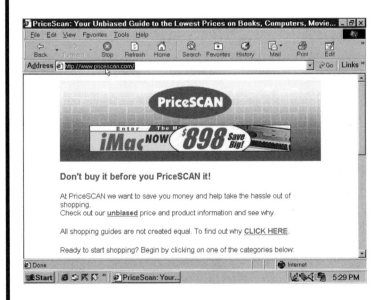

Pricescan (www.pricescan.com) compares prices from dozens of online stores.

With Price Watch (www.pricewatch.com), you can click in a category of computer product to get all the prices, or enter a customized search.

range you want. The results list includes the model number, the vendor name, and a selection of dealers along with their prices.

With the online service Price Watch (www.pricewatch.com), as shown in the figure above, you can click on a category of computer product to get all the prices, or enter a customized search. You can also search for the best price on a particular product from a particular manufacturer.

Covering hardware, software, and components (such as generic memory), StreetPrices (www.streetprices.com) "sniffs out the best consumer prices on the Web." It updates its index hourly.

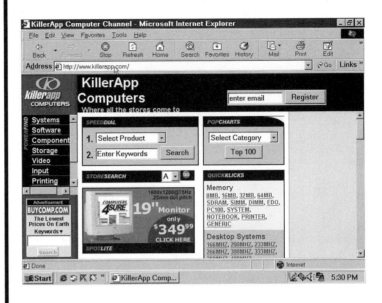

Killerapp Computers (www.killerapp.com) calls itself a computer-shopping channel.

Killerapp (www.killerapp.com), as shown in the figure above, calls itself "a shopping channel for computers." It helps you pick the right product at the best price and most convenient location. You can select a product area, then enter your keywords to drill down to exactly what you want. You can see lists of the hundred most popular products in a wide variety of categories. You can get detailed contact information on hundreds of computer dealers nationwide. Killerapp also lets you create your own personalized page for tracking prices of products that you are interested in buying.

Online Computer Superstores

The online computer superstores may have some related editorial content or point you to reviews, but their main function is to make it easy for you to buy comphuter items after you have already decided what you want.

- Computer Shopper (www.computershopper.com), as shown in the figure below, is the online equivalent of the monstrously large print publication you see on magazine racks in grocery stores. Published by Ziff-Davis, the magazine is stuffed with page after page of ads and price lists—which are probably far more in demand that the editorial content. This publication is the one to which you should turn when you've already done your homework, know exactly what you want, and want to find the best price for it. Computer Shopper's online version is a shopping site—a computer superstore, with links to related classified ads and auctions. The online site,

The popular magazine, The Computer Shopper, *has an online equivalent, overflowing with product ads and links to popular hardware, software, and computer accessories.*

however, does not sell any items, nor does the magazine. Computer Shopper simply links you to the vendor who is selling the desired product, and makes no endorsement regarding the reliability of those who place advertising in the magazine, as well as on its Web site.

- Cyberian Outpost (www.outpost.com) provides the usual product lists of hardware, software, and accessories, so that you can both search and browse this site's inventory. This site also offers advertised specials and software downloads. Cyberian Outpost also has a "Manufacturer Stores" section, with selected products from a couple dozen vendors. If you want an item delivered overnight, this online store claims that if you place your order before midnight EST, you can receive the goods the next day via an overnight shipping service.

- CompUSA (www.compusa.com) is keeping its physical stores going, with fix-it and installation services, as well as training. Check its leasing program. The Web site lists the physical store locations and helps promote advertised specials that only apply at the physical stores. But a wide range of products are available for purchase directly online, including complete systems made to order for you, based on your responses to its online configuration capability. It will be interesting to see how this business evolves—whether or not CompUSA's online site and its physical retail locations can complement one another, and how. (Was Egghead brilliant or foolish to jettison its physical stores?)

In addition to selling the same hardware, software, and accessories online that it used to sell through physical stores, Egghead (www.egghead.com) runs two related online businesses. SurplusDirect (www.surplusdirect.com), as shown in the figure below, is an "online liquidation center," a place for manufacturers to get rid of excess inventory—not just for computers and software, but also for jewelry, luggage, home and garden products, and other merchandise categories. And Egghead Auctions (www.surplusauction.com) uses an online auction mode to sell computer hardware and software, both new and used/reconditioned, and also sells a variety of consumer products.

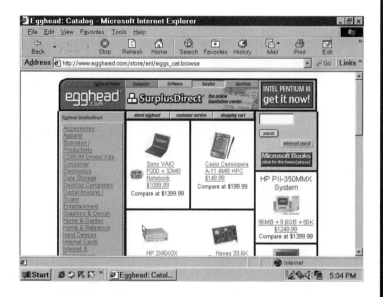

Egghead operates SurplusDirect (www.egghead.com/store/ ent/eggs_cat.browse), which is an online liquidation center for computers and software, as well as jewelry, luggage, home and garden products, and a variety of merchandise in other categories.

- Circuit City (www.circuitcity.com) currently uses its Web site just to provide information about the products it sells, and to point visitors to its physical stores. You can't buy online yet, but it's hard to imagine that it won't move in that direction soon.

- Micro Center (www.microcenter.com) calls itself "the computer department store." Its Web site points visitors to its chain of physical stores in 10 states across the United States. Like Circuit City, Micro Center does not yet sell directly online.

- In addition to being an online technology superstore, Necx (www.necx.com) also has an outlet center, mainly to sell "end of life, open boxed, and demonstration models." (See the figure below.)

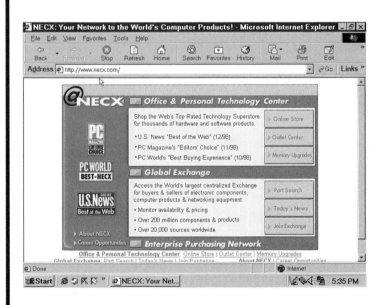

Necx is both an online technology superstore and an outlet center for liquidating out-dated, open-boxed, and demonstration computer items.

Necx also maintains a centralized exchange for buyers and sellers of electronic components and computer products, listing over 200 million items from over 20,000 sources.

- Computer Discount Warehouse (www.cdw.com) focuses on sales to businesses rather than individuals, as this site's slogan, "computing solutions built for business," indicates. That means that in addition to hardware and software, it also has a "solutions" section, and you will not find any articles or help geared for "newbies." But many of the products for sale here are the same as the ones you see at other computer superstores; if you have done your homework (or need the products for work at home), this online site may be a good place to look for a bargain.

- Buy.com (www.buy.com), shown in the figure on page 160, runs half a dozen online superstores, one of which (www.buycomp.com) focuses on computer hardware, and another of which (www.buysoft.com) sells software. Price comparisons by way of Pricescan often show products from here near the top of the list.

- Selling only software, Beyond.com (www.beyond.com) is set up to handle the needs of computer novices, as well as general shoppers. In the "Customer Service" section, you'll find a step-by-step guide on how to shop with Beyond.com, details on how to track your order, and information about hundreds of software publishers. The site also offers

IF YOU'RE SO
INCLINED

A wide variety of simple, inexpensive gadgets designed just to get you connected to the World Wide Web are just now becoming available. If accessing the Web is all you want to do, check out WebTV (which uses your television set instead of a monitor), and also take a look at televisions that have Web access built into them.

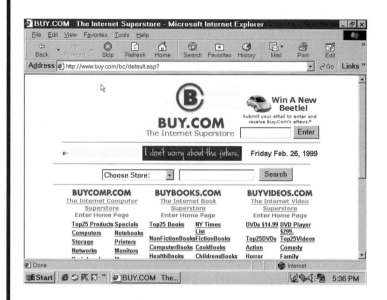

Buy.com (www.buy.com) has a section that sells computer hardware (www.buycomp.com) and a section that sells software (www.buysoft.com).

a recommendation guide and a gift center. While many software sites are set up just for techies, Beyond.com looks and feels like a superstore.

Chumbo.com (www.chumbo.com) also sells software in superstore style. It has a section that describes new games that have not yet been released but are likely to be in short supply when they do come out. Chumbo.com lets you preorder for shipment on release day.

Despite its name, Buysoftware.com (www. buysoftware.com) sells computers, accessories, peripherals, and training, in addition to software.

PC Connection (www.pcconnection.com), as shown in the figure on page 161, is a long-time mail-order catalog company, now using the Internet to sell the same technology products. The site has separate areas for clearance sales and auctions. PC Connection promises to deliver everything overnight, even when orders are placed as late as 2:45 a.m. EST. In addition to offering a 30-day money back guarantee on many of its products, this online store also offers technical support and operates a factory-authorized repair center.

▩ Value America (www.valueamerica.com) has the look and feel of a major department store, with one area of the store dedicated to selling computers. The site encourages visitors to "become members" at no cost. Members get discounts and

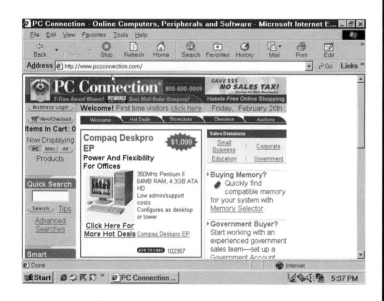

PC Connection (www.pcconnection.com) promises to deliver anything you order from them overnight, even if you place your order as late as 2:45 a.m. EST.

QUICK ⊙ PAINLESS

earn "ValueDollars" that can be spent on future purchases. ValueDollars represent at least 1 percent of an item's price, and they can be used for up to 50 percent of a future order. Also, if you are a member, Value America keeps receipts of your purchases on file as documentation for warranties and rebates. This site can track a shopper's important personal dates like anniversaries and birthdays by sending the shopper automatic reminders of those dates.

- iDOT.com (www.idot.com) calls itself "PCs for Smarties." The site has sections set up as Community Stores for "gamers," college students, and small business owners. The iDOT site also highlights low-cost machines in its "UnderGrand Store." You can sign up to get this site's free e-mail newsletter, and also to get early notification of upcoming product specials. Once you've picked a base computer model, you can "Go Configure" to put together a complete system. You can also use iDOT's configuration tool to select the right upgrade for your existing system.

- Insight (www.insight.com), as shown in the figure on page 163, bills itself as "your discount source for computers, hardware and software." It offers over 80,000 brand-name products at discount prices. Expect a no-frills approach, with special discounts available for business, education, and government customers.

- BuyersZone (www.buyerszone.com) is set up to serve the office needs of businesses. This site acts as an intermediary between buyers and vendors.

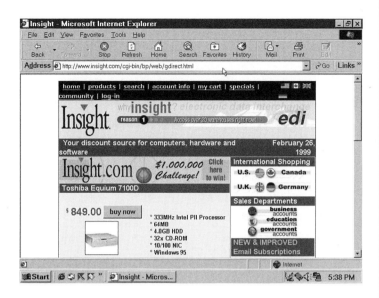

Insight (www.insight.com) considers itself to be the best discount source for complete computer systems, other hardware, and software.

BuyersZone has numerous categories, including computers, and provides online tools for you to "learn what you need to know before you go buying," compare products, and get quotes from vendors linked to this site.

- J&R (www.jandr.com) sells computers and software, as well as consumer electronics gear, music, and movies. Here you are buying systems "off the shelf," as is, rather than configuring them. But if what they have happens to be what you want, the price might be good, and you could buy it with a minimum of hassle.

- If you want commercially published game software for your PC, check out Game Lord (www.babbages.com) for reviews and demonstrations.

If and when you install a new operating system (such as Windows 95 or 98), you'll find that you need new driver software for your existing printer to work properly. Go to AltaVista (www.altavista.com), and enter in the query box the model name of the printer and the word driver (e.g., +bj200+driver*). You are likely to find the software you need at one of the pages near the top of your results list.

THE MAKERS AND SHAKERS

The computer retail business is incredibly competitive. Anybody can assemble a system from parts made by many different sources, not just companies that are known as computer manufacturers. Computer stores, too, can assemble and sell their own complete computer systems. Every time you pick up a computer magazine, you'll see advertisements from new sources selling complete computer systems.

For instance, just before Christmas 1998, a new company soared out of nowhere to grab a significant chunk of the PC market. emachines (www.e4me.com), as shown in the figure on page 165, currently sells new, fully equipped, powerful 300Mhz computer systems (including the monitor, 24X CD-ROM, 56K modem, 3+G hard drive, and 32 MB RAM) for less than $500—less than half the cost other competitors were selling comparable systems for at that time.

You might be reluctant to deal with a newcomer because of questions regarding reliability and support—will they be around if and when it breaks? But if the system is built from standard commodity pieces, any computer fix-it shop should be able deal with it, and third-party service contracts (such as those offered by some computer stores) should be able cover it. If you have any doubts about a particular company or system, ask for advice from the people you would normally turn to for fix-it help.

With prices dropping at that rate, don't be surprised if some of the old established computer system

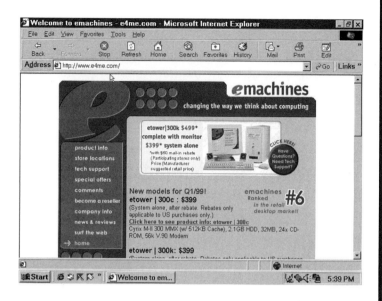

The online computer retailer emachines (www.e4me.com) sells new, fully equipped, powerful computer systems for as little as $500.

manufacturers with easily recognized names soon disappear. (I worked for Digital Equipment for 19 years. Ten years ago, Digital was the second largest computer company in the world. Today, Digital doesn't even exist anymore, having been swallowed up by Compaq.)

However, you should still check not just the online stores, but also the computer manufacturer Web sites, where you may find better special deals on select products. Also, the larger, Internet-savvy computer makers, like Dell and Gateway, are likely to have a wide range of products available directly through their Web sites. You may want to use their configuration tools, have them put together your dream system, and take advantage of their creative financing options.

QUICK ☜☞ PAINLESS

If you visit an online superstore and find an attractive system made by a company you know little about, you should definitely go to the manufacturer's Web site to do some additional checking before making your purchase. What else does this manufacturer offer? How does the company represent itself? How does it try to differentiate itself from competitors? Also, be sure to check how easily you will be able to get follow-up information and service, should you decide to buy a computer from this manufacturer.

Dell (www.dell.com), as shown in the figure on page 166, seems to be the current online computer sales leader, both in terms of volume of business and its Web site's ease of use. This PC manufacturer has a lease program that's available for individuals as well as businesses, with a calculator to figure out if leasing a PC is the right option for you. Dell has "employee purchase" agreements with corporations, schools, and federal agencies, so you might be able to get a special price on your personal purchase if you work at the right place. Dell also sells refurbished and guaranteed products at substantial discounts. You can buy online or call a toll-free number. Dell's advertisements appearing in magazines typically include an "E-Value" code that you can enter at Dell's Web site to take advantage of advertised offers.

Dell provides clear explanations of delivery time and shipping options so that you have a good understanding of what to expect when you purchase a PC. After you place an order for a computer with Dell, its online order status system lets you check continually to see what's

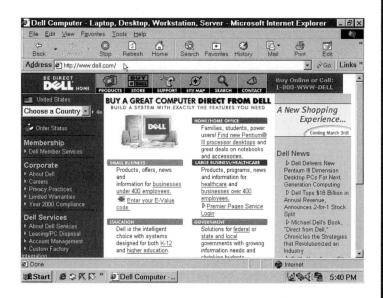

Dell (www.dell.com) is the current online computer sales leader.

happening with the custom computer they are assembling for you until the time you receive your PC.

If you click Dell's "contact" option, you'll see an extensive list of choices organized by the types of questions you might have, each of which has an e-mail address and phone number.

When you enter Dell's site, the choices you first see are arranged by how you might want to use their products. If you click on the Home option, then Dell displays a Web page that lists notebook computers, desktop PC systems, software, and accessories. Go another level deep into these nested options, and you will be able to pick a "recommended" configuration, or choose to build a PC customized to your needs. With Dell's configuration tool, you can select your basic PC style, and then add all the options you might want: processor speed, hard disk storage space, modem, amount of RAM, etc. With each selection, you will be able to see how each choice changes the computer's overall price.

If the components you choose might not work well together, the configurator displays a symbol to alert you to that possibility. Then, if you are an expert, you can research the details and make your own decision; or, if you are an ordinary shopper, you can select other components to remedy the problem. Once you put your choice in the "shopping cart," you also can click on Request Sales Help, and someone will—if you like—step you through your final purchasing steps to make sure what you are ordering matches what you want and need. No wonder Dell reportedly sells over $10 million worth of products per day over the Web.

Gateway (www.gateway.com), as shown in the figure on page 169, offers an option to trade in your PC after two years, and provides financing so you can pay monthly rather than all at once. This computer manufacturer has had a successful mail- and phone-order business before the dawn of the Web. Recently, they opened a nationwide chain of stores at which you can see, touch, and test the products you are interested in buying. (Gateway opened its physical stores at the same time that Egghead closed its stores.) Gateway also now makes good use of the Internet to provide technical support for its customers. Before the Web, if you called Gateway for technical support, you would most likely have to stay "on hold" for over two hours, waiting to talk to a support

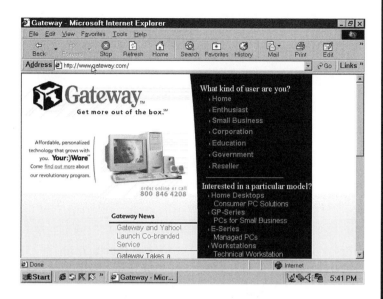

Gateway (www.gateway.com) lets you trade in your PC after two years for a new one.

person. (Oftentimes, you might not be lucky enough to get through to Gateway at all). Now you can get answers to many of your questions with quick searches through the Web site's Q&A section.

Because of competitive pressure, expect other computer makers, like those in the following listing, to imitate and improve the kinds of features and service that Dell and Gateway offer today.

- Compaq (www.compaq.com)
- Fujitsu (www.fujitsu-pc.com)
- Hewlett-Packard (www.hp.com)
- IBM (www.ibm.com)
- Micron Electronics (www.micronpc.com)
- microworkz (www.microworkz.com)

- Sony VAIO Direct (www.sony.com/vaiodirect-800)
- Toshiba (www.toshiba.com)
- WinBook (www.winbook.com/wbcommerce/index.htm)
- UMAX (www.umax.com)

For links to sites devoted to every imaginable computer-related specialty—from handheld computers, to storage devices, to internal components—check the lists at major directories such as Yahoo! (www.yahoo.com) and LookSmart (www.looksmart.com).

THINK SMALL

A new submarket recently emerged for palm-sized computers, dominated today by 3Com's PalmPilot. The PalmPilot comes with a docking station and infrared port, so you can synchronize your files with those on your desktop or notebook computer. And two of these gadgets can link with one another by way of their infrared ports to "exchange business cards."

PalmPilots have no keyboard. You input information using a touch screen that understands a shorthand code. You "scribble" what you want to remember with a pen-like device. The palm-sized computer later displays the information in a neat and readable font. It can even come with a modem, for connection to the Internet.

These machines don't replace desktop or notebook machines. They are so small that you carry one in your pocket and pull it out when you need it to check phone numbers, appointments, and reminders. Some people even use these little PCs to keep track of golf scores while

IF YOU'RE SO
INCLINED

Free-PC has joined forces with Compaq to offer free computers to "people who agree to share personal data about themselves and be exposed to Internet advertising." Consumers must agree to use the free computers at least 10 hours a month and allow the machine to download advertising that is displayed in a strip on the right side of its screen. For details, check www.free-pc.com.

Palm-sized PCs may be your next computer hardware "necessity." You can see details at www.palm.com.

on the course. These palm-sized PCs are yet another class of product that eventually you'll probably "need." For details on palm-sized PCs, visit the Web site www.palm. com, as shown in the figure above.

The popularity of palm-sized computers has fostered an entire range of specialized software and related gadgetry. If you are looking for palm PC-related products, you will usually find these items listed separately at computer superstores. PalmPilot Gear HQ (www.palmpilotgear.com), as shown in the figure on page 172, currently sells over 2,000 different software packages for PalmPilot machines. You can buy an expense report desk accessory, an aviator pocket reference, programs to keep track of your bank accounts, arcade-style games—there is an immense variety of applications.

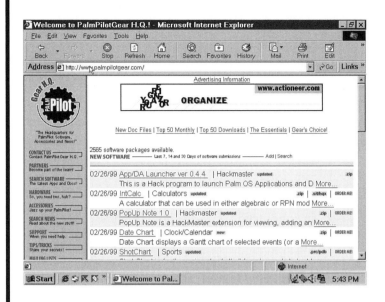

PalmPilot Gear HQ (www.palmpilotgear.com) currently sells over 2,000 different software packages for PalmPilot PCs.

GOING SOFT

Many of the online computer superstores previously mentioned in this chapter also sell software. Some online stores, like Beyond.com, even specialize in software. In addition, another set of sites operate as software download centers. The online stores sometimes give you a choice of buying software in tangible form (such as CD-ROM) or downloading it from their site. You could, in some cases, get the same products at either an online store or a download center, but the download centers cater to the folks who are more technically inclined and usually don't handle tangible media. With a software download site, you won't put your choices in a "shopping cart" and pay for your selection by credit card.

Instead, you immediately download to your computer a trial copy of the software you want to buy. After using the trial version of the software, if you decide you want to buy it, you then pay the software publisher through an online transaction. Typically, trial software versions have built-in time limits, which make the software fail to operate after 30 or 60 days, unless you either pay to license the software, obtain from the publisher a code to unlock the version in which the timer has expired, or get authorization to download a registered version.

You can also get what's known as "shareware," which is software you try out first and then pay for later, if you like the product. With shareware, your trial version won't time out, but it may come with limited functionality—just enough to whet your appetite and

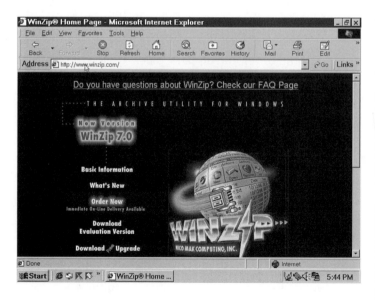

Award-winning products like WinZip (www.winzip.com) are available as "shareware" for download over the Internet.

make you want to buy the full-blown version. Or the version you download for free works very well indeed, but to get any future upgrades, you'll need to pay to register your copy. One fine example of this type of product is the award-winning WinZip file archiving utility (www.winzip.com), written and distributed by Nico Mak Computing, Inc., as shown in the figure on page 173.

Other software, called "freeware," is completely free. The authors of freeware write the software for the fun of it, for the general good of computer users, and for the chance to demonstrate their software writing skills. Often, the developers insist on having their names attached and restrict the software to noncommercial use, then retain the intellectual property rights while letting people freely copy the software. With terms like that, if the freeware turns out to have potential, then the author retains the right to turn it into a commercial product. Still other developers place their freeware in the public domain, and welcome others to develop improvements and create variations of the original freeware, with all the freeware developers working together as part of an online community.

You'll find try-it-before-you-buy-it software, shareware, and freeware at the same download sites.

Keep in mind that whenever you download software, you are at risk of bringing a virus into your computer, which could cause a nuisance, erase files, or completely disable your computer. Imagine your computer is about to have sex with another machine, and exercise appropriate precautionary measures. You are most likely—but never guaranteed—to be safe down-loading software from trusted sites. You should also have anti-virus software on your PC that automatically checks any new programs before you run them. Ideally, you would want antivirus software which automatically updates itself over the Internet as new viruses are dis-covered, like Norton AntiVirus from Symantec.

If you are new to downloading software, you should read the introductory article, Free (and Nearly Free) Stuff and Where to Get It, by Gail Shaffer. You can find this article at *PC Magazine's* Web site (www.zdnet.com/pcmag/pctech/download/best/index.html). (See the fig-ure below.)

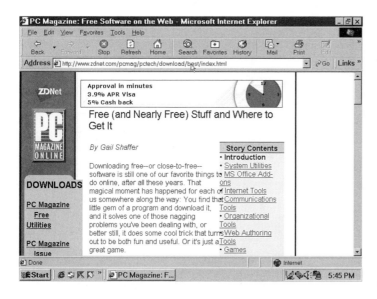

You can find the helpful article on software downloading, Free (and Nearly Free) Stuff and Where to Get It, by Gail Shaffer, at PC Magazine's Web site (www.zdnet.com/pcmag/pctech/download/best/index.html).

If you are interested in finding out what shareware and freeware is available in any particular category, use Softcrawler (www.softcrawler.com). (When you enter this URL, the site displays a page for you to first select your language selection.) This site searches simultaneously across eight major download sites. You just enter what type of software you are looking for and get a list of what's available from these sites:

- CNET's Shareware.com (www.shareware.com)
- CNET's Gamecenter.com (www.gamecenter.com)
- CNET's Download.com (www.download.com)
- Ziff-Davis' Software Library (www.zdnet.com/swlib)
- FreeWare32.com (www.FreeWare32.com)

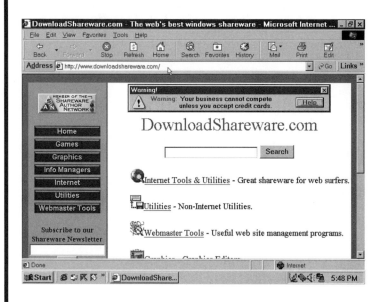

The shareware site DownloadShareware.com (www.downloadshareware.com) offers an enormous number of downloadable software programs for your selection.

- Albert's Ambry (www.alberts.com)
- FileMine (www.filemine.com)
- FilePile (www.filepile.com)

Also check DownloadShareware.com (www. downloadshareware.com), as shown in the figure on page 176, Tucows (www.tucows.com), and Newapps Software Archive (www.newapps.com), all of which have an enormous number of downloadable software programs available.

FOR THE ADVANCED COMPUTER BUYER: NEWSGROUPS, CLASSIFIEDS, AND AUCTIONS

Folks who are knowledgeable about computer hardware and software can find the best bargains in new and used computer gear through newsgroups, classified advertisement Web sites, sites that focus on used equipment, and auction sites.

The pricing of computers is based on rapid advances in technology, which lead to predictable improvements in computer speed. As a rule of thumb, a machine that's 18 months old should be worth only half what it originally sold for because you could buy one twice as fast for the same price today. One that's 3 years old should be about a quarter its original value. And many people with perfectly good equipment feel compelled to sell their old machines and buy new ones to run the latest and greatest new software. So if the computing tasks you want to accomplish do not require the latest and greatest

IF YOU'RE SO
INCLINED

You could save yourself some money by asking around the office or your neighborhood to see if you can find a friend, neighbor or relative who just upgraded to the latest and greatest computer and wants to unload his old one. Stick with someone you trust who can also help you as you get started.

computer hardware, and if you know enough about computer hardware to be confident about making purchasing decisions and evaluating used hardware, you could come up with some serious computer hardware bargains.

As you try to navigate your way through this difficult and complicated territory, turn to newsgroups and e-mail discussion lists for advice and tips, as well as announcements of items offered for sale.

As discussed in Chapter 2, there are literally thousands of computer-related newsgroups, each focused on a different area of interest. Go to DejaNews (www.dejanews.com), and search for items directly related to your computer and software shopping questions. Then get involved in that newsgroup's discussion, asking for help when you need it and providing help to others when you can. Similarly, check and become involved in e-mail discussions, a list of which you'll find at Liszt (www.liszt.com). Also, check the major classified sites, like Classified2000 (www.classified2000.com).

For used and refurbished equipment, consider the Advantage Computer Exchange (www.computerpricing.com), as shown in the figure on page 179. This site features both PC and Mac price indexes, which reflect nationally tracked used computer sales, indicating low (the average buyer's bid), high (the average seller's ask), and close (the average sales price) for every item. Computer Exchange also provides links to PC and Macintosh user groups. User groups are geographically centered organizations of computer users with common

YOU'LL THANK YOURSELF LATER

For information about computer-related flea markets that are held in the physical world, perhaps near where you live, check KGP Productions (www.pcshow.com).

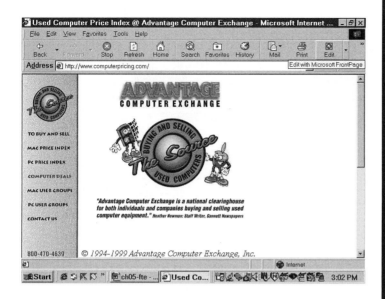

For the online leader of used and refurbished equipment, consider the Advantage Computer Exchange (www. computerpricing.com).

ongoing computer interests. These groups can be drawn together by a common hardware platform (PC or Macintosh) or by a particular software interest (for example, an operating system like Windows or UNIX), or a particular software application (like FrontPage, QuarkXpress, or Office). These user groups usually conduct physical meetings on a regular basis.)

Also consider the refurbished offerings of major computer companies like Dell and Compaq. Last summer, I bought a notebook computer for my daughter at Compaq Works (www.compaqworks.com), as shown in the figure on page 180, at an excellent price, with an extended warranty and service agreement. Some configurations and special deals are in short supply, and

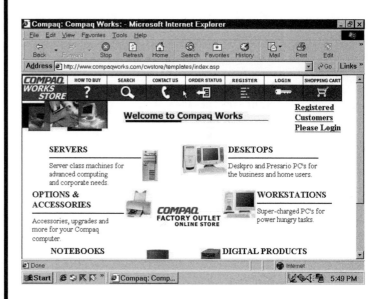

You can buy refurbished computers at a great savings from Compaq Works (www.compaqworks.com).

Compaq Works updates its offerings throughout the day. I found it best to check the listings online, then call Compaq Work's 800 number and talk to a knowledgeable salesperson who understood what each hardware package actually included. The salesperson may also know of other choices which have not yet appeared in the Web site listings, and may alert you to a better deal than the one about which you were inquiring.

The Boston Computer Exchange (www.bocoex.com) works primarily with companies that want to buy and sell excess inventory and idle assets. Continually checking with this Web site can result in a bargain or two.

Some computer auctions sites sell only new and refurbished equipment, and deal directly with you, the buyer. Each computer is offered for bid online for a certain length of time. When the specified bidding time has expired, the person with the highest bid is notified by e-mail and pays the company running the Web site by credit card. The auction site then ships the hardware.

In Spring 1994, the Internet Shopping Network (www.internet.net) was the first store to sell computer products directly to the public over the Web. After just a few months, Barry Diller, of Home Shopping Network fame, purchased the company. Today the Web site points visitors who are looking for a computer superstore to the Cyberian Outpost. But the Internet Shopping Network still sells computers and related gear auction-style at First Auction (www.firstauction.com). (See the figure below.) This auction site offers "flash auctions" throughout the day—auctions in which the bidding starts at just $1, and

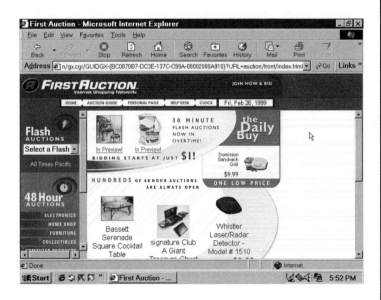

First Auction (www.firstauction.com) offers fast-paced "flash auctions" throughout the day, as well as slower-paced auctions for new computer hardware.

the total bidding time is less than 30 minutes. After the 30-minute bid time expires, the highest bidder gets the product offered through auction, and the merchandise is new, not used. First Auction also has less frantic 48-hour auctions, with a wider selection of goods for sale. If you are lucky, you might pick up a complete, well-equipped, new computer system for $200–$300.

Other auction sites of this kind include:

- Egghead Auctions (www.surplusauction.com)
- Onsale.com (www.onsale.com)
- Ubid.com (www.ubid.com)

Other auctions link up buyers and sellers of new, refurbished, or used equipment, like a dynamic version of classified ads. For instance, the Used Computer

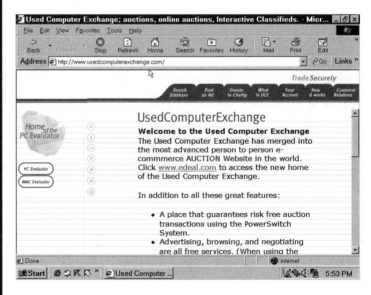

The Used Computer Exchange (www.usedcomputerexchange. com) runs an auction site that links sellers and buyers of used computer equipment.

Exchange (www.usedcomputerexchange.com), as shown in the figure on page 182, runs an auction site that links sellers and buyers of used computer equipment. This business is designed to foster the trust that is essential for them to succeed as liaisons between buyer and seller. The Used Computer Exchange can act as an auction agent to hold the buyer's money in trust while running diagnostics on the seller's computer. It also guarantees that sellers get their money, and the site carries a 30-day warranty on every computer that is sold.

Getting Time On Your Side

	The Old Way	The Lazy Way
Driving to and from the store	30 minutes	Not needed at all by doing it *The Lazy Way!*
Walking up and down aisles, reading prices and checking capabilities	30 minutes to consider the couple dozen products in stock	10 minute search covers hundreds or thousands of products
Waiting in line for a chance to talk to a salesperson	10 minutes	Not needed
Going to a second, a third, and a fourth store to check their prices for comparable systems	2–3 days	5 minutes, using a price-comparison site
Seeking out and talking to knowledge-able friends for advice	1–2 weeks	1–2 days, using newsgroups, chat rooms, and forums
Waiting in the checkout line	10 minutes	2 minutes (posting order)

Chapter
six

Buying Time:
Shopping For Travel

Are you planning a trip? If so, your plans trigger a set of related needs: transportation, a hotel room, maybe a rental car, and probably information about local entertainment and other activities. Because anyone shopping primarily for one kind of travel service is likely to need others as well, the companies providing these services tend to ally with one another (that is, when they don't directly compete).

In addition to wanting to catch your attention when you are thinking about travel, these companies have a lot in common. They sell time-contingent services, rather than products. The seats on planes, the rooms in hotels, the cars at the rental lots, even seats at a theater are all limited. You need to reserve the space in advance to be sure you'll have it when you need it. And if a given space is not taken for a given time slot, the vendor will get nothing for it.

A time slot is an asset before the time arrives. The value rises with the scarcity. Then once the time has passed, the asset simply disappears.

Hence the travel industry is subject to wild time-contingent shifts in supply and demand. The vendors would love to be able to change prices rapidly to take advantage of fierce competition for the last few seats, or to sell off remaining inventory with special offers before it becomes worthless.

"Travel" is a business model—the business of matching limited, time-dependent resources with customers (as opposed to businesses where the availability is unlimited, such as pay-per-view TV). The short-term car rental business has more in common with the airline business than with a car sales/lease business. The time-share condo business and the vacation home rental business have more in common with the hotel business than the buying and selling of real estate.

What matters is not the physical product, but how customers relate to the product in a time-limited way. The vendor sells the time slot, not the physical product. The vendor sells an intangible—"ownership of time," or "the experience of your life," whichever way you perceive it.

The Internet's ability to match remote buyers and sellers can help the vendors maximize their profits, while at the same time enable shoppers to find lower prices than they might ever before have imagined.

In the past, a major constraint on the ability of the market to operate efficiently was the difficulty involved in getting the right information and then making the necessary transactions. Especially with airlines, the information was so complex that only a limited set of trained specialists (travel agents) had access to the schedules and pricing of all vendors, along with the authority to make reservations and issue tickets. Now ordinary travel shoppers like you can access all that information in simple, easy-to-understand form, and can make reservations and buy tickets over the Web.

As more and more people realize that they have this direct power, travel agents need to redefine their role and provide services that today's travelers would be willing to pay them for providing.

At the same time, airlines and other travel service companies are scrambling to create alliances, including special package offers and interlocking reward programs. Such programs are aimed at repeat customers and tied in with efforts to balance demand (like seasonal pricing) to avoid empty seats and rooms. Travel agencies may take the packaging to another level, including deals with resorts and entertainment events—for the Super Bowl or DisneyWorld, or guided tours, or scuba diving, golfing, or skiing vacations.

With travel, rewards programs not only encourage customers to come back to the same vendor to accumulate points, they also create opportunities to create different classes of service. Your repeat patronage can earn you gold or platinum membership which qualifies you for special privileges and also insulates you from the common hassles and inconveniences of travel. With the right membership, you'll get first shot at the best seats or rooms, you'll get to board your airplane first, and you'll even earn more points each time you return than the

ordinary customer does. In the past, long lines, poor service at airports, and crowded coach compartments on planes might have prompted you to fly another airline the next time. Today, when airline conditions seem awful in general, the annoyances serve as an incentive to concentrate your travel on a single airline, or go out of your way to earn credits from their allies, and thereby earn the right to better service in the future.

As you enter into the world of online travel shopping, remember that every "deal" is also a temptation. Yes, if you planned to travel, shopping online can help you get the best prices, perhaps allow you to get the reservations you want at the time that you want, and arrive at your destination so armed with information that you needn't waste time on logistical nuisances. But by opening yourself up to all this information about opportunities you otherwise would never have heard of, you may well end up traveling more often and spending more (albeit more effectively) than ever before.

DO-IT-ALL TRAVEL SITES

Web sites that provide information and services related to one aspect of travel naturally expand, through alliances, to cover them all, bringing all your travel options to your attention at once. Today's major "do-it-all" travel Web sites include:

- Microsoft's Expedia Travel (expedia.msn.com)
- Travelocity (www.travelocity.com)
- Yahoo! Travel (travel.yahoo.com)

- Travelbase Internet Travel Planning (www.travelbase.com)
- The Trip.com (www.thetrip.com)
- Preview Travel (www.previewtravel.com)
- Travel.com (www.travel.com)
- Atevo (www.atevo.com)
- Flifo (www.flifo.com)
- TravelScape (www.travelscape.com)
- Travel Quest (www.travelquest.com)
- Internet Travel Network (www.itn.net)
- Biztravel.com (www.biztravel.com)
- 1travel.com (www.1travel.com)
- Travelzoo (www.travelzoo.com)

Let's take a look at what they have to offer.

When you enter Microsoft's Expedia Travel (expedia.msn.com), as shown in the figure on page 190, you are presented with three main choices: book a flight, reserve a room, or rent a car. To get full access to all of the site's features, you need to fill out a registration form, and get a username and password. Then you can search for flights by lowest published airfare or by preferred travel times and airline. If you sign up for "fare tracker," this site will send you e-mail messages about best price offers for specific trips that you are planning. Expedia's hotel lookup feature provides detailed information on over 38,000 hotels. The map area provides driving directions, as well as local maps. "Expedia Magazine" has travel-related articles. "Communicate" is an area where you

IF YOU'RE SO
INCLINED

Do you like ghost movies? If so, maybe you would like a night at a ghost-infested hotel. Check out the article "The Suite Hereafter" at Yahoo! Travel (travel.yahoo.com/Destinations/Activity/Cruises_and_Adventure_Tours/Paranormal_Phenomenon/).

With Microsoft's Expedia travel site (expedia.msn.com), you can book a flight, reserve a room, or rent a car.

can discuss matters of common interest with other travelers in forums (bulletin-board style) or live chat. The car rental section includes nine companies: Advantage, Alamo, Avis, Budget, Dollar, Hertz, National, Sears, and Thrifty.

In Expedia's "Vacation Shopping" area, you can check out "Vacation Packages," "Cruises," "Resorts," "Sports and Adventure," and "Special Deals." But these sections could use more content. There are only five resorts and eight cruise lines. And the section labeled "Trains, Buses, and Charters" actually has no buses, just Amtrak and AirCharterNet.

For information about local events and attractions, Expedia points you to Microsoft's Sidewalk City Guides (expedia.msn.com/daily/sidewalk). These sites cover

Boston, Denver, New York, San Francisco, Sydney, Chicago, Houston, San Diego, Seattle, Twin Cities, and Washington.

Travelocity (www.travelocity.com), as shown in the figure below, claims its site provides "access to more travel providers than any other Internet site." This site includes the flights of over 700 airlines (400 bookable online), 50 car rental companies, and 40,000 hotels. Travelocity processes your airline reservations through SABRE, the same system used by 40,000 travel agents. When you buy a ticket, you have three delivery choices: electronic ticket (you just have to show your ID at the airport), postal mail, or travel agent.

Keep in mind that each of these major travel sites will have its own "special deals" section, with some

IF YOU'RE SO *INCLINED*

Would you rather go by bus? Surprisingly, bus companies get short shrift or no shrift at all at travel-related Web sites. If you want to check this low-cost alternative, you can get a list of bus company Web sites at Yahoo! (dir.yahoo.com/Business_ and_Economy/Companies/ Transportation/Buses/ Bus_Lines).

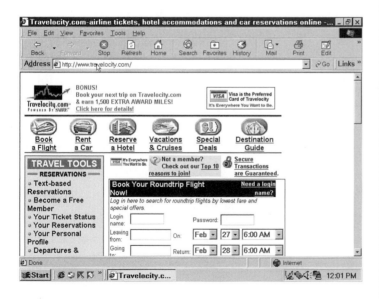

Travelocity (www.travelocity.com) claims to offer access to more travel providers than any other Internet site.

overlap. So if deals are what you are looking for, you should keep checking rather than latching on to the first one you see.

Travelocity also has a destination guide with details about all countries and major cities. This site's bed and breakfast section profiles 19,000 individual bed and breakfasts and inns in North America, and another 1,700 in the rest of the world. The listings call out "ski resorts" separately and provide details on dozens of them. Additionally, this site provides maps, weather, a currency converter, frequent traveler information, and seat maps for a dozen airlines.

Yahoo! Travel provides the same basic services (plane, rental car, and hotel search and bookings), but it looks like an excellent place to window-shop—to poke around for ideas when you know that you want to travel, but aren't sure where you want to go. Here you can search by "lifestyle," which includes business, family, lesbian/gay/bisexual, Jewish, naturalist/nudist, singles, seniors, special needs, women, and vegetarian. You can also research your trip by destination, including by country or activity of interest (arts and education, cruises and adventure tours, resorts, and sports and outdoors). You'll find tremendous variety here, from safaris to whale watching to paranormal phenomena. Here, too, you can join scheduled chats on travel topics or open-ended chat sessions, or participate in message boards (forums) organized by activities and interests, destinations, and lifestyles.

YOU'LL THANK YOURSELF LATER

Want to see some background on the travel company you are about to do business with? Then check the "scorecard" on 22 top travel sites at Gomez Advisors (www.gomezadvisors. com).

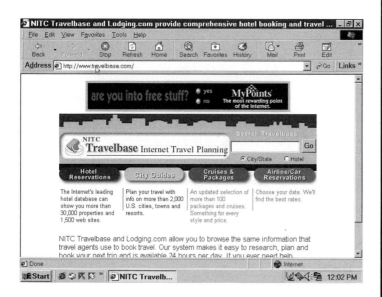

With the Travelbase Internet Travel Planning Web site
(www.travelbase.com), you can search or browse the database of 30,000 hotels, or obtain a password to access the
airline and car rental section.

Travelbase Internet Travel Planning (www.
travelbase.com), as shown in the figure above, lets you
search or browse through its database of 30,000 hotels,
1,500 of which have Web sites. You can click on a state
and then on a city or area, then select either only hotels
with Web sites or every local hotel. Some of the hotels
allow you to book online. This is a good place to check if
you want to see the Web site of a hotel but don't know
if it has one or what the Web address is. You need to sign
up and get an ID and password to use Travelbase's airline
and car rental system. This Web site also has a toll-free
phone number to call for help.

In addition to the usual do-it-all travel-site capabilities, Trip.com, as shown in the figure on page 195, has some very interesting guides and tools. For instance, with its "flight tracker," you can pick a particular flight that is now in the air and see its plotted course on a small-scale map, then view its current position over a large-scale map, and also see its present speed, heading, and altitude, together with the takeoff time and scheduled landing time. You can also request e-mail notification when a particular flight lands.

Trip.com's "airport guides" offer airport maps, regional maps, and terminal views for all major airports. You can sign up for "Trip.com," a free weekly e-mail newsletter with tips, trends, and deals, or for "Deals-2-U," which is e-mail notification of special low fares on routes in which you are interested.

A downloadable "world clock" makes it easy for you to display on your PC the current time at any cities of ongoing interest to you. For travel-related information and articles, you can check its online magazine, "The Complete Traveler," or Trip.com's "News and Community" section.

Preview Travel (www.previewtravel.com), as shown in the figure on page 196, claims to have over 6 million registered users, which is probably due in large part to its extensive destination guides. For each major destination, you can read about attractions and activities, accommodations, restaurants, when to go, arriving and departing, getting around, practical information, and

QUICK ⬤ PAINLESS

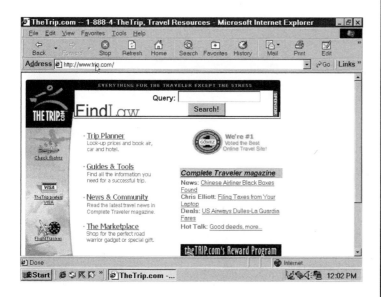

With Trip.com (www.trip.com), you can make all the usual travel arrangements offered by the site, and you can also track a particular airline flight and receive e-mail notification when the flight lands.

special interests. In addition, you can take a look at a photo gallery, a video clip gallery, and related vacation packages for each destination. Preview Travel also lets you create your own custom mini-guide, with selected portions of its online content packaged neatly for you to print out and take with you on the trip.

If you aren't sure where you want to go, you can use Preview Travel's "vacation finder" to help make up your mind. You can check a wide range of vacation and cruise packages by region.

Getting ready to go, you can check Preview Travel's packing list suggestions, for each of about a dozen categories of trips. If you want to buy any clothing or

Preview Travel (www.previewtravel.com) claims to have over 6 million registered users.

luggage online or toll-free by phone, you can do so from the site's TravelSmith store (travelsmith.previewtravel. com). Preview Travel's "business" travel section provides you with a different arrangement of the same underlying tools and options.

Are you getting a little overwhelmed with the wealth of possibilities? It's not over yet. Take a look at Travel.com (www.travel.com). There you'll find the usual 500 airlines, 33,000 hotels, 50 rental car companies, 3,000 bed and breakfasts, and miscellaneous cruises and vacations. But here, too, you'll find links to other travel-related Web sites, carefully arranged in 3,500 categories. You'll also find links to non-Microsoft guides to New York City, Las Vegas, Los Angeles, Chicago, and St. Louis. From this site, too, you can access the "discounted hotel inventory" provided by Hotel Reservation Network. And, of course, you can access maps, get e-mail notification of drops in airfares, and read an online travel magazine.

Atevo (www.atevo.com), as shown in the figure below, offers "content, community, and commerce," including the usual suspects (airlines, hotels, and destination information). This site's National Parks section, organized by state, provides a wealth of detail on U.S. parks. Atevo also makes it easy to interact with fellow travelers, offering you free personal Web space to set up as "Your Travel Page," in addition to the opportunity to participate in travel-related message boards (forums).

Flifo (www.flifo.com), as shown in the figure on page 198, has an international flavor. This site gives you a

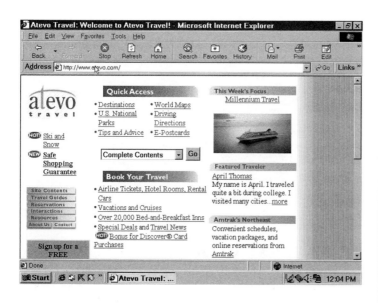

The Atevo travel Web site (www.atevo.com) has a National Parks section.

choice of having your tickets delivered in the United States, United Kingdom, Canada, or Australia. With this site, too, you can book flights, hotel rooms, and rental cars; but Flifo offers very little else—none of the usual destination information and related links. Flifo, however, does offer discounted rates on flights abroad.

TravelScape (www.travelscape.com) is a subsidiary of Las Vegas Reservation Systems, and has special relationships with hotels in that city, in addition to offering the typical do-it-all travel-site services. (See the figure on the top of page 199.)

Travel Quest (www.travelquest.com), as shown in the figure on the bottom of page 199, has all the usual services, plus a "Rail Services" section with links to Amtrak, to the train that links England and France through the

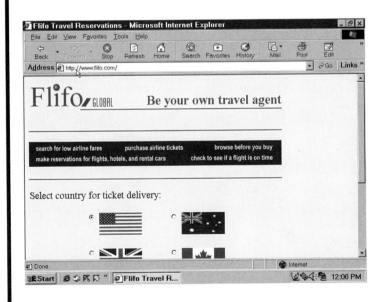

The Flifo travel Web site (www.flifo.com) has more of an international flavor than the other travel Web sites.

TravelScape (www.travelscape.com) is a subsidiary of Las Vegas Reservation Systems, and has a special relationship with hotels in that city.

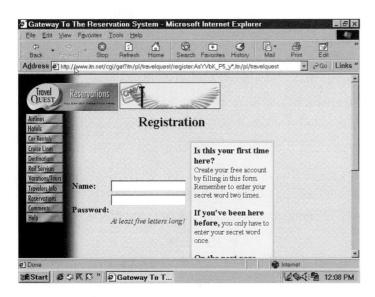

With the Travel Quest Web site (www.travelquest.com), you can access information on Amtrak, rail travel from England to France via the Chunnel, and other specialty train services.

Chunnel, and to specialty train services. Don't be intimidated by the registration form on the home page. If you are still window-shopping, just click on one of the choices in the left column, and you'll bypass the registration area.

The Internet Travel Network (www.itn.com), as shown in the figure on page 202, boasts over 4 million registered users. Along with vacation packages and deals, it offers travel guides to over 4,000 destinations, known as "Rough Guides." From there, you can choose "Rough Takes," which consists of biweekly updates on travel events and trends. Why does the Internet Travel Network get so many users when there are so many other sites providing similar services and information? By offering a variety of reservations systems designed both for large and small companies, employees can easily book travel arrangements and get the best corporate discounts. It also offers reservation services from other companies that operate networks of travel agencies. In addition, the network partners with non-travel companies that want to offer travel-booking services from their Web sites. If you run a Web site, just plug in their reservation services and you're in the travel business. Visitors to your site can book their flights and hotel rooms without leaving your site. Apparently, Uniglobe, CNN, and Ticketmaster all use this service.

The biztravel.com site (www.biztravel.com), as shown in the figure on page 201, acts as a do-it-all site for the frequent business traveler. This site helps you maximize your frequent flier miles and your credits in frequent "stayer" programs by guiding your choices in booking flights, hotels, and rental cars. It also helps you keep track of all your credits in those reward programs in one place. The "Cityinfo" section serves as a guide to hotels, restaurants, airports, weather, etc., in major U.S. and international cities. If you need to plan meetings, conferences, and shows, "Event Source" lets you search through a database of 9,000 meeting hotels and sites worldwide.

Biztravel.com's "Pager Alert" service lets you receive flight status, gate info, and weather conditions at your destination by e-mail delivered via any pager service that provides an e-mail interface. You can sign up to receive automatic upgrades from coach if and when you are eligible. You can also use its services to track flights in

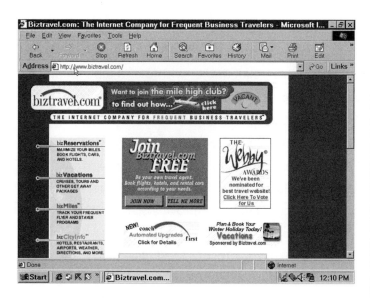

The biztravel.com travel site (www.biztravel.com) is the do-it-all site for the frequent business traveler.

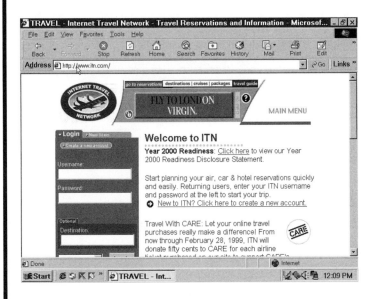

The Internet Travel Network (www.itn.com) boasts over 4 million registered users, as well as travel guides to over 4,000 destinations known as "Rough Guides."

route, plan a group event, find a trade show, charter a flight, and read world travel warnings. It also has a page of great travel-related links with useful descriptions. To access these travel-related links, click on the Other Valuable Sites option from the Biztravel home page.

More? Yes, don't stop now. The variety and richness of these sites is amazing. 1travel.com (www.1travel.com) provides a large collection of classified ads posted by travel agencies and travel providers. You'll be delighted at choices you never knew you had. Want to stay in a log home? Want a tour to the Seychelles Islands or to the Czech Republic? How about an Alaskan cruise or language study trip or a casino vacation? This site offers discounted fares on international reservations departing from 21 countries, from a database of over 3 million fares. They also offer special service if you are planning a multi-city (five or more) or multi-country (three or more) trip. (See the figure below.)

How would a newcomer ever hope to get a foothold in a market so remarkably well served as this one? When Travelzoo.com (www.travelzoo.com), as shown in the figure on page 204, launched its "do-it-all" travel site in April 1998, the Travelzoo management offered visitors part ownership in the company, just for visiting. As the company's senior management explains on the Web page www.travelzoo.com/story.htm, "Travelzoo.com soared in popularity this summer (of 1998) by adopting a unique, never-before-seen ownership concept. Netsurfers were invited to become co-owners of the

1travel.com (www.1travel.com) provides a large collection of classified ads posted by travel agencies and travel providers.

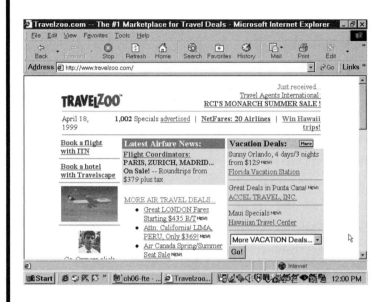

When Travelzoo.com (www.travelzoo.com) launched its "do-it-all" travel site in April 1998, the Travelzoo management offered visitors part ownership in the company, just for visiting.

Travelzoo.com site. Within three months, 700,000 people had signed up. And with that, the company's ownership goal was reached. As co-owners, these 700,000 netsurfers have an incentive to visit the site again and again, and to encourage others to do the same. This has led to a major boom in visitor traffic to Travelzoo.com. And as the number of hits increases, so do the advertising dollars the site can command."

ONLINE TRAVEL AGENCIES

The Internet is transforming the role of travel agents. With travelers able to do extensive research and book planes, hotels, and rental cars quickly and on their own, why use an agency? TravelHUB (www.travelhub.com), as shown in the figure below, answers, "Do you know that...airfare prices change daily? That great deal you found on your own today may be old news tomorrow! A difference of one day in departing or arriving dates can save you hundreds? Certified travel agencies will often work for you for FREE? Travel agencies often have first-hand experience with the places they recommend? Certified travel agencies have a lot more leverage than individuals when settling disputes with airlines and travel suppliers? You can have a team of 'insiders' working for you."

TravelHUB hosts a worldwide directory of travel agencies, categorized by specialty. The specialties include: airfare only, adventure, business, cruise,

TravelHUB (www.travelhub.com) is an online travel agency that promises you a team of "insiders" working to make your travel hassles easier.

ecotours, family, alternative lifestyle, handicap, seniors, singles, sports, student, specialty travel, and by geographic location. (If you want to travel in New Zealand, you might want to have a local agency plan the details for you.) TravelHUB provides the address and phone number of each agency, plus a link to the agency Web site and a button to click to bring up a form to request its services.

TravelHUB also brings together in one place the travel specials of over 500 travel agencies, and lets you sign up to receive daily travel-special alerts by e-mail.

In addition, TravelHUB purports to have the "largest online database of international discounted airfares (consolidator fares)." According to TravelHUB, consolidator fares are airline tickets purchased by airline wholesalers and resold to travel agencies at discounts of up to 70 percent off regular rates. Some of these fares are for charter flights, but most are with regular airlines. They recommend that you first check the latest deals on scheduled fares, then come here to see if you can do better with a consolidator rate. They also warn that cancellation fees for consolidator fares are high—up to 50 percent of the fare price—so make sure your plans are definite before buying tickets this way.

Uniglobe Travel (www.uniglobe.com) runs a retail travel franchise with 1,100 locations. (See the figure on page 207.) The Web site allows customers to book their own flights, pick vacation packages, etc., with the local agencies getting credit for the sale. Visitors can search for affiliated agencies in their area. Uniglobe also runs a

A COMPLETE WASTE OF TIME

The 3 Worst Things to Do When Traveling:

1. Forget your tickets.

2. Forget your passport.

3. Forget your 6-year-old and leave him home alone.

Uniglobe Travel (www.uniglobe.com) runs a retail travel franchise with over 1,100 locations, linked by this Web site.

proprietary intranet Web site, which links these agencies so that they can work together to assemble unique travel packages.

Some of the larger agency Web sites, like Global Online Travel (www.got.com), as shown in the figure on page 208, provide the same kinds of services as the do-it-all sites, letting you book your own flights, hotel rooms, and rental cars. But they focus on their special deals, vacations, and cruises; and they also provide phone numbers for you to talk directly with travel professionals, if you'd like. (Global is backed by Signature Travel Services, a chain of travel agencies.) The do-it-all sites list specials and packages, too, but with nowhere near the variety of choice that the agencies offer, and without the option of direct contact that the agencies are equipped to provide.

Traveler's Net (www.travelersnet.com), as shown in the figure on page 209, provides do-it-all site type resources, acts as an agency, and gives you a rebate on agency fees that it receives from travel providers. As explained at the site, "When you do the planning and furnish us with the information necessary to book your trip, we share the commission that is paid to us by travel suppliers." They have detailed tables showing you how much you get back on the purchase of airline tickets and vacation packages, based on the price. The sums are not princely, but this is "found money"—money back after you paid the best price you can find. Traveler's Net's lists of travel links (www.travelersnet.com/links) are also quite rich, and well worth exploring.

Global Online Travel (www.got.com) is a large travel agency Web site that concentrates on special deals, vacation packages, and cruises.

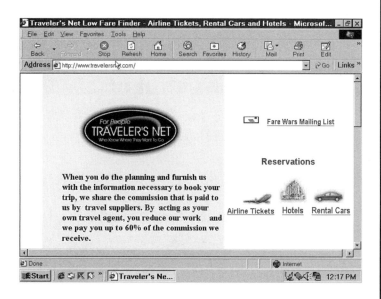

Travelers Net (www.travelersnet.com) is an online agency Web site with lists of travel links that are rich and well worth exploring.

Many agencies seem to focus on vacation travel, putting together a unique variety of packages in which they have worked out all the details and negotiated discount prices with all the vendors.

Bon Vivant (www.bvt-usa.com), as shown in the figure on the top of page 210, is a travel agency headquartered in Pennsylvania. It specializes in vacation packages and has a wide variety of offerings. For instance, under "exotic," you can choose among Africa, Galapagos Islands, and Antarctica. Under Africa, Bon Vivant has 16 safaris to choose from, and under Antarctica, you choose from among four different itineraries. Bon Vivant provides preferred discount rates at 12,000 hotels and inns.

Bon Vivant (www.bvt-usa.com) is an online travel agency that offers "exotic" vacation packages including ones to Africa, the Galapagos Islands, and Antarctica.

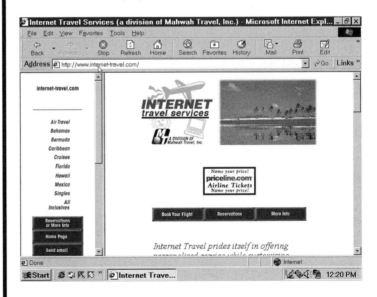

Internet Travel Services (www.internet-travel.com) is an online travel agency that specializes in "dream vacations" and "hassle-free business trips."

Internet Travel Services (www.internet-travel.com) as shown in the figure on the bottom of page 210, is an online travel agency that specializes in "dream vacations" and "hassle-free business trips." When you click on Air Travel, you connect with Priceline for airline tickets and hotel rooms. Major areas of this site focus on the Bahamas, Bermuda, the Caribbean, cruises, Florida, Hawaii, Mexico, and singles.

The Travel Network agency (www.travelnetworkinc.com) operates out of Florida and has a franchise business in 15 countries. The site includes cruises, honeymoons, packages and tours, and specials.

For escorted tours at discount rates, check Pennsylvania Travel (www.patravel.com). On its opening page, it is explained how the discounts work—basically, you get back part of what would have been booking commission.

For a two- to four-week European vacation based in "your own private apartment or house," check Untours (www.untours.com). (See the figure on the top of page 212.) According to the site, "Before your trip, our well-trained staff helps you select the right country, area, apartment, and length of stay, (and) reserves and purchases the most convenient and economical air and ground transportation.... Upon arrival our carefully-selected European staff meets you at the airport (standard group arrivals only), escorts you or gives you detailed self-escort directions to your apartment, invites you to a group orientation session to help you decide what to do during your stay and how to do it, hosts a

IF YOU'RE SO
INCLINED

Might you be interested in a train ride through South Africa on a steam locomotive? Check a site run by individuals who want to preserve the tradition of train travel in South Africa (www.ru.ac.za/departments/iwr/staff/daf/tt/timetabl.html).

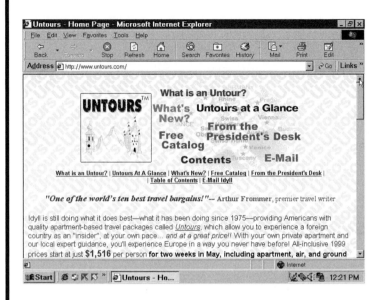

Untours - Home Page - Microsoft Internet Explorer

File   Edit   View   Favorites   Tools   Help

Back   Forward   Stop   Refresh   Home   Search   Favorites   History   Mail   Print   Edit

Address   http://www.untours.com/

What is an Untour?

UNTOURS™

What's New?   **Untours at a Glance**

Free Catalog   **From the President's Desk**

Contents   **E-Mail**

What is an Untour? | Untours At A Glance | What's New? | Free Catalog | From the President's Desk |
| Table of Contents | E-Mail Idyll

"One of the world's ten best travel bargains!" — Arthur Frommer, premier travel writer

Idyll is still doing what it does best—what it has been doing since 1975—providing Americans with quality apartment-based travel packages called *Untours*, which allow you to experience a foreign country as an "insider", at your own pace... *and at a great price!!* With your own private apartment and our local expert guidance, you'll experience Europe in a way you never have before! All-inclusive 1999 prices start at just **$1,516** per person **for two weeks in May, including apartment, air, and ground**

Internet

Start   Untours - Ho...   12:21 PM

For a two- to four-week European vacation based in "your own private apartment or house," check Untours (www.untours.com).

special group event..., and is available by telephone throughout your stay if you need additional assistance."

IS THE PRICE RIGHT?

Several large travel sites have tried to carve a niche for themselves in the area of low rates. Both Lowestfare.com (www.lowestfare.com) and Cheap Tickets (www. cheaptickets.com) focus on that end of the market.

Priceline (www.priceline.com), as shown in the figure on page 213, takes a unique approach to pricing. You post a request for air travel with them, indicating where you want to go and when and how much you are willing to pay. You guarantee your offer with a major credit card. Then Priceline seeks a seller willing to fill that

Want to plan some special nights out at restaurants during your vacation or business trip? Check DineNet Menus Online (www. menusonline.com) for a national restaurant directory, with full menus.

request. With Priceline, "there is no auction, no bidding and no back and forth. Simply name your price and let Priceline find a seller." Recent advertising blitzes by well-known personalities like William Shatner and Rush Limbaugh have made Priceline a well-known online travel service. Priceline has also recently added hotel rooms to its online offerings.

CHECK THE AIRLINES

Don't presume that you will always get the best deal from a travel do-it-all site or a travel agency site or even Priceline. If you are interested in air travel, check the airlines as well. They, too, have their specials; and many also give extra discounts or other benefits for buying your ticket online at their site. Some, like Continental and

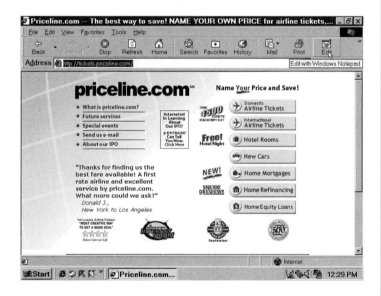

With Priceline.com (www.priceline.com), you name your own price for airline tickets and hotel rooms.

American, offer e-mail alerts of special deals. Many will let you check your frequent flier miles and cash them in for travel directly at their site. In addition, you can read at these sites all the complex rules about how you can use your miles, how you can earn bonus miles, and what kinds of added benefits you get from accumulating enough miles to become a higher class of travel citizen (e.g., Gold or Platinum). Also, the recent trend toward "ticketless" systems makes buying and changing tickets online far easier, since you don't need a physical printed ticket to board your plane.

Here are the addresses of the major U.S.-based airlines. You'll note that unlike most stores, where the address is basically the company name, these companies tend to have unexpected URLs that you probably couldn't guess.

- American Airlines (www.aa.com)
- Northwest Airlines (www.nwa.com)
- Continental Airlines (www.flycontinental.com)
- Delta Airlines (www.delta-air.com)
- Southwest Airlines (www.iflyswa.com)
- Trans World Airlines (www.twa.com)
- United Airlines (www.ual.com)
- US Airways (www.usairways.com)

To find the Web sites of other airlines, go to www.yahoo.com and enter "airlines" in the search form.

QUICK ⬤ PAINLESS

Need to phone home? Rent cellular and satellite phones, worldwide, at Action Cellular Rent-a-Phone (www.globalphone. net).

PLAYING THE INCENTIVE GAME

Frequent flier miles have become a kind of alternative currency. Hotels and car rental companies offer credit on airlines and visa versa. Businesses of all kinds make deals with airlines to offer frequent flier miles as an incentive to do business with them. You get offers for thousands of miles as a bonus for switching phone companies. You can sign up for credit cards that include a promotion whereby every dollar you spend is worth a frequent flier mile.

If you are a collector of frequent flier miles, then you can and should consider a few new reward programs linked to your online behavior. On the Internet, you can get credits which can be exchanged for

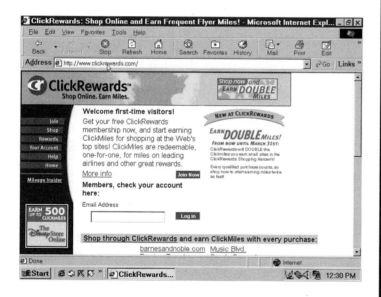

Sign up at ClickRewards (www.clickrewards.com), and get credits that you can exchange for frequent flyer miles by shopping at associated online stores.

frequent flier miles by signing up at ClickRewards (www. clickrewards.com), as shown in the figure on page 215, and shopping at associated online stores. You can also sign up at Bonus Mail (www.bonusmail.com) or My Points (www.mypoints.com) and earn rewards (exchangeable for frequent flier miles) for receiving and reacting to e-mail ads.

SITES THAT STRIVE TO DO ONE THING AND DO IT WELL

While the do-it-alls cover everything, some travel sites focus on particular niches based on the kind of activity, or characteristics of the traveler (such as age or occupation). For instance:

- The same company that produces Golf Travel Online (gto.com) and Ski Travel Online (skito.com), also plans to launch a travel site that focuses on "destinations" (www.destinations.com).

- New Choices (www.newchoices.com) focuses on people age 50 to retirement.

- Green Travel network (www.greentravel.com) provides adventure and "eco" travel packages.

There are literally thousands of such specialized travel-related Web sites. To explore further, check the links at such do-it-all sites as Travel.com and Travelernet.com, or go to LookSmart (www.looksmart. com) and click on Travel and Vacations.

ANY ROOM AT THE INN?

The do-it-all sites seem to have hotels well covered, with tens of thousands of listings and online bookings. But, especially if you are collecting frequent "stayer" credits with a particular chain, you should check that company's Web site to learn about their latest special deals. To learn their Web addresses, check Yahoo! (http://dir.yahoo.com/Business_and_Economy/Companies/Travel/Lodging/Hotels).

Also, there are a few hotel specialty sites that offer unique services. For instance,

▪ Hotel Wiz (www.hotelwiz.com) lists 43,000 properties worldwide and offers up to 40 percent discounts on 15,000 of them. It has an easy-to-use search engine, and allows online booking. It also provides hotel reviews.

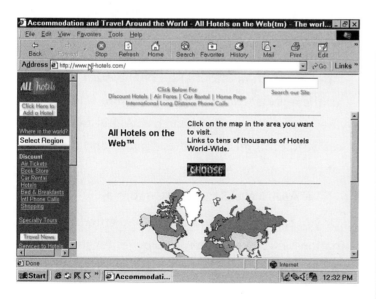

All Hotels (www.all-hotels.com) boasts links to virtually all the hotels on the Web.

IF YOU'RE SO
INCLINED

Would you like to see wildlife in its natural habitat? How about an excursion to Mongolia? Check World Wildlife Fund Travel (www.wwfus.org/travel).

- Hotel Express International (www.hoteldiscount.com/anglais/index3.htm) operates as a hotel discount club, offering 50 percent off on accommodations in 3,500 hotels in 72 countries. Membership currently costs $200 a year.

- All Hotels (www.all-hotels.com) boasts links to tens of thousands of hotels worldwide—virtually all the hotels on the Web. (See the figure on page 217.)

DON'T FORGET YOUR TRADITIONAL SOURCES

As you explore the new online travel resources, don't forget the companies you've often turned to in the past for similar services and information. With very few exceptions, you'll find them on the Web. Consider, for example:

- The large local branches of AAA Travel Services have their own Web sites, and some of them (like California at www.aaa-calif.com/travel/services.html) offer a wealth of information online, such as local traffic reports. Call your local branch to find out if they are online, or do a search at AltaVista (www.altavista.com) for AAA Travel Services and the name of your state, for example

    +"AAA Travel Services"+California

    Or you can go to www.aaa.com and enter the destination zip code to locate Web pages for the closest AAA office.

- Youth Hostels International (www.iyhf.org) can hook you up with hostels in any country.

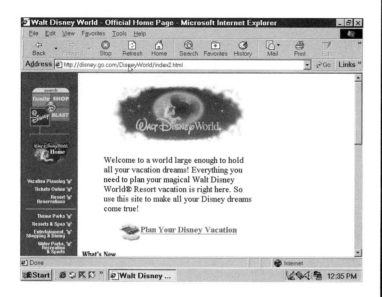

Walt Disney World has its own Web site at www. disneyworld.com, which provides all the information you would even need to plan a family vacation with Mickey and all his friends.

- Club Med (www.clubmed.com) provides info on all its resorts from a central site.
- Walt Disney World (www.disneyworld.com), as shown in the figure above, and Disneyland (www.disneyland.com) both offer special travel packages.

Also, consider the travel magazines, both the online versions of print ones and the new ones that have been exclusively created on the Web. For a list of these sites, go to LookSmart (www.looksmart.com), and click on Entertainment & Media, then News & Magazines, then Magazines by Subject, then Travel Magazines. Near the top of the list you'll see a hybrid magazine, *Epicurious*

Do you want to save postage on postcards? Go to Travel Preview (www.travelpreview.com) and send digital postcards for free from their site. The recipient gets e-mail saying to check a specific URL where they'll find the photo you chose, together with your personal message. To be wickedly lazy, send the postcards before you leave on your trip—take care of your social obligations quickly and easily, and then you can forget everyone but yourself while you're gone.

Epicurious Travel (travel.epicurious.com) is an online hybrid magazine with content taken from over half-dozen print publications like Conde Nast Traveler, Brides, Gourmet, Allure and Vogue.

Travel (travel.epicurious.com), as shown in the figure above. This is an online magazine with content gleaned from half a dozen print publications (*Conde Nast Traveler, Brides, Gourmet, Allure,* and *Vogue*). And if you are into exotic travel and love great photography, check the online version of National Geographic (www.nationalgeographic.com).

THE LAST WORD

While not technically a magazine, The Mining Company (www.miningco.com/travel) provides similar information and advice. Like a magazine, this site is supported by advertising, rather than by selling you travel services directly. Volunteer guides/experts scour the Web for interesting news and sites in their area of interest and share their findings with you in the form of articles and categorized lists of links. In their "Resources" section, you can find eco-tourism, travel with kids, United States National Parks, elegant resorts, etc. And in their "Vacations" section, you'll find backpacking, bicycling, birding, camping, canoeing/kayaking, cruises, fly-fishing, freshwater fishing, gold, honeymoons, hunting, power boating, sailing, saltwater fishing, skiing, spas, and theme parks. The approach here is direct and personal, rather than "corporate," and there are opportunities to share your thoughts and insights with other travelers.

Getting Time On Your Side

	The Old Way	The Lazy Way
Checking airline schedules	2 hours on the phone or half an hour at a travel agency	5 minutes
Finding the lowest fare	2 hours, and still not sure that there isn't a better deal	30 minutes to check for best deals at several major sites, or 5 minutes signing up at Priceline
Picking the right vacation resort for your family	Weeks gathering brochures and comparing sparse information and misleading photos	One day checking dozens or hundreds of resorts and related hotels
Getting hotel and rental car reservations	30 minutes on the phone, and you're not quite sure what you signed up for	5 minutes at a major travel Web site, with all your options made clear to you
Planning what you'll do once you get there	Buy 3 books (1 hour at physical book store), then take 2 weeks to read them, and only get info that's, at best, a year old.	5 hours, checking the latest info on all the local events, activities, and restaurants.

Chapter
seven

Bringing Home the Bacon, and Healthy Food, Too

The major online grocery supermarkets are set up to provide the most benefit to those who buy a lot of items at a time and return frequently. They offer convenience and time savings, at reasonable but not cut-rate prices. And, typically, delivery charges more than wipe out the savings from any "specials" unless your order is large enough to qualify for free delivery.

If you are the sort of person who doesn't put much value on time savings, uses lots of coupons, and goes to two or three different real-world grocery stores a week in order to chase the lowest prices, don't bother with the online supermarkets. Do it your way.

If there are gourmet treats that you crave for yourself or would like to buy as a gift, and that aren't available locally, check the online specialty food shops. Once again, you aren't likely to find bargains. A discount of 20 percent off doesn't mean much for relatively low-priced items if you then have to add shipping charges. But you might be able to quickly and conveniently purchase merchandise that otherwise would be very hard to find, except by catalog or while traveling.

GETTING STARTED: INDULGE YOURSELF WITH A GOURMET TREAT

An online shopping trip for hard-to-find foods would be a good way to get started. Once you've bought a few items of this kind, you will probably feel far more comfortable trying an online supermarket for your regular weekly groceries.

The International Gourmet's World of Cheese (www.igourmet.com) is an online specialty shop for the cheese lover.

For the cheese lover, consider International Gourmet's World of Cheese (www.igourmet.com), as shown in the figure on page 224. There you can sign up for the Cheese of the Month and get "a different, exciting world-class gourmet cheese at the beginning of every new month!" You can also order individual items, check cheese-related recipes, and chat with other cheese lovers.

For fresh or smoked seafood shipped overnight from Florida, check Shore to Door Seafood (www.shoretodoor.com), as seen in the figure on top of page 226. That's where you can find Atlantic salmon, swordfish, yellowfin tuna, etc. Shore to Door also offers almost every type of fresh seafood you could ever crave, from stone crab claws in season, to Gulf-fresh shrimp, to live Maine lobster. All items are shipped fresh to your door for a truly gourmet treat. What's your preference?

If you are more interested in health than taste, and if you are particularly concerned about the use of pesticides and other chemicals, you should take a look at the vegetables and fruits available from Diamond Organics (www.diamondorganics.com), shown in the figure on the bottom of page 226. There you can take a guided tour of the family farm, and meet the family as well as view the produce. To get started, you can order a variety of samplers for about $50, including overnight Federal Express delivery.

Do you crave the perfect cut of beef? Then consider specialty grocers Dean & Deluca (www.dean-deluca.com). At this Web site, you can find a 12-lb., bone-in rib

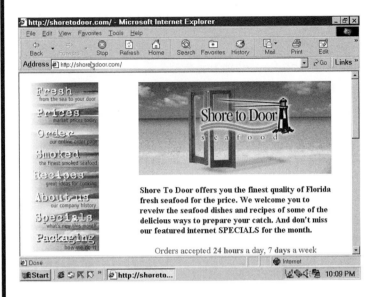

Florida's Shore to Door online seafood market sells ocean-fresh shrimp, crab, lobster, and even stone crab claws in season.

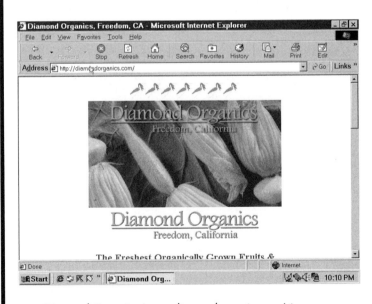

Diamond Organics (www.diamondorganics.com) is a family-owned farm featuring a variety of organic fruits and vegetables shipped fresh to your door.

roast for $150 or six 10-oz. filet mignon steaks for $80. (See the figure below.) You'll have to add on shipping, of course—$10 for standard 7–10 day delivery of that filet mignon and $30 for UPS next-day delivery. Dean & Deluca also offers caviar, smoked fish, cakes, pastries, fruits, and many other items. If you are a connoisseur of fine apples, perhaps you'd like their apple sampler (10-lb., 12 apples) for $45, plus shipping.

Are you just dying for goat cheese in oil or white truffles? Then try the "Delicacies" area at Balducci's (www.balducci.com), shown in the figure on page 228. You can also get canned anchovies in their "Specialties" area and a wide variety of homemade pastas and sauces in their "Pasta" section.

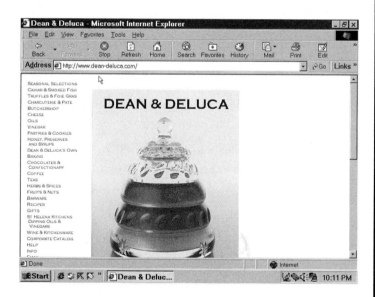

Dean & Deluca (www.dean-deluca.com) offers some of the finest cuts of beef, as well as hard-to-find olive oils and other specialty and ethnic foods.

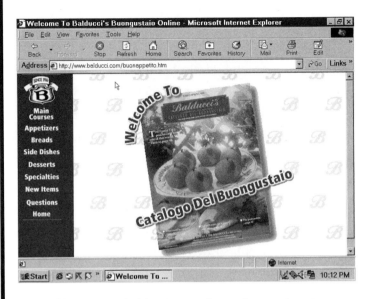

Balducci's (www.balducci.com) is known for a wide variety of homemade pastas and sauces.

In addition to pastas, Balducci's also offers completely prepared entrees, like rack of lamb or chateaubriand, ready to put into your oven and complete with the necessary instructions to finish cooking the entrée items. Buying ready-to-cook gourmet items changes the whole process for busy people who like to entertain.

For more exotic recipes, like potato-and-goat-cheese galette, check Cooking.com (www.cooking.com). This site provides complete cooking instructions, including steps and related details, as well as nutritional analysis. The figure on page 229 shows the recipe for White Chocolate Coeur a la Crème. Unfortunately, you'll have to shop for the ingredients elsewhere. While the site does sell some specialty foods, including pastas, herbs, salsas, and dips, these ingredients are not correlated with the recipes. Cooking.com's main line of products appears to be cookware, tableware, and cookbooks.

Frieda's (www.friedas.com) offers Asian and Latin produce, along with exotic fruits and nuts from around the world.

GreatFood.com (www.greatfood.com) lets you browse by category, brand, review, or meal occasion (such as "back packing, barbecue, beach party..., cocktail party). The figure on top of page 230 shows the results of a search for "beach party." This site also has a gift finder where your choices are arranged by price range, in case you'd like to send some Beluga caviar to your aunt in Poughkeepsie.

For herbal tea, including a Tea of the Month offer, visit Snowbound Herbals (www.sbherbals.com). This site's related products include herbal oils, salves, and massage

The cooking site Cooking.com (www.cooking.com) provides visitors with complete cooking instructions and nutritional information.

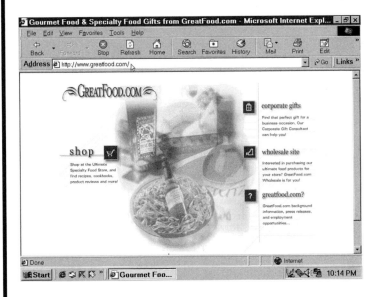

GreatFood.com's (www.greatfood.com) search capabilities let you search by special occasion, like beach party, and find all the items you'll need to buy from them to have a great time.

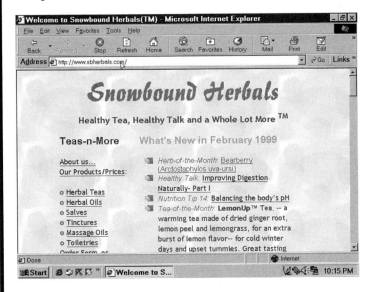

Snowbound Herbals offers not only tea, herbal and massage oils, and salves, but it also features articles on how to use these products.

SHOP ONLINE The Lazy Way

oils. (See the figure on the bottom of page 230.) Here you'll also find lots of articles related to herbs and teas and how they can benefit your health.

If you want to buy wine or beer online, keep in mind that all deliveries will require an adult signature. As they say at Virtual Vineyards (www.virtualvin.com), seen in the figure on page 232, "Someone of legal age must be at the shipping address during the day to sign for and accept the packages. Packages cannot be left without the signature of an adult." This procedure is intended to prevent minors from buying alcoholic beverages online, and is necessary to comply with state laws. Other online wine dealers include K&L Wine Merchants (www.klwines.com) and SendWine (www.sendwine.com), which are set up primarily to handle gift purchases and corporate or multiple orders.

To find an online store that offers the specialty that meets your individual taste, try going to Yahoo! (www.yahoo.com); in the query box on the opening page, type the name of the item you want. For instance, enter "Amish food" and then click on the first link, and you'll get three choices—one in Pennsylvania Dutch country and the other two in Illinois. Or enter "lobster" and click on the first link, and you'll get a list of dozens of suppliers. As an alternative route, you can go through the cascade of menus at Yahoo!, clicking first on Business and Economy, then Companies, then Food, and continue down whatever path strikes your fancy. To browse for gourmet, special food, wine, and beer stores at Looksmart (www.looksmart.com), click on Shopping, then Food & Wine.

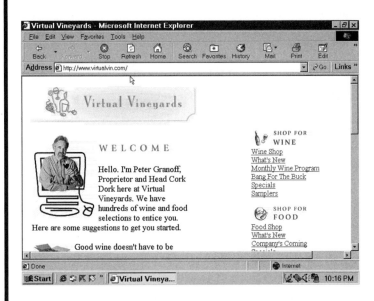

Virtual Vineyards (www.virtualvin.com) lets you search for your favorite but hard-to-find California Cabernet Sauvignon or Merlot.

BUYING YOUR WEEKLY GROCERIES

Why would you ever want to do your regular grocery shopping on the Internet? The store you always go to is only half a mile away, and you know where—aisle and shelf—to look for just about everything you are likely to buy. You could dash over there, fill up your cart with a week's worth of groceries, get through the checkout line, load the bags into your car, get home, and unpack everything in just an hour or two (depending on how crowded the store was and how long the lines were).

An hour or two? What else could you be doing with that time? And how often do you end up making quick trips to the store to pick up items you forgot the last time or things you ran out of unexpectedly? For me, it's about two or three times a week. Of course, those short trips don't take as long as the main one. But that does add up to a total of over three hours a week, every week (even when I'm on vacation!), just grocery shopping. And every time I walk into a supermarket, I end up coming out with more than what I intended to buy. I'm a sucker for well-packaged, well-placed, and well-priced impulse items.

What's the alternative? Shopping online, of course. Some Internet-based grocery services are nationwide and use shipping companies for delivery. But most are local or work in partnership with local supermarkets. Today, your choices will depend largely on where you happen to live.

The Grocery Shopping Network (www. groceryshopping.net/storelocator.htm), which recently merged with eGrocery, provides a service that helps

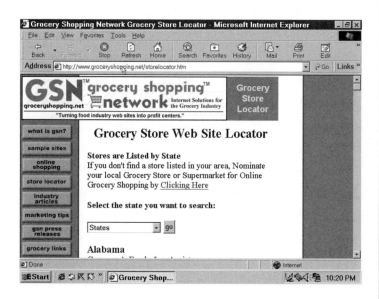

The Grocery Shopping Network (groceryshopping.net/ storelocator.htm) has a store locator to help your find a store near you that provides online grocery shopping.

existing grocery stores with physical sites to also do business online. With their store locator, shown in the figure on page 233, you can browse through a list of hundreds of stores, scattered across most states in the U.S.

Once these services reach volume, they are likely to thrive and spread rapidly. This business is tough. The vendors are ramping up for what should become a very lucrative market ($85 billion by 2007, according to articles at the Grocery Shopping Network). But at the moment, they all seem to be losing money. They need to attract enough customers to reach the volume that will make them profitable. In the meantime, if you are fortunate enough to have a local service, try using it immediately. These new companies are doing everything they can to attract and keep customers like you.

The online-only businesses buy food at wholesale prices, just like the local grocery stores do, but operate with far less overhead than physical stores, which have to invest in and maintain attractive store space and have higher payrolls, with cashiers and others involved in face-to-face customer interaction. Hence, online grocery service could become extremely profitable. But to reach volume, they need to induce ordinary people like you to change long ingrained grocery-buying habits. That's difficult, despite the promised convenience and time savings.

So expect the online supermarkets to keep coming up with new services and tempting special offers and discounts. Now is a great time to be an online consumer.

TODAY'S TOP CHOICES

Let's take a look at a few of today's services to give you an idea of what's available and what's typically involved. Remember, on the Internet, details change often. Check specific Web sites for the most up-to-date information.

- NetGrocer (www.netgrocer.com), as shown in the figure on page 236, delivers throughout the U.S. (except Alaska and Hawaii) by way of overnight delivery. Delivery takes two to four business days and costs $2.99 for orders under $50 and $4.99 for all orders over $50. However, this service doesn't provide fresh produce and meat—just packaged and canned goods.

- Peapod (www.peapod.com) works in partnership with supermarket chains—Jewell Osco in Chicago, Stop and Shop in Boston, Tom Thumb in Dallas, Safeway in San Francisco and San Jose, Randalls in Austin and Houston, and Kroger in Columbus. At its Web site, you enter your zip code to get specific information about terms in your area. Professional shoppers shop at a supermarket for you. The price you pay is what you would pay if you went to the store yourself (including in-store specials and redemption of coupons). Peapod offers next-day delivery ("in most cases") seven days a week, and you can choose a two-hour delivery slot that's convenient for you. There's a $7.50 delivery charge for orders under $60, no charge above that. To place your orders, you can use your Web browser, or with

IF YOU'RE SO
INCLINED

Some online stores offer enormous selection—more brands and sizes than you are likely to find in a typical supermarket. Just once, take the time to consider options you've never tried before, and add the good ones to your regular list.

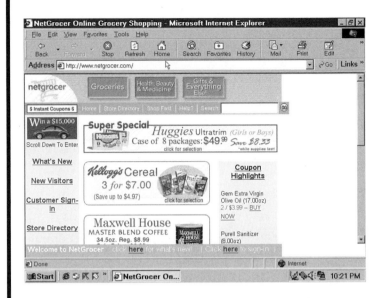

*NetGrocer (www.netgrocer.com) delivers groceries through-
out the United States, except in Alaska and Hawaii.*

Windows software you can download the catalog
from the Peapod site. This site acts more like a local
grocery shopping service than a regular online store.
Also, remember that this service is available only in
certain major metropolitan areas; but as the popularity of on-line grocery shopping increases, look for
this site's service to be expanded and similar services
to become available in yet uncovered areas.

Serving the Boston area, Hannaford's HomeRuns
(www.homeruns.com) purportedly charges prices
comparable to supermarkets, offers next-day delivery to homes in its service area, and has a double-
your-money-back guarantee on its products. The
minimum order is $30 with a delivery charge of $10.
There are no delivery fees for orders over $60.
HomeRuns sends out a printed catalog to customers

twice a year (the latest is 97 pages long, with over 5,000 items). You can order over the Internet or by fax or phone. The service charge is $5 to process phone and fax orders, but processing is free on the Web. (See the figure below.)

- Another Boston-area service, Groceries To Go (www.gtg.com), takes orders over the Internet and by fax. It experimented with home delivery (in partnership with a local milk company) and probably will again. But, for now, it delivers to the parking lots of large corporations at the end of the work day and has a central pickup facility. There is a $25 minimum order. Groceries To Go's online recipes ("Shop by Meal") are sorted by cuisine (e.g., Italian, Chinese, Mexican, etc.) and by preparation time.

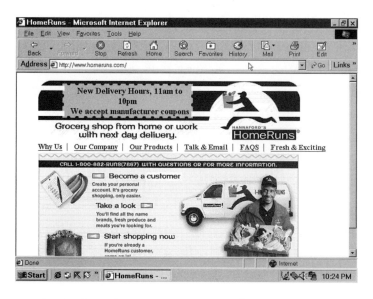

Serving Boston's area, HomeRuns (www.homeruns.com) sends out a printed catalog twice a year and will process your order for free on the Web.

Also serving the Greater Boston area, ShopLink (www.shoplink.com) not only does groceries, they also handle dry cleaning, video rentals, prepared foods, bottle and can redemption, shoe repair, and UPS shipping. ShopLink is trying to be your overall convenience service. Other online grocery services are on an ad hoc basis—come and shop when you want, and all you need is your browser. When you sign up for ShopLink, you get specialized software on a CD-ROM, and you pay them on a monthly basis. There are two service levels: $25/month for weekly delivery, and $39/month for weekly delivery plus one special delivery per month.

HOW TO FIND TOMORROW'S CHOICES

Complete grocery services—ones that will provide you fresh produce and meat along with everything else—tend to be local. To find one that could work for you, check your local shopping sites for links. Typically, this would be through your local newspaper, or at one of Microsoft's sidewalk sites (such as www.boston.sidewalk.com, as seen in the figure on the top of page 239.) And stay alert for ads in traditional media.

You can also check the major directories—LookSmart (www.looksmart.com), as shown in the figure on the bottom of page 239, and Yahoo!—and browse through their lists of food stores in hopes of finding one or more in your area.

IF YOU'RE SO INCLINED

Find and buy all the cookbooks you could ever imagine at Amazon.com, or at an online store that specializes in your favorite kind of food and style of cooking.

One of the Microsoft sidewalk sites, Boston.sidewalk.com (www.boston.sidewalk.com) can provide you with information about online grocery shopping in your area.

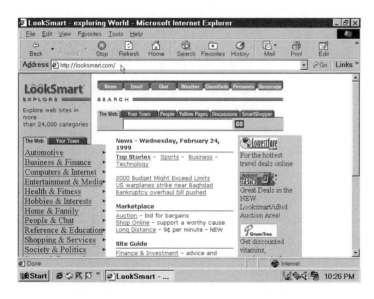

You can browse LookSmart's (www.looksmart.com) lists of online food stores to see whether one is operating in your area.

FINDING THE SERVICE THAT'S RIGHT FOR YOU

Select an online grocery service for convenience. The meaning of "convenience" depends on your lifestyle. While one service may be perfect for you, another might end up being more hassle than it's worth. If you don't find one that seems right for you today, check again in a couple months. New services are opening at a rapid rate. Look carefully at the details:

Delivery

- Delivery location (to your home or a pickup spot). If you live in an apartment or in a neighborhood where you don't feel comfortable leaving anything of value on the back doorstep, you might prefer to pick up your groceries at the parking lot at work or at a drop-off point that's on your way home.

- Delivery frequency (how many times a week). You need some items, like milk and bread, more than once a week. And you can't always foresee what you'll want a week in advance. If you can get deliveries two or three times a week, that will save you trips to the store.

- Delivery time (when during the day you can expect to receive the orders). You might prefer to get your deliveries in the morning before you leave for work, like the milkman and bread man in bygone days. Or you might prefer that the deliveries come shortly before you arrive home from work, so there would be less time for them to sit unattended as a temptation to curious neighborhood kids, or less time before you can put them in the refrigerator. Perhaps you might want to find a service that delivers in the evenings and on weekends.

- Lead time (how long in advance do you have to submit your order). With some stores you can submit your order the day before you want it. With others you have to give two days or more notice. In most cases, the shorter the lag time, the better.

Ease of Composing an Order

You've been buying groceries in supermarkets all your life and probably take for granted all the time-consuming steps involved. Now that you're shopping a totally new way, you'll be going through new steps that will feel awkward until you've repeated them often enough for them to become routine. That's when you will begin to see the real time savings.

You'll find that the different services, under the pressure of competition, tend to provide similar shopping experiences. Nearly all will provide you with a choice of ways to find the items you want. For instance, you should be able to search by generic names of foods and by brand name. You should also be able to browse through categorized lists of items. Choose a method that matches your way of thinking and remembering, and build your new routine around that. Given your style, you may find it particularly important to be able to:

- Type want you want in plain English and see what the service matches. Perhaps you'll be supplied with

YOU'LL THANK YOURSELF LATER

Consider the value of time saved—especially in mid-winter when the weather is horrendous and the traffic impossible, or in the fall and spring, when your kids are heavy into school activities and you just don't have time to go to the store. Or when you are just plain too tired.

QUICK ⬤ PAINLESS

Having easy access on-line to lists of what you have bought each week, you can see what you have spent and what you have spent it on, helping you to better plan and manage your money over extended periods of time.

information about serving size and price per serving, or with the pricing quickly translated to terms that are easy to compare (like price per pound) so you can make quick choices concerning brand and size.

- Access your previous orders and build a new order by editing them rather than starting from scratch.

- Select a recipe, indicate the number of servings, and see a list of what you would need to buy, in a form that's easy to add your order.

- Sort your choices by their fat content or other dietary factors.

ANOTHER SELECTION CRITERION: THE TYPES OF FOOD THEY CARRY

Do they offer fresh produce, or only canned and packaged foods? Much of the convenience of online shopping comes from getting everything or just about everything from a single service. Watch out if there's a category of food that the online services don't carry and that you need all the time. These are some good questions to ask:

- Do they offer fresh meat? Unless you are a vegetarian, that will be important.

- What happens to fresh meat and vegetables if I'm not home when they deliver? Perhaps you remember when the milkman deposited milk in an insulated box on your porch, usually before you got up in the morning, and you'd pop it in the refrigerator before you went to work. Today's grocery services will probably deliver perishables in throw-away insulated containers, packed with refrigerants, or they'll provide you with a large durable plastic cooler for you to keep on the porch. You'll have to decide if the temporary storage provided is appropriate for the kinds of foods you plan to buy and the length of time they are likely to sit before you bring them in. (If worried about theft, choose a service that lets you pick up your groceries or that can guarantee delivery at a time when you are home.)

- What about the quality of the selection? "I have no problem ordering canned and packaged goods— they are all the same," you say. "But I'm not about to trust a stranger to pick my meat or even my tomatoes." In fact, that's the first question I asked when my wife wanted to try one of these services. I simply couldn't imagine that a stranger could select fruit that was ripe but not too ripe, and good but low-cost cuts of meat. So as a test, I ordered peaches and top-round steak. The peaches arrived unbruised, firm, and juicy. The steak had little fat, was marked with a "buy by" date like at the supermarket, and tasted fine. Now I'm a believer.

Try it, and you'll like it—unless you are extremely difficult to please. Remember, these outfits desperately want to win and keep your business. The people they have selecting fresh food for you are likely to be far more selective than you are. Will the service level decline when these businesses reach volume? I don't think so. As

YOU'LL THANK YOURSELF LATER

You probably already have a to-do list on your computer. Now keep a grocery list, adding to it whenever you run out of something that you use regularly. That will make it a snap to compose your online order.

more people like you get used to online grocery shopping, you can expect all physical supermarkets to open online services. They'll need to for survival. And you can also expect lots of newcomers to the business, with much lower barriers to entry since they don't need to build fancy stores. That means you can expect to see lots of competition for the foreseeable future, and your satisfaction will be essential for their success.

MAKE UP YOUR MIND AND GO FOR IT

If you decide to grocery shop online and pick a service that works for you, stick with that service. For other kinds of shopping, it may make sense to hop from one online store to another, aiming for the best price. For regularly weekly groceries, the best strategy is to find one service that works for you and learn how to get the most out of it.

You might want to store-hop and comparison shop for specialty and gourmet items, but for your standard milk, bread, soda, snacks, meat, and vegetables—the foods that are on your shopping list week after week—stay put, unless the store has done something that undermines your loyalty. You have made an investment of time to figure out how their Web site works and learned to find and order the things that you want. Don't throw that away by trying out one service after another. Rather, learn to use one very well, and take advantage of all the convenience features.

Grocery shopping isn't a matter of buying one or even half a dozen items and lingering to make sure that each is "just right." Rather, you need dozens, perhaps even a hundred items every week. You are not a professional shopper. You have a life to live. You want to get this over with, quickly and efficiently. And because you will incur service and delivery charges if your order is below a minimum (typically around $60), there's not much to gain from item-by-item price comparisons from one store to another. In fact, being too choosy about prices will end up costing you not only time but money, since you'll have to pay for multiple deliveries.

GETTING OVER THE FIRST-TIME BLUES: COPING WITH ONLINE CATALOGS

The first time you try to place an order for a week's worth of groceries, you'll curse me. "What kind of nonsense is this?" you'll say. "What idiot put this catalog together? I don't think this way. I don't shop this way. I've been sitting here for over an hour, clicking from one blankety-blank list to another, and I still don't have my whole order in. Where's the convenience? Where's the time savings? I've been ripped off."

Actually, the experience is not that different from your first time through a new supermarket "superstore." You are faced with aisle after aisle after aisle, and nothing seems to be organized the way it was at the store you used to go to.

In both cases, there's a learning curve. It's far easier the second time. And eventually the organization of the store becomes part of the map of your mind, and you

QUICK ⊕ PAINLESS

At most online supermarket sites, you can see the total of your order as you go along by taking a look at your "shopping cart." That is the page that summarizes the choices you have made. At that page, you can easily delete or substitute products to stay within budget and see the adjustment to your total each time, rather than guessing as you typically have to do at your neighborhood store.

know without even thinking about it just where to find what.

Actually, an online store is likely be very systematic, following a strict hierarchy of categories. In contrast, a physical store is laid out for efficiency of the operation (such as placing refrigeration units next to the wall), and to tempt you with impulse items up front near the check-out counter.

But there is no getting around the fact that new-comers will find it tedious to fight their way through the online grocery catalogs. This is a major barrier, and the vendors are scrambling to find solutions.

For instance, NetGrocer lets you type in your shop-ping list, however is natural to you, and tries to auto-matically match what you've typed with what it has in its catalog.

HomeRuns prints its complete catalog and periodi-cally sends it to customers by snail-mail. They do that in part because their business isn't only on the Web—you can also phone (800 number) or fax. But the printed ver-sion of the catalog can come in handy for online shop-pers as well. The organization is the same as on the Web, and you can flip through and get a feel for the whole thing, rather than stepping through one Web page at a time. You can check off the items you want while on the train or subway to and from work, while waiting for an appointment, or during a boring meeting. Then, once you've made your choices, transferring the information to the Web is a breeze.

YOU'LL THANK YOURSELF LATER

It's going to take awhile to learn what's where, and how to click your way through to a com-pleted order. So make your first trial runs when you have time to spare—for instance, when you call for ser-vice and are put on hold, when you have to wait for a repair person to arrive, or while wait-ing for your 6-year-old to complete his video game and get ready for bed. Later, when you need to order groceries in a hurry, you'll be prepared.

GO BACK TO THE CORNER STORE OR LOCAL SUPERMARKET WHENEVER THAT MAKES SENSE

Remember, choosing to go online, you don't sign a contract. You don't make a vow to be forever virtual. Do what's natural and convenient in every instance.

If you suddenly run out of a couple items, like milk and bread, or you unexpectedly learn you'll be having guests for dinner, forget the Internet. Just pick up what you need at a local store.

The Internet makes sense for groceries:

- when you need to buy a lot of stuff, or

- when there are items you need repeatedly at regular intervals so you could set up a standing order.

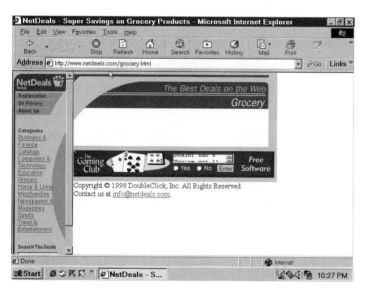

You can use the NetDeals Web site (www.netdeals.com/ grocery.html) to print coupons on your printer and then use them in local supermarkets that participate in the NetDeals program.

IF YOU'RE SO
INCLINED

If you really like to use coupons, CoolSavings (www.coolsavings.com), as shown in the figure on this page, offers coupons for retail locations other than grocery stores. Some of their deals are offered by K-mart, Kids "R" Us, and H&R Block.

CoolSavings (www.coolsavings.com) offers coupons for areas other than groceries.

Otherwise, the lead time from when you place the order to when it's delivered is simply too long to be convenient. (Remember, you are doing this for convenience, not just so you can brag to your neighbor that you are Internet-savvy.)

The exception is if and when there's a convenient pickup point (e.g., your company's parking lot) and your Internet grocer lets you pick up the same day you place your order. Eventually, that kind of service may be commonplace; it may take service like that to move large numbers of grocery shoppers to the Internet. But today, that kind of service is very rare.

USING THE INTERNET TO AVOID HAVING TO SHOP

Maybe you don't really need to shop today. Take a quick look at what you have in the refrigerator; maybe you could quickly combine those miscellaneous items into a tasty meal. Of course, you'd never be able to find the recipe in a cookbook because you would never know the name of it (or at least I wouldn't). So let the Internet perform a little magic for you.

Go to AltaVista Search and click on Advanced Search. In the top box, just type in an ingredient, like chocolate, for example. You can also enter a list of ingredients. Don't worry about punctuation—just enter the words. Then in the bottom box (the big one), enter the word

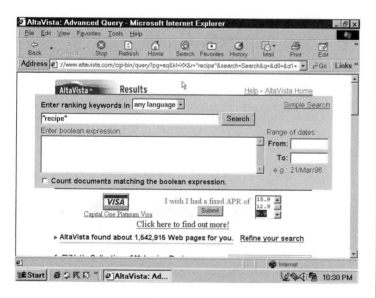

Using AltaVista's Advanced Search option, enter the word "recipe," and click Search to get a listing of Web pages that feature recipes.

QUICK ◖▥▸ PAINLESS

If you do have same-day delivery to a convenient pickup point, you can, from the office, prepare for the guests your spouse just invited to dinner. Just choose a recipe and let the online service calculate what you need and assemble the order for you.

"recipe" (without the quotes). (See the figure on page 249.) Click on Search. In a second or two you should see a list of Web pages that mention the word "recipe" and that also have those ingredients, with the pages that have all those ingredients at the top of the list. Click on the ones that look interesting. With a little luck, that could be your next meal—without your having to go to the store.

FUND-RAISING FOODS ON THE NET

If you are a community-oriented person, you may want to try a variety of high quality, mostly frozen foods sold by Market Day (www.marketday.com, seen in the figure below.) This shopping service is really a fund-raising

Market Day (www.marketday.com) offers high-quality, mostly frozen foods as a fund-raiser for private schools and similar organizations.

organization for private schools and other types of related organizations. Once a month, Market Day supplies a convenient four-page brochure from which you can make your selections. Market Day then delivers the ordered items by truck monthly to the school or organization using the food sales service as a fund-raiser. All foods offered are of restaurant quality, although some are packaged in larger-than-usual quantities. If you are not sure of a school or organization in your area that is part of the Market Day program, contact the Web site, and they will be able to locate the nearest member of their fund-raising network.

Getting Time On Your Side

	The Old Way	The Lazy Way
Travel	20 minutes	0 minutes
Picking week's groceries	1 hour	20 minutes
Checking out	10 minutes	0 minutes
Makeup trips to the store	1 hour, 30 minutes	30 minutes
Talking to folks you don't want to talk to	30 minutes	0 minutes
Exercising to shed pounds gained from eating impulse food	2 hours	0 hours

Money, Money, Money: Shopping for Banks, Loans, Insurance, and Investments

Shopping for money? Yes, indeed. Ten or 20 years ago that term would have sounded very strange—at least for ordinary folks like us. But today, if you don't shop for the best bank, the best loan rate, the best prices on insurance, the best retirement plan, the best way to reduce your income tax, and the best investments, you are throwing your money away.

The Internet offers hundreds of quality Web sites that deal with every aspect of your personal finances. If you are a fully functioning member of society (not in prison and not under age), you are almost certain to find information and advice on the Internet that can save you or gain you money—significant sums of money, not only for today, but for tomorrow and the next day, too.

When you are talking about money, having the right information or lacking it can make a huge difference in the amount you can save, gain, or lose. What you don't know about finance issues can cost you big time, both in the realm of personal finances and in the realm of investing.

Unless you are an expert investor, you most certainly can find new ways over the Internet to save or gain money that you've never before considered. Once you have tasted the fruit of knowledge regarding money, you must taste again and again and again. Your days of blissful ignorance will be over. You will not be able to rest until you have checked all likely sources of advice and information before making an important financial decision. You will read article after article, even when they are on the same subject because one article may have an unexpected detail that makes all the difference in your unique case.

It's no wonder that Web sites featuring financial information are multiplying like gerbils. One individual Internet user with an important pending financial decision might easily look at dozens, even hundreds, of screens a day. And people who use the Internet and get hooked on investing for gain will be tempted by the wildly fluctuating market, the ease of online trading, and the low online transaction fees to buy and sell, and buy and sell, over and over again. With the wildly increasing interest in online money activities, every online financial company is crazily fighting to gain every possible customer's attention and win that customer's loyalty.

As we take our online shopping tour of Web sites that relate to money, we'll first consider sites that focus on personal finances and teach you how to manage your money well. Then we'll look at those sites that focus on what you can do if you have money to spare and are anxious to get a piece of the fast-paced online investing action.

DOING THE MOST YOU CAN WITH THE MONEY YOU HAVE

Be forewarned that the online realm you are about to enter is enormous. Because there are so many Web sites that deal with managing personal finances, begin by scouting the online territory to get a sense of what type of information is available and how it might help you. To get you started in the right direction, first take a quick look at three sites designed for the beginner:

- Quicken.com (www.quicken.com): This site, produced by the makers of Quicken software, focuses on "Making the Most of Your Money." It has sections on investments, home and mortgage, insurance, taxes, banking and credit, small business, retirement, life events, saving and spending, and financial forums (for discussion of common concerns with other visitors).

- MoneyCentral, Family Finance (moneycentral.msn. com/family/home.asp): The family section of this Microsoft site deals mainly with "life events"— marriage, raising kids, coping with separation, caring for parents, saving, and selecting and paying for college. Other sections you can access off the main page (moneycentral.msn.com) include "Retirement and Wills," "Real Estate," "Smart Buying," "Investor," "Money and Banking," "Taxes," and "Insurance."

▨ The Mining Company Guide to Personal Finance (pfinance.miningco.com): This site features many informative money management articles and lots of links to related money management sites.

Quicken and MoneyCentral have a multitude of articles and "calculators"—online programs that help you figure out what money management considerations are best for you. These programs ask you questions about your personal financial situation, and, based on your

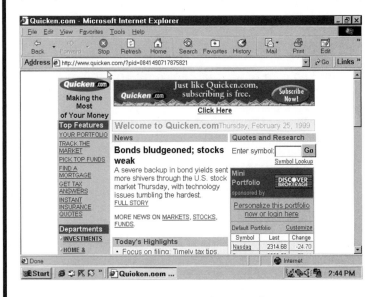

The Quicken Web site (www.quicken.com) features an important section called "Life Events," which can assist you in planning for important milestones you'll probably encounter.

responses, the program calculates the financial conse-quences and points you toward possible alternatives to your current approach. At Quicken, look especially at the section "Life Events," which is shown in the figure on page 256.

The Mining Company provides volunteer "guides" for each of hundreds of different subject areas on the Internet. These guides scour the Internet for information related to their subject, and provide helpful links and articles for their visitors. Personal finance is one of the subjects they handle extremely well.

When you enter the Mining Company's personal finance section, as shown in the figure on page 258, you'll notice that the Web site isn't as polished and flashy as the Quicken and MoneyCentral Web sites. But the articles and links you find there, as well as the site's opportunities for discussion with other online people in situations similar to yours, will probably prove more valuable to you in the long run.

When you visit the MoneyCentral Web site, check the "Banking" area (moneycentral.msn.com/banking/home.asp), and click on Manage Debt. In that unlikely place, you'll find several very helpful calculators. Of par-ticular interest is the calculator called the Instant Budget Maker, which you will find in the "Create a Budget" sec-tion, shown in the figure on page 259. Enter your family income and a few other facts, and you'll get back a detailed list of how much the average family like yours pays for housing, transportation, food, etc., based on federal statistics. Taking a look at what other families spend is a good, realistic way to start your budget.

IF YOU'RE SO
INCLINED

For fun ways to teach kids about money and invest-ments, check Kiplinger's Kid's and Money (www.kiplinger.com/kids) and also Kids' Money (pages.prodigy.com/kidsmoney).

Although not as polished and flashy as some personal finance Web sites, the Mining Company's personal finance section (pfinance.mimingco.com) has features that are an important part of personal money management.

If you have a pressing financial problem, first focus on that problem, of course. If, however, you are fairly worry free, approach the Internet's personal finance information with an open mind and explore finance-related Web pages links that grab your fancy. Keep an eye out for an unexpected financial benefit, a money choice you didn't know you had, or a piece of personal finance information that you had no idea was available. Take brief notes about each of these three introductory sites: what sections look interesting, what articles you might want to read, what calculators you might want to use. But don't try to read and do everything now on your first visit; otherwise, you'll never have time to familiarize yourself with all the other financial resources available on the Web.

When you have checked those first three recommended Web sites, you should next check out the advice at the following additional sites, similarly taking notes as you go:

- Cheapskate Monthly (www.cheapskatemonthly.com): At this online newsletter Web site, see the rapid debt repayment plan calculator, which is shown in the figure on page 260.

- The Dollar Stretcher (www.stretcher.com): Check this Web site for important weekly tips and advice.

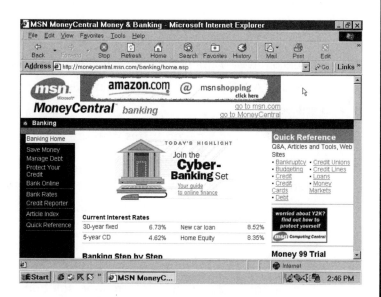

At the MoneyCentral Web site (moneycentral.msn.com/ banking/home.asp), you can start working on your own budget by trying the "Instant Budget Maker" online calculator.

The Cheapskate Monthly features a rapid debt repayment plan calculator.

- Kiplinger.com (www.kiplinger.com): When you visit this site, try "Ask Kiplinger" for common questions and answers.

- Money.com (www.money.com): This Web site is an online version of *Money* magazine.

- Financenter.com (www.financenter.com): At this Web site, you can find information about loans, credit lines, insurance, retirement, and budgeting.

Remember, in the Web's vastness, you no longer have to settle for a "one size fits all" information solution. You might very well spot a Web site that offers the perfect information for you. If you continue to research the lesser-known Web sites and follow uncommon links, you'll find that the potential savings and peace of mind are well worth your extra effort. So, don't stop with the most common and best-known sites. As you continue to see what financially related information is available on the Web, also scan the names of the sites linked to:

- Looksmart (www.looksmart.com): At this site, click Home and Family, then select Personal Finance. There you can choose among dozens of choices in the following categories: "Best of the Web," "Banks and Credit Unions," "Car Finance," "Credit and Debt," "Estate Planning," "Insurance," "Mortgages," "Retirement Planning," "Software," "Taxes," and "Tools and Calculators."

- Lycos (www.lycos.com/money): At the Lycos site, check out the "Life Events" section in particular, which includes tips on paying for college, taxes, buying a car, death, divorce, financial aid, kids, making a will, marriage, when you're just starting out, and worker's comp.

- Yahoo! Finance (quote.yahoo.com): At Yahoo!, you can get information about loans (credit reports, mortgage quotes, auto loan rates), insurance (quotes on auto, life, home, and renters insurance), and taxes (online tax filing, refund estimator, and tax organizer).

BANKING OVER THE INTERNET (A FEW OF THE MANY)

The Internet gives you an opportunity to take charge of your personal finances, in unique ways and with a

YOU'LL THANK YOURSELF LATER

You can also use the Web to get related information from the United States government in print form. Check the government site called Money (www.gsa.gov/staff/pa/cic/money.htm), which lists numerous free and cheap booklets about personal finance.

degree of control never before possible. With the wide range of online banking services now available, you can shop for the best financial services, compare options, and readily change services that you could not easily change before the advent of Web banking.

Today, nearly all traditional banks have Web sites. Some of these Web sites are simply online brochures, featuring only static marketing content. Increasingly, many bank Web sites now provide methods for customers to perform online tasks without having to visit a branch or make a phone call. With most bank Web sites, you can get account balance information, transfer money from one account to another within the same bank, and apply for loans and credit cards. You can have your salary automatically deposited in your account. And, with your permission, the bank can automatically deduct loan payments from your account. Some bank Web sites provide your account information in a form that you can directly download into your computer's personal finance software, like Quicken or Microsoft's Money.

Just keep in mind that a handful of banks insist that their customers use the highest available level of encryption security when accessing their files online. If that's the case for a bank that you want to use, you will need to download the "strong encryption" (128-bit) version of your favorite browser, as discussed in Chapter 1.

If you would like to find an online bank, the best place to start is to check out banks with branches in your area. You can search the Internet for Web sites of the local banks you know by name, often just by entering "www.name.com" in your browser's address window, where "name" is the actual name of the bank. Be sure to compare each bank's services and offers to find the best deals.

After you have checked the Internet for local banks with Web sites, you should also check the banking section at

MoneyCentral (moneycentral.msn.com/banking/home. asp) to compare the rates offered by various (but not all) online banks. You can also check the Security First Network Bank (www.sfnb.com)—the first bank to exist only on the Internet, operating without any physical branches. (See the figure below.)

The Security First Network Bank (www.sfnb.com) is the first bank to exist only on the Internet, without any physical branches.

Before you decide on an online bank, you should also check several banks that have gained a reputation for their use of the Internet:

- Wells Fargo (www.wellsfargo.com)
- Citibank (www.citibank.com)
- Bank of America (www.bankamerica.com)

Remember, you don't have to do all your banking with the same institution. One bank might offer you free checking and free ATM service. Another might have the lowest mortgage rates. Still another might pay the highest rates on IRAs. Check the lists later in this chapter for sites that provide you with advice, calculators, and price/rate comparison in such areas as loans and retirement.

BEWARE OF ONLINE BILL-PAYMENT SERVICES

When it comes to online banking, you need to be cautious about one important area. If you are tempted by a bank's online bill-paying service, take a very close look at the terms and details before you sign up. When you first consider online bill paying, it's natural to assume that when you enter an order for your bank to pay a bill, the bank pays the bill automatically, electronically, and instantaneously. However, some online bill-paying services hold your payment money for as long as two weeks, aggregating the payments made by you and others to the same business, and then sending paper checks by regular postal mail to pay all the bills at once. This method of bill paying can cause severe problems in potential past due bills.

I was stung by this very problem last year around Christmas time. Proud to be taking advantage of the latest technology, delighted not to have to pay for postage, and believing that I now could keep tight control on my checking account, maximizing the "float" available to me, I paid dozens of bills online. The next month, I got socked with dozens of late charges from those companies I had paid with such pride and satisfaction. My online bill-paying service had lumped my payments with those of other individuals using their service to pay the same debtors, and then issued paper checks to those debtors. With the slowness of Christmas mail, the paper checks arrived after the due dates. As a result of this situation, I wound up with late charges and a messy-looking credit record that took many phone calls and letters to correct.

As more and more people pay bills online, this "delay-to-pay" method used by some online banks is certain to change, making direct electronic payment to businesses of all kinds widely available. But until that time, watch out for services that just mail checks the old-fashioned way.

FRIENDS, ROMANS, BANKERS, LEND ME YOUR MONEY

Many financially related Web sites offer several different types of information. If you are looking for a competitive mortgage rate, check the do-it-all real estate sites discussed in Chapter 10. And when considering a loan, the more well-known personal finance sites discussed in this chapter also include loan-related information. But several other Web sites are dedicated to helping you determine your loan needs and provide you with advice on comparison shopping for the best rate and terms. Here is a list of suggested loan-related sites:

- GetSmart (www.getsmart.com): This site is a borrower's marketplace. For example, you can search through thousands of credit card offers to compare terms and conditions.

- MortgageAuction.com (www.mortgageauction.com): At this site, mortgage lenders can bid for your home loan business.

- E-loan (e-loan.com): With E-loan, you can search for lenders and rates. This site also features articles on loan information.

- Quicken.com Home and Mortgage (www.quicken.com/mortgage): This popular site offers several different loan calculators, as well as a good selection of loan-related articles. (See the figure on page 267.)

- QuickenMortgage (www.quickenmortgage.com): This site offers mortgage-shopping tools.

- MortgageQuotes (www.mortgagequotes.com): At this site, you can compare mortgage rates from over 1,000 lenders nationwide.

- Credit.com (www.credit.com): With Credit.com, you can search for credit cards and loans and apply for mortgages. The site also offers credit-related advice.

IF YOU'RE SO
INCLINED

Do you have children in college or nearing college age? Check the Financial Aid Calculators at the College Board (cbweb1. collegeboard.org/finaid/ fastud/html/fincalc/ fcintro.html). With this online calculator, you can quickly figure out how bad off you'll be once your children hit college age.

*At Quicken.com's Home and Mortgage (www.quicken.com/
mortgage), you can use several different loan calculators.*

- Priceline.com (www.priceline.com): This site offers a
"name-your-own-rate" service to help you find
mortgages.

The major credit card companies also have their own
Web sites. Here is a list of those sites:

- MasterCard (www.mastercard.com)

- Visa (www.visa.com)

- American Express (www.americanexpress.com)

- Discover Card (www.discovercard.com)

To check your personal credit reports, consider a
credit monitoring service like ConsumerInfo.com
(www.consumerinfo.com), as shown in the figure on
page 268, or go straight to the major credit rating companies. These sites typically charge a subscription fee for

To check your personal credit report, try ConsumerInfo.com
(www.consumerinfo.com).

their services, but they may offer free samples (e.g., 30 days).

Here is a list of the major credit rating companies:

- Experian (www.experian.com)
- Trans Union (www.tuc.com)
- Equifax (www.equifax.com)

INCOME TAX SURVIVAL KITS

How many times have you been in the midst of your last-minute tax calculations only to discover that you need some form that you don't have, or that you need to read some IRS booklet to figure out what you need to do next? Perhaps these needs finally drove you to pay for a tax book with lots of forms printed in the back or to hire a tax preparation service.

With the IRS's Web site, you can now print out tax forms and booklets provided directly from the Internal Revenue Service (www.irs.ustreas.gov), as shown in the figure on page 270. To be able to read and print IRS forms and booklets, you will need "Adobe Acrobat" software. If you don't have this plug-in, you can download it for free from the IRS site and follow the installation instructions.

In addition to the information provided at the IRS site, the following sites will provide you with tax advice and information. Another set of sites provides massive lists of links to sites with still more information—enough to meet every imaginable tax-related need. Some of these are maintained by companies, others just by knowledgeable individuals who scoured the Web for this kind of information for their own purposes and provide the lists of links for the benefit of all.

Additional Tax-Advice Sites

- Taxweb (www.taxweb.com): This site is a consumer-oriented source for federal, state, and local tax developments.
- Tax Analysts Online (www.tax.org): From this Web site, you can access worldwide tax-related news.
- MoneyCentral Taxes (moneycentral.msn.com/tax/home.asp): The MoneyCentral Taxes section offers several financial calculators and tax-related articles.

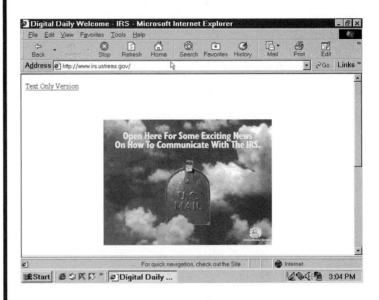

From the IRS site (www.irs.ustreas.gov), you can print tax forms and booklets with your printer.

- Warren Gorham & Lamont (www.wgl.com/tax/tax.html): This site offers information on all kinds of taxation issues.

- H&R Block (www.handrblock.com): The Web site is official site of the H&R Block tax preparation service.

Lists of Tax-Related Links

- Tax Resources (www.taxresources.com)

- Tax and Accounting Sites Directory (www.taxsites.com)

- Will Yancy's Home Page (www.willyancey.com/index.htm)

- Tax Resources on the Web/Alan G. Kalman Home Page (pages.prodigy.net/agkalman)

If you make good use of these online resources, you should be able to do your taxes yourself, or at least help your tax preparer by making better tax-related decisions and doing a better job of recording, documenting, and organizing information.

While you are gathering tax information, you might also consider buying a PC tax preparation program and filing your taxes online. If trying this approach appeals to you, consider

- Intuit's TurboTax (www.turbotax.com)
- Kiplinger's TaxCut (www.taxcut.com)
- SecureTax.com (www.securetax.com)

REDUCING THE RISK OF BUYING THE WRONG INSURANCE

In the past, you might have felt dependent on an insurance agent to provide you with advice on what you might need in the way of life, home, automobile, or health insurance. You might have felt a bit uncomfortable about how much you were paying, unsure as to whether you were overinsured or that the companies your agent represents don't offer the best rates. Now you can do some research on your own, and either use the facts as a new basis for negotiation with your agent or buy insurance directly from the insurance company.

The Internet's insurance-related Web sites can help you learn what your options are and also will provide comparative pricing information. Some of the best insurance information Web sites are:

QUICK ◖▪▪◗ PAINLESS

Considering buying some software to help manage your finances? Check the sites, which are suggested by LookSmart (www.looksmart.com). To see this site's list of recommendations, click on Family and Home, then select Personal Finance, and then select Software.

- Quicken InsureMarket (www.insuremarket.com): Quicken's "personal insurance service" offers real-time quotes, connection with agents, articles, and insurance-related calculators.

- Insweb (www.insweb.com): This site offers quotes, calculators, and articles on all insurance types so that you can comparison shop for the best deals.

- MoneyCentral Insurance (moneycentral.msn.com/insure/home.asp): MoneyCentral's insurance section offers insurance calculators and magazine-style articles.

- QuickQuote (www.quickquote.com): This Web site is an insurance-comparison system and purchasing service for term life insurance and annuities.

If you are considering doing business with a company you never heard of before, you might also want to check Weiss Ratings (www.weissratings.com), which is shown in the figure on page 273. This consumer-advocate site rates the financial strength of 16,000 institutions, many of which are insurance companies.

RETIREMENT PLANNING AND ADVICE

Increasingly, individuals are taking control over the investments being made with their retirement funds. Stocks and bonds and mutual funds aren't just for the rich. They are also for folks who have retired and depend on them for their only income. Hence, sooner or later, we'll all need to learn about investments, especially long-term ones.

QUICK  PAINLESS

Dynamically calculate your mortgage repayments at Kal Jeacle's Mortgage Calculator (www.jeacle. ie/mortgage). With this calculator, you can either type in your numbers or drag sliding bars with your mouse, and immediately see the impact of your choices shown in graphs and tables.

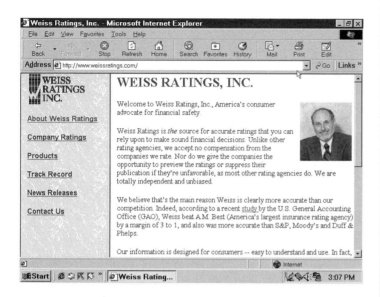

The Weiss Web (www.weissratings.com) site is a consumer-advocate site that provides the financial strength ratings of over 16,000 financially related institutions, mostly insurance companies.

Quickly, can you tell me the difference between a traditional IRA, a Roth IRA, a 401(k), etc.? If you have one of these plans, what investment funds should you select to maximize your return or to maximize your security?

To help you sort your way through these complex and changing issues on which your financial future depends, consider visiting these Web sites:

- New Choices (www.newchoices.com): This site offers advice for people from age 50 to retirement.

- The Mining Company (retireplan.miningco.com): The Mining Company's retirement planning section features retirement-related articles and links.

- Financial Engines (www.financialengines.com): This site provides advice for 401(k) plan participants.

- Social Security Online (www.ssa.gov): The Social Security online site provides information on all aspects of Social Security, Medicare, etc. (See the figure below.)

- Quicken.com (www.quicken.com/retirement): Quicken's retirement section features retirement-related articles.

- MoneyCentral Retirement (moneycentral.msn.com/retire/home.asp): The MoneyCentral Retirement section has retirement-related calculators and magazine-style articles.

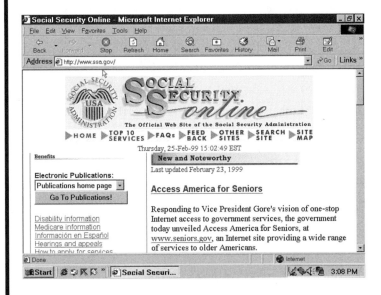

With the Social Security's online site (www.ssa.gov), you can easily find information on social security, Medicare, and other related government programs.

INVESTING FOR GAIN—IF YOU HAVE MONEY TO SPARE AND ARE WILLING TO RISK IT TO GET MORE

You'll find that it's a short step from shopping for the best loan and insurance rates to shopping for mutual funds for your retirement plan, and from there to dabbling in online trading. With online trading, what had been a game for the rich is now a game for the masses. If you try the online trading game, just be sure you are using money you have to spare, not the weekly food money. With online trading, there are no guarantees that you'll do well with your investments, even with the very best information and advice.

Win or lose, the online trading experience can become addictive, bordering closely on the realm of gambling. The ease of action, the real-time now-or-never thrill of catching a fleeting piece of information, and acting instantaneously bears little resemblance to the realm of carefully thought-out and slowly executed long-term investment.

Yes, with online trading, money is won and lost, but at lightning speed. And the online trading experience itself is likely to become an emotional one as well as a form of live entertainment, where the objective is not to earn money so much as it is to experience that winning sensation.

The Internet has a large number of high-quality online trading sites. This fact alone should give you a clue that lots of people hope to make money from your online trading activities. Remember that someone will

Take a break. Go to the Mining Company's Personal Finance section (pfinance.miningco. com) and click on Financial Funny Bones. At this location, you'll find links to five sites packed with money-related jokes.

The Lazy Way

Are you curious about a key personality at a company you are interested in investing in? Want to know what other businesses this person is involved in? Check www.edgar-online.com/people. This site is the best privately managed online source for information and documents recorded and maintained by the Securities and Exchange Commission (SEC).

win in the online trading experience, even if you don't, so proceed with caution as you trade online. Many of these sites are news-related because timely and accurate news is so important in the online trading game.

Investment Advice, Stock Prices, Information about Companies, and Financial News

Some sites provide a wide range of information from purportedly unbiased sources:

- Dow Jones Business Directory (bd.dowjones.com)
- Quicken.com (www.quicken.com)
- CBS MarketWatch (cbs.marketwatch.com)
- MoneyCentral Investor (investor.msn.com/home.asp)

Other sites provide a personal touch, with the unique perspective of individuals who have gained a reputation for "betting on the right horses":

- The Motley Fool (www.fool.com), as seen in the figure on page 277
- TheStreet.com (www.thestreet.com)
- Armchair Millionaire (www.armchairmillionaire.com)
- Financial Pipeline (www.finpipe.com)

The online versions of well-known magazines and newspapers provide another rich resource for finance-related news. In most cases, the current issues are available for free. At some sites, you have to pay a subscription fee to get full access to resources (including searching through back issues).

The Motley Fool (www.fool.com) is an investment-related site that promises "to educate, amuse, and enrich."

- *Wall Street Journal* (www.wsj.com)

- *Smart Money* (www.dowjones.com/smart)

- *Barron's Online* (www.barrons.com)

- *New York Times* (www.nytimes.com)

- *USA Today Money* (www.usatoday.com/money)

- *Financial Planning* (www.fponline.com)

- *Newsweek* (www.newsweek.com)

- *Fortune* (www.fortune.com)

- *Business Week* (www.businessweek.com)

- *Forbes* (www.forbes.com)

- *Mutual Funds Online* (www.mfmag.com)

- *Online Investor* (www.onlineinvestor.com)

Some people prefer not to have to look for news, but would rather have news directly delivered to them, in real time. If that's your style, go to PointCast (www.pointcast.com) and download the site's software. PointCast replaces your screen saver and continuously delivers the latest headline news to your PC, so long as you remain connected to the Internet.

You can also subscribe to personalized news services (for free or for a fee), which provide you with pre-filtered feeds of the kinds of news you say you want.

- Newshound (from Knight Ridder) (www.newshound.com)
- NewsEdge (formerly Individual, Inc.) (www.newsedge.com)
- PointCast (www.pointcast.com)

Some of the hottest stocks today fall into the "Internet" or ".com" category. Several sites focus on that set of companies and related trends.

- The Internet Stock Report (www.isdex.com)
- Internet World (www.iw.com)
- NewsLinx (www.newslinx.com)

Some sites focus on global economic trends and how they are likely to affect markets:

- The World Bank (www.worldbank.org)
- The Economist (www.economist.com)
- Financial Times (www.ft.com)

The major stock exchanges also have their own sites, with a variety of information related to the markets they serve.

- American Stock Exchange (www.amex.com)
- NASDAQ-Amex (www.nasdaq-amex.com)
- New York Stock Exchange (www.nyse.com, as seen in the figure on page 279)

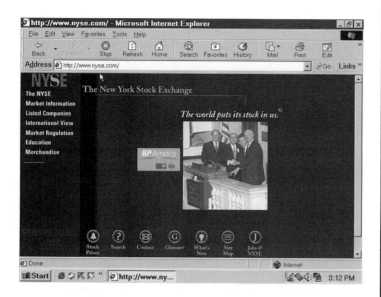

The New York Stock Exchange's Web site (www.nyse.com) offers an online version of the famous stock exchange's excitement.

- Boston Stock Exchange (www.bostonstock.com)

- Chicago Board Options Exchange (www.cboe.com)

- Chicago Stock Exchange (www.chicagostockex.com)

- Chicago Mercantile (www.cme.com)

- Pacific Exchange (www.pacificex.com)

- Philadelphia Stock Exchange (www.phlx.com)

In addition, an enormous variety of sites take unique approaches that, depending on your individual circumstances, could prove very valuable to you:

- Invest-o-rama (www.investorama.com): This site is an online directory of investing sites, and also provides tools for investors.

You just heard about a "hot" Internet stock. To get the company's domain name, go to AltaVista and enter into the search window the query:

host:domainname.com

to see how well indexed the company's pages are, and how easy they are to find. Then enter

+host:domainname.com - link:domainname.com

to see how many other Web sites think highly enough of that company to link to it.

- The Investment FAQ (www.invest-faq.com): Investment FAQ provides answers to common investment-related questions.

- The Young Investor (from Liberty Financial) (www.younginvestor.com): This site offers financial training for kids, including financially related games.

- Gomez Advisors (www.gomezadvisors.com): This site features investment news and personal financial advice.

- Quote.com (www.quote.com): Quote.com offers quotes, news, research data, and advice.

- StockMaster (www.stockmaster.com): This site provides quotes, research data, and investment advice.

- Yahoo! Finance (quote.yahoo.com): This site offers quotes and links to finance-related resources, as well as message boards, stock chat, net events, and finance clubs.

- Hotbot (www.hotbot.com): At this site, go to the "Manage Your Money" section and click on Finance to get stock information and prices.

- AltaVista Finance (www.altavista.com): At the AltaVista Finance site, click Stock Quotes for current trading prices and information.

- Go Money (money.go.com): This site offers quotes and investment news.

- Edgar (www.edgar-online.com): This site features filings submitted to the Securities and Exchange Commission and information about every publicly traded company in the United States.

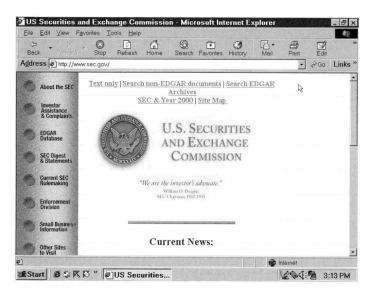

The U.S. Securities and Exchange Commission has an online site at www.sec.gov.

- U.S. Securities and Exchange Commission (www.sec.gov): At this site, you can file complaints. (See the figure above.)

- FinanceWise (www.financewise.com): This search engine focuses on Web sites and links to the entire financial world.

- The Syndicate (www.moneypages.com): This site offers financial news and advice.

- NVST.com's Private Equity Network (www.nvst.com): This site provides information on mergers and acquisitions, as well as venture capital.

Online Trading

If and when you are ready to begin trading, you should check the top trading online companies, each of which offers their members a variety of information resources along with the ability to buy and sell rapidly, at low cost, over the Web.

- Ameritrade (www.ameritrade.com)

- BEST Direct (www.pfgbest.com): This site features information on commodity futures.

- Charles Schwab (www.schwab.com), as seen in the figure below

- Datek Online (www.datek.com)

- Discover Brokerage (www.discoverbrokerage.com)

- DLJdirect (www.dljdirect.com)

- E*Trade (www.etrade.com)

- Fidelity Investments (www.fidelity.com)

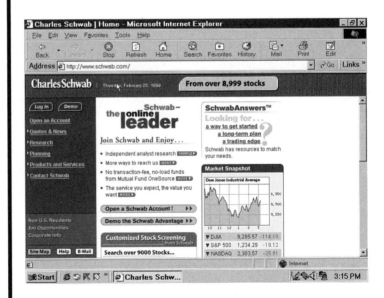

At the Charles Schwab online Web site (www.schwab.com), you can buy and sell stocks, as well as get important trading advice.

- Quick & Reilly (www.quick-reilly.com)
- SiebertNet (www.siebertnet.com)
- Waterhouse Securities (www.waterhouse.com)

Before diving in, you should check an excellent tutorial, The Gomez Advisors Investor's On-Ramp, an "online investing primer." This series of files begins at www.quote.com/gomez/content/step1.htm and covers opening an account, researching a stock, entering your order, and reviewing your account.

Also, keep in mind that online trading involves rapid-fire action, and you don't want your gun to jam just when you "see the whites of their eyes." When evaluating online trading companies, carefully consider their reputation for allowing their customers access during busy times. The information might be great, the look and feel of the site just what you want, and the transaction fees amazingly low. But when the market goes crazy, the traffic to that site will go crazy, too, and that's when you absolutely positively need to be able to connect. The top companies appear to do this very well, in most circumstances. Beware of the newcomer who looks good on the surface, but may not yet be equipped for crisis mode. You don't want to get locked out due to a traffic problem at the very moment you have to buy or sell.

Full-Service Brokers and Money Management Companies

Depending on your time frame and how much money you have to invest, you may also want to consider the

traditional full-service brokers and money management companies, all of which also have a presence on the Web.

- Merrill Lynch (www.merrilllynch.com)

- Morgan Stanley Dean Witter: (www.ms.com)

- Paine Webber (www.painewebber.com)

- Salomon Smith Barney (www.smithbarney.com)

WHAT'S GOING ON? WHY IS ALL THIS GREAT INFO AVAILABLE FOR FREE? WILL IT CONTINUE?

When you realize how much excellent information is available for free at finance-related Web sites—information that used to be closely held for members only, or sold at a high price—you begin to wonder, "What's going on?" Your first guess might be that this is like the grand opening of a department store or a mall, with lots of free offers to draw crowds. Then once the hoopla is over, the free stuff disappears. That is very unlikely in this case. Expect more, not less, great information and online calculators and decision-support tools. Expect more finance-related Web sites and the further growth of the ones that are there.

These sites are supported—very well supported—by advertising. When you visit a major money-related site, you'll see bright-colored flashing banners intended to tempt you to click to other money-related sites. The revenue from these banner ads pays the way for financial sites to provide you with all this diverse, rich information for "free."

If you buy a house, the folks in the real estate business might see you again in a decade. If you buy a car, you might come back again in three years. But if you choose an online bank or buy an online stock, these financial sites might see you again tomorrow and the next day and the next day, for the rest of your life.

To win your repeat business, online trading companies like E*Trade and Charles Schwab are reportedly spending as much as $250–$300 in advertising for each new customer they acquire. A single company like that might spend $150 million a year for advertising. And there are many companies competing for your attention in this same arena, driving each other's advertising spending upward.

Who is the target audience for their advertising? Primarily, these companies want to reach people who are already online and who are already looking for financial advice. That means you are a hot investment for them. Likewise, insurance companies, mortgage companies, banks, and other financial services companies all want your business. When you visit a Web site that provides good, free financial advice, you may be trying to make key financial decisions. It's no coincidence that you find these flashy banner ads located right at the Web sites maintained by the kinds of companies that can help you with these critical financial issues.

A typical ad rate on the Internet today is about $25 per 1,000 page views or about 35¢ per click-through. In other words, every time you look at a Web page with an ad on it, the company providing you with that "free"

information may be getting about $2\frac{1}{2}$¢ just because you clicked on the ad. Or in the alternate payment approach, every time you click on a banner ad, the company who created that page gets somewhere on the order of 35¢ because you decided to take a look at the advertiser's site. The information provider can attract more traffic and hence more advertising revenue by providing good and useful content. The likelihood that people will click through to the advertiser site is increased by closely matching the content of the ads and the content of the Web pages where they appear.

In other words, don't expect this bonanza of information to go away any time soon. Rather, expect, enjoy, and profit from enormous quantities of high quality, useful information, advice, and tools.

Getting Time On Your Side

	The Old Way	The Lazy Way
Driving your car to the bank branch	10 minutes	0 minutes
Waiting to talk to the assistant manager	30 minutes	0 minutes
Asking the assistant manager about your best IRA choices	15 minutes	0 minutes
Waiting while the assistant manager tries to find answers for you	15 minutes	0 minutes
Waiting while the assistant manager answers the phone instead of continuing to talk to you	10 minutes	0 minutes

Chapter
nine

Car Shopping Tour: Worry-Free Wheeling and Dealing

If you haven't shopped for a car online, you probably haven't bought the right one (except by chance) because there's no way you could have been aware of the range of choices or had access to the data necessary to make a truly informed decision.

When it comes to buying cars, we're not just talking about saving time and money. For these purchases, if you shop the traditional way, you're wearing a blindfold and playing spin the bottle or pin the tail on the donkey to make your vehicle choice. You have well over a thousand makes and models of new cars from which to choose. And for each of those cars, you can pick from a multitude of combinations of options and colors. For used cars, the range of choices is even far greater, and so are the risks.

Before the Internet craze, ordinary consumers simply had no way to access to all the relevant information on car selection. Even if you had access to the resources of a professional car buyer, you could never have manually and rationally sifted through them all in a reasonable amount of time.

Today, even if you don't find the car you want online, you definitely should take advantage of the Web's complete, convenient information and research tools to guide you through the car decision-making process.

WHERE TO START LOOKING FOR A NEW CAR?

If you are looking for a new car, your first step should be to clear your mind of preconceived notions that could get in the way of making the right decision. Does it really have to be American made? or a Toyota Camry? or red with racing stripes? Do you really need to buy it from the same local dealer where you got the last one? Does it really have to look just like the one in the commercial with the bikini-clad girls draped around it?

Unless you live downtown and depend on public transportation, cars are an inextricable part of your life. They are probably your main means of getting to work, to stores, to entertainment, and to friends. (You might say they are the forerunners of the Internet—taking you where you need to go physically, whereas the Internet gets you there electronically.)

Your first notion of what type of car you might want to buy for yourself comes from what you have previously experienced: the cars your parents owned as you were growing up; the ones you've previously owned yourself; the ones you've seen driving by or parked; the cars owned by friends, rivals, and neighbors; the cars you've rented when traveling. Additionally, you see cars constantly in movies and on television and in advertising—everywhere you look.

By the time you decide you need or can afford to buy a car, you have already seen thousands of possibilities, and you probably have a pretty good idea of what might suit your tastes and your budget—perhaps too good of an idea. In other words, you have probably formulated a vision of your perfect car, and following your traditional shopping method, you would go to local dealers to compare your mental image of that perfect car with the cars you see on the lot.

If you were to use the Internet instead of physically going to the car dealer, your first inclination would be to go to the Web site of the car manufacturer whose ads have come closest to matching your perfect car image.

I'm asking you now to forget these traditional approaches. Try to erase that picture you have of your perfect car and free yourself to consider the full range of choices that would really make sense for you.

To select your car the online way, start by using one of the dozens of car-buying decision tools available on the Web. I recommend starting with PersonaLogic (a division of AOL) (www.personalogic.com), which is shown in the figure on page 292. In addition to cars, PersonaLogic also provides decision guides for bikes, camcorders,

A COMPLETE WASTE OF TIME

The 3 Worst Things to Do When Buying a New Car:

1. Fall in love at first sight with a car you see in an ad.

2. Settle for a vehicle that the nearest dealer happens to have on the lot.

3. Pay sticker price.

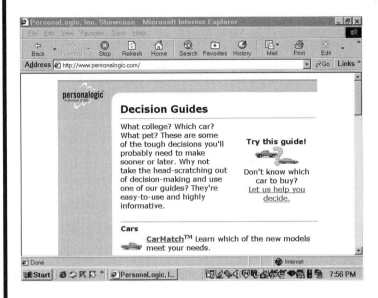

If you are looking for a new car, try starting with the PersonaLogic decision guide (www.personalogic.com).

cities, colleges, cruises, and dogs. Guides like this appear to be unbiased, but some sites might charge manufacturers who want their products to be included.

From the PersonaLogic home page, click on "CarMatch" for a car-buying decision guide that includes over 1,200 new car models, leaving out the most exotic and expensive vehicles, and including nearly all those that ordinary people are likely to buy. You can select a typical profile—Commuter, College Freshman, Executive, Soccer Mom, Sport Driver, or Weekend Warrior. Or you can click on Need Help Picking the Perfect Car and enter car type (including vans and trucks), model year, price (with a calculator to help figure out what you can afford), size, safety features, technical matters, manufacturer, etc. Once you've entered your selections, you can weigh these factors according to how important they are for you. Your final list of matches will include a "score" for each make and model, indicating how well each vehicle compared with the profile you created. Now, with the PersonaLogic-generated preliminary list in hand, you can click to get to detailed information on any car on that list. The figure below shows PersonaLogic's list of four-wheel drive sport utility vehicles under $25,000.

Now, return to the page that shows your matches. Click on Compare with Another Car, and indicate which of the competitors you want to see compared one-on-one with your original selection. PersonaLogic then generates a comparison Web page, as shown in the figure on page 294. While the comparison data may contain hidden biases, the basic facts about other vehicles in the

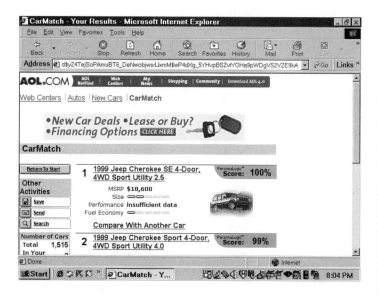

With the search criteria set to look for four-wheel drive sport utility vehicles, PersonaLogic made these recommendations.

same model category can be very helpful, making you aware of other choices.

The original list and the comparison lists that PersonaLogic provides for you will likely include models you may have never heard of or have certainly never considered. They also may not include the car you thought you were in love with. If your perfect car doesn't appear, double-check your choices. You also might want to redo the selection options to see what other cars PersonaLogic suggests when you make even subtle changes in selection criteria. After you have several recommendation lists, you can then ask for one-on-one comparisons between your perfect car and the cars at the top of your list of recommendations.

Once you are comfortable with the results and certain that they accurately reflect your budget and tastes,

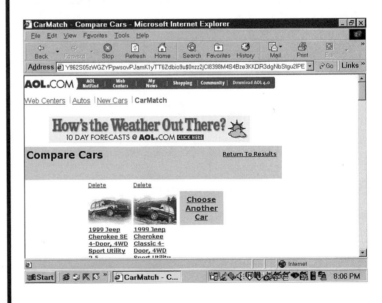

The PersonaLogic car decision tool also compares competitors in a particular model category.

you should print the list. This list can then serve as a primary reference as you use other online auto shopping resources.

You'll most likely be surprised at the widely differing results you'll get using other online decision guides. Presenting you with different questions can lead you down different paths with very different conclusions. Hence, you should be sure to use more than one online car-selection tool.

Even if you tend to make snap decisions and your first online car-selection exercise has provided you with a candidate that you are sure you want, your work still isn't completed. One way or another, you will eventually need to contact a specific dealer to select options, get a final price, and learn about delivery.

ELECTRONIC WINDOW-SHOPPING

Some people window-shop for cars, trying on possible new identities long before they are actually ready to buy. They collect brochures from dealers and compare the choices of styles, colors, and options, imagining what their perfect car would be like.

That kind of comparison is much easier if you use the Web's resources. All the major car manufacturers have their own Web sites, and each is packed with slick photos, fancy graphic effects, and brochure-style copy. (Porsche's manufacturer Web site, www.porsche.com, is shown in the figure on page 296.) If you like the selection list you got from one of the sites like PersonaLogic, search the Internet for the manufacturers' Web sites.

YOU'LL THANK YOURSELF LATER

After you've narrowed your search for that much wanted and needed auto, but before you have solidified your choice, you need to check the online information about rebates and specials. Lycos has a good list of these resources at www. lycos.com/wguide/wire/ wire_484433_71892_ 3_1.html.

Porsche's Web site (www.porsche.com) shows eye-catching graphics and all the details contained in the manufacturer's paper brochures.

Each will be brimming with colorful, compelling online brochures for every model they make.

The following list features the URLs for all the major automobile manufacturers:

- Audi (www.audi.com)

- BMW (www.bmwusa.com)

- Chrysler, which includes Chrysler, Dodge, Jeep, Mercedes-Benz, Plymouth, Pontiac, and Smart (www.chrysler.com)

- Ford, which includes Ford, Lincoln, Mercury, Jaguar, Aston Martin (www.ford.com)

- General Motors, which includes Buick, Chevrolet, Oldsmobile, Saturn, and EV1 (an electric car) (www.gm.com)

- Honda, which includes Honda and Acura (www.honda.com)

- Hyundai, which includes Accent, Tiburon, Sonata, and Elantra (www.hyundai.com)

- Isuzu, which includes VehiCROSS, Rodeo, Trooper, Amigo, Ombre, and Oasis (www.isuzu.com)

- Lexus (www.lexususa.com)

- Mazda, which includes Miata, MPV, Protege, Millenia, and 626 (www.mazdausa.com)

- Mitsubishi, which includes Debonair, Diamante, Galant, Carisma, Lancer, Mirage, Minica, Aspire, GTO, Eclipse, FTO, and Legnum (www.mitsubishi-motors.co.jp)

- Nissan, which includes Altima, Maxima, Pathfinder, Quest, Frontier, and Sentra (www.nissanmotors.com)

- Porsche (www.porsche.com)

- Saab (www.saabusa.com)

- Saturn (www.saturn.com)

- Subaru, which includes Forester, Legacy, Impreza, and Outback (www.subaru.com)

- Suzuki, which includes Grand Vitara, Esteem, and Swift (www.suzuki.com)

- Toyota, which includes Avalon, Camry, Camry Solara, Celica, Corolla, 4Runner, Land Cruiser, RAV4, Sienna, Tacoma, and T100 (www.toyota.com)

- Volkswagen, which includes Golf, Jetta, Cabria, GTI, Passat, EuroVan, and the New Beetle (www.vw.com)

- Volvo, which includes the C70, V70, S70, and S80 (www.volvocars.com)

YOU'LL THANK YOURSELF LATER

Check search engines and print ads to see if there might be a car-related site that serves your geographic area. If you search online for the site, you'll get all the information about all the potential dealers within driving distance from you. For instance, The Digital Dealer (www.digitaldealer.com) covers Washington, D.C.

Each manufacturer's site typically provides a lookup guide so that you can find dealers in your area. Some manufacturers' sites feature online tools to help you make decisions about which of their models you might want to buy and which of their financing plans you might choose. You may even be able to configure your particular car online, with the manufacturer's Web site automatically calculating your new car's total price with all the options you've selected. The figure below shows the Ford Motor Company's Web site.

Today, however, you cannot yet buy your new car completely online. Yes, Saturn's television ads give you the impression you can just click your way through their site, and someone comes to your door with the keys. In fact, Saturn's site (www.saturn.com) lets you configure

The Ford Motor Company (www.ford.com) offers lots of online auto-shopping options.

your options, calculate your payments, and apply for financing. But the price you see is just the Manufacturer's Suggested Retail Price (MSRP). Your last online step is to use Saturn's lookup guide to find the dealer nearest to you, or to request a dealer contact you. When you talk to the dealer, you then get to find out about "retailer installation charges." With this final bit of information in hand, you can negotiate your final price. The dealer's invoice pricing featured by the online research sites can become extremely helpful to you as you close in on a final purchase price.

When you surf the Internet to visit the auto manu-facturers' sites, realize that these sites tend to have fancy dancing-prancing graphic effects, which take a long time to load and display on your computer. Some of these graphics effects are so complicated that they may crash your browser or your computer system. If you experience this problem, don't panic. Just reboot your computer or restart your browser, and steer clear of that site. (You can probably get good information about that manufacturer's cars at more user-friendly, do-it-all car purchase-related Web sites.)

If you are looking for a car that is more exotic than those manufactured by the automakers we have dis-cussed so far in this chapter, try to locate that company on the Web by turning its name into a URL (e.g., Alfa Romeo becomes www.alfaromeo.com). If this suggestion doesn't work, then try searching a directory like Yahoo! (www.yahoo.com). If you are looking for a truly rare and ridiculously expensive vehicle, then a dealer specializing

QUICK PAINLESS

Once you've found a dealer, go to Mapquest (www.mapquest.com). At this site, you can enter your address and the address of the dealer. Mapquest then gives you detailed directions on how to get to that dealer, including the distance from your house.

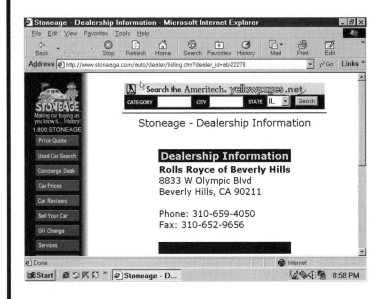

If you are hoping to add a Rolls Royce to your car collection, try contacting Rolls Royce of Beverly Hills at www.stoneage.com/auto/dealer/home.cfm/ABI22278.

in that type of car may be more helpful than the manufacturer. Dealers of such specialty cars are often able to track down the one-of-a-kind gem you seek; an example is Rolls Royce of Beverly Hills at www.stoneage.com/auto/dealer/home.cfm/ABI22278, as shown in the figure above.

GET THE DEVIL OUT OF THE DETAILS

For folks like me, a car is a basic necessity, and buying a new one is a traumatic, time-consuming hassle. I just want to get the purchase over with, with reasonable confidence that I have paid a fair price for a car that I can count on to get me where I need to go. The do-it-all car sites seem designed for me, simplifying and speeding up the entire car-buying process at all stages—even trade-in, financing, and insurance.

These are the Web's most popular do-it-all car-buying sites:

- American Car Buying Service (www.acscorp.com)
- Autobytel (www.autobytel.com)
- Autoconnect (www.autoconnect.com)
- AutoWeb (www.autoweb.com)
- Carpoint, which is owned by Microsoft (http://msn.carpoint.com)
- Carsmart (www.carsmart.com)
- Dealernet (www.dealernet.com)

Each of the major Web portals has business relationships with one or two of the do-it-all car sites, as well as numerous specialty car sites. And the do-it-all sites also have relationships with specialty car sites, embedding their content into the overall experience that they provide—trying to keep you occupied and happy, right where you are.

Although each site features a distinctive overall look and feel, once you dive into the site's information, you'll find significant overlap. What appears like hundreds of different resources are actually hundreds of different paths to the same pool of car-buying information.

All of these sites strive to provide you with every scrap of information you might need while buying a car. They make their money both through advertising and through business relationships with auto dealers and

IF YOU'RE SO
INCLINED

Ever tempted to get into the car business? Today, Acura is the first choice you see in the pull-down selector menus at all the major car sites, simply because it's first in the alphabet. To beat them out, name your car the Aardvark.

manufacturers. And once these sites catch your attention, their goal is to keep you at their specific site, searching through that site's plentiful and useful resources until you've made an auto purchase decision.

By the way, some of these "do-everything" car sites have business arrangements with dealers, so that when you use that site's decision tool, you can connect with a nearby dealer, usually one who has the car you want in stock. Then you can head over there for a test drive, check the options and final pricing, and decide whether to make this purchase.

In the past, when you were ready to make a car purchase, you probably put your dream aside, went to the dealer, and tried to save money by buying one of the cars that they already had in stock. On the Internet you can probably find a dealer that has a car that is very close to what you want—hence getting you selection, a good price, and fast delivery.

THE INS AND OUTS OF TRADE-INS AND OTHER FINANCIAL OPTIONS

If you plan on trading in your current car, you can use the Internet's online resources to help you with this part of the process, too. For example, at Carpoint (www.carpoint.com), seen in the figure on page 303, you can use the online version of the Kelley Blue Book to determine the trade-in value of your old car, what it might be worth if you try selling it yourself, and what a dealer would charge for the same car. This valuable information can help you determine if your old car is worth fixing or how much money you might get for it as a trade-in.

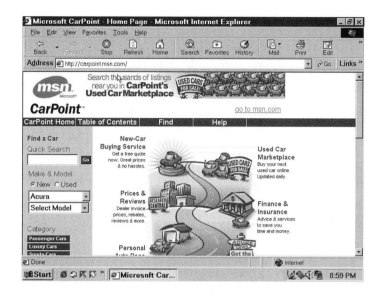

CarPoint (www.carpoint.com) contains valuable information regarding used cars. Among the information offered at this site are details you can use to determine whether you should sell your used car yourself or trade it in.

Carpoint also provides detailed reports on recalls, repairs, and reliability ratings for any of the cars you might consider. With Carpoint, you can also check the used car prices for previous years of the model for which you are looking, to help determine the resale value and also to decide if you might be better off buying a used rather than new car.

Carpoint lets you check financing options, too. The site gives you an interactive quiz to help decide whether to buy or lease, to compare competitive interest rates from various lenders, and to get advice when shopping for a car loan. Carpoint also features an online payment calculator to help you determine whether you can afford that monthly payment.

YOU'LL THANK YOURSELF LATER

Ever consider leasing rather than buying? Confused by the deals and the terms? Quickly educate yourself on the lease-versus-buy subject at Leasesource (www.leasesource.com) before you start talking to a dealer.

At Autobytel.com, shown in the figure below, you can also consider the pros and cons of purchasing an extended warranty. Once you've made all the remaining decisions about your potential car purchase, you can submit your request to buy, finance, or lease a new or used car. Autobytel will forward your request to an "accredited" dealer in your area, who will then contact you by phone and quote a "firm, low, no-haggle, no-hassle price with the understanding that you are ready to buy and that you are an information-empowered consumer." Just remember that even though Autobytel has given you this "firm" price, you still haven't settled on options, dealer charges, and delivery. Even at this point, you still have some important issues to discuss with the dealer who contacted you.

At the Autobytel.com Web site (www.autobytel.com), you can consider the pros and cons of purchasing an extended warranty.

FINDERS KEEPERS: REAPING THE REWARDS OF DEDICATED RESEARCH

For some people, selecting a car to buy is a challenging research project. These buyers want to learn everything they can about the quality, reliability, gas mileage, maintenance, repair issues, resale value, and so on, of all the models they are considering. Armed with tons of information, the well-researched buyer goes to the dealer for a face-to-face confrontation in hopes of negotiating the best price for that desired car. If you operate this way, then the mass of auto-purchasing information on the Web will make you feel like you are in heaven.

After you have exhausted the information sources we have discussed in this chapter so far, if you still want to do more research, check out the Internet's online car magazines and car electronic book sites:

- *Autopedia* (www.autopedia.com), shown in the figure on page 306, is a site containing voluminous reference material on everything that has to do with cars.

- *AutoWeek* (www.autoweek.com) is currently a site with very little content, serving as just an online ad for its print publication. On the other hand, this site should soon grow because it plans on adding a collection of its back issues.

- *Car and Driver Magazine* (www.caranddriver.com) features articles, a buyers' guide, road test data, and information on car shows.

- *Consumers Digest* (www.consumersdigest.com) offers advice on the best car buys, car care, and auto safety.

If you want to buy a new car, but would like more than a test drive before making your final decision, find a car rental place that offers cars of that kind. Rent one for a getaway weekend, and let the entire family go for a trial ride.

The Lazy Way

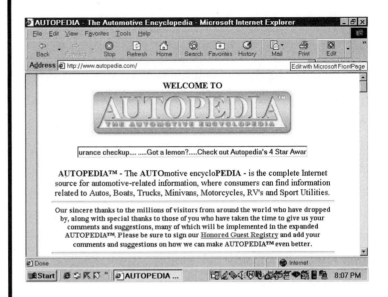

Autopedia (www.autopedia.com) is an online encyclopedia for everything about cars.

- *Consumer Reports* (www.consumerreports.com) is the online version of the well-known publication. To be able to benefit from its online research, however, you have to pay $2.95 per month for a subscription.

- *Motor Trend Magazine* (www.motortrend.com) features articles galore and a "carwizard" to check prices for both new and used automobiles.

ADDITIONAL DECISION TOOLS AND PRICING

The Web also offers a variety of tools to help you with auto pricing and various car-related decisions. The following Web sites offer help ranging from browsing makes and models to determining book value for used cars and trucks:

- Autolocator (www.autolocator.com) allows you to browse this Web site by make and model, or by car type/category. The site also features a listing of certain dealerships. Note that not all dealerships are included.

- Autosite (www.autosite.com) has facts and pricing for a wide range of new cars. This site also includes side-by-side comparisons of models, a loan/lease calculator, information about the latest rebates and incentives, and expert opinions about which cars are best in each car class.

- Edmunds (www.edmunds.com) offers advice, road test data, pricing information, alerts on rebates/incentives, and a discussion area to exchange information on common car-buying issues with experts and other car buyers.

- Just the Facts (www.intellichoice.com/jtf/) is a service provided by IntelliChoice After you have gotten the details on a particular model from the PersonaLogic decision tool, click on Just the Facts for even more details. And should you be a glutton for data, pay the Just the Facts folks $4.95 to get a comprehensive collection of information regarding your car choice.

- Kelley Blue Book (www.kbb.com), shown in the figure on page 308, is the online version of the "bible" of used car prices.

- Kiplinger (www.kiplinger.com/cars) is yet another new car selection/decision tool.

YOU'LL THANK YOURSELF LATER

Do you buy cars frequently? Then consider the "Mobalist Rewards Program" at Autobytel (www.autobytel.com). By buying a car at participating dealers, you earn a significant discount on your next purchase or lease of a vehicle through Autobytel.

Kelley Blue Book (www.kbb.com) is the online version of the "bible" of used car prices.

FINANCING AND INSURANCE

Naturally, no car purchase is complete without going through the difficulties of obtaining financing and new auto insurance coverage. How do you know that you've gotten the best percentage rate and terms? And when it comes to buying auto insurance, who can tell what coverage is best for the amount? Don't worry because the Internet offers you several sites to make you feel better about making those decisions. Some of those Web sites are

- CarFinance.com (www.carfinance.com) offers financing rate and payment choices, with an instant calculator, and related articles on auto financing.

- Pace Buyer's Guides (www.carprice.com) provides you with even more prices, payment calculators, and information about auto financing. The figure below shows carprice's home page with a link to its payment calculator.

- InsWeb (www.insweb.com) offers comparative auto insurance quotes from State Farm, Progressive, Nationwide, CNA, Liberty Mutual, and other companies.

Other Web sites offer additional specialized information related to car buying:

- Autohelper (www.autohelper.com) features pointers to thousands of Web sites related to car buying.

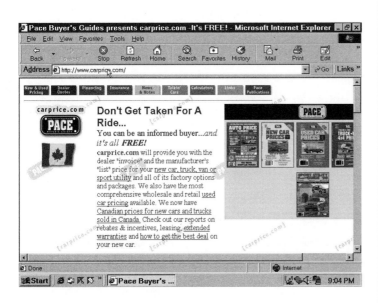

With Pace Buyer's Guides' carprice.com's payment calculator (www.carprice.com), you can see how much per month that new Corvette will cost you.

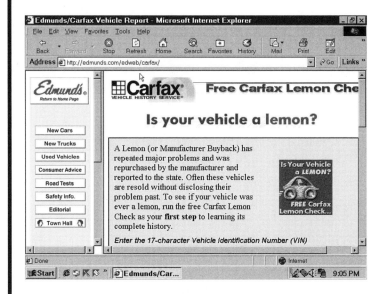

Ever wonder if your used car was declared a lemon? Use Carfax Lemon Check (www.edmunds.com/edweb/carfax/) to confirm or dispel your suspicions.

Carfax Lemon Check (www.edmunds.com/edweb/carfax/) is a Web site where you can check to see whether your car has ever been declared a lemon. Just enter your vehicle identification number, as shown in the figure above, and discover your car's history.

IF YOU DON'T TRUST A USED CAR SALESMAN FACE-TO-FACE, WHY TRUST ONE ONLINE?

For most consumers, trust and choice are the two major factors to consider when buying the right used car. Internet Web sites can help immensely with the making the choice part of the used car-buying process. With the

Internet, you have easy access to information about many, many used vehicles.

In the past, to buy a used car, you might have scanned your local newspaper's classified ads, with their brief descriptions laced with bizarre abbreviations. You considered potential purchases from used car dealers and private individuals within 5–10 miles from your home.

With the Internet's wide-ranging search powers, you can now get detailed information—in plain English—on vehicles almost anywhere. With this range of search capability, you might consider going to a dealer located 50 or even 100 miles away, and maybe even farther.

When searching for a used car in the past, if you saw a newspaper ad for a car that interested you, you went to the dealer to ask about that car. Often the car was gone by the time you got there. Maybe the car had been ridiculously low priced just as bait to get lots of people to drive to that used car lot, so that the dealer could then convince the disappointed buyer to consider another, more expensive car (the old "bait-and-switch" routine). With the Internet, however, you can have a clearer idea of what types of used cars are available, and you might even be able to put a "hold" on the car of interest until you've had a chance to see and test drive it. Changes in how used car dealers conduct their business make it more likely that you'd be willing drive a longer distance to evaluate a potential purchase.

But when you arrive at this used car dealer's lot—no matter the distance—will you trust the person who is

IF YOU'RE SO
INCLINED

If you are a car collector, check Swapmeet (www. mm.com/swapmeet/) for information about buying, selling, swapping, and auctioning classic vehicles. Also look at *Jalopy Journal* (www. jalopyjournal.com), a magazine about classic cars, with classifieds for buying and selling.

selling the used car? Regardless of whether the seller is a dealer or private individual, you do not have much information about who is trying to sell you the car.

Over the last 10 years, I bought five used cars that I found online at the company where I worked (Digital Equipment). I was very satisfied with the price and reliability of all of them. At Digital's peak of success, the company had over 120,000 employees. The people I bought those cars from lived in different towns than I did, and were total strangers to me. But we worked for the same company and operated in a common environment of trust and honesty. If I had any follow-up questions, I knew that I could easily contact this person at work by phone or e-mail. And all of Digital's employees knew that any rare instance of unfairness would be discussed openly in the very same notes conferences where I had learned that the used cars were for sale. Sellers tended to include complete detailed descriptions of any defects, and they also priced their vehicles fairly and lower than they would if they were selling the cars in other ways. These people knew they could sell their used cars via the Digital network in just a few days, at no cost to them and with a minimum of hassle.

But buying a used car from a public forum like the Internet changes completely the complexion of the transaction. The Internet's online used car services that match sellers to buyers are challenged to establish trust. These used car sites do so by providing the buyer access to the best available data and advice, so that the buyer can make confident, informed decisions about his or her purchases. Through policies, procedures, certification programs, recommendations, guarantees, and the like, these used car Web sites attempt to build trust between seller and buyer, with a safety net for the buyer. The sites might list hundreds of thousands of vehicles, but only certify or recommend a subset of cars. The sites also might list only cars sold through dealerships—dealerships with which they have business relationships that include some sort of guarantee.

Most of the Internet's major do-it-all car sites include used as well as new car listings, and all the tools and information you'd need to make your decision for either. Sites like Autoconnect (www.autoconnect.com) boast over 600,000 used car listings. At Carpoint (www. carpoint.com), you need to get a plug-in to your

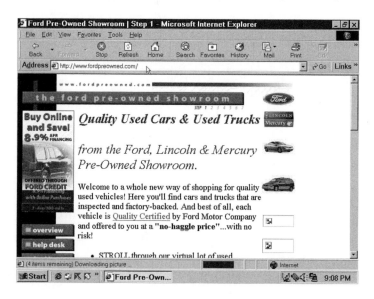

The Ford Motor Company stands behind the used cars at the Pre-owned Ford Web site (www.fordpreowned.com).

browser to view that site's used car listings. Just follow the Carpoint Web site instructions. Downloading the plug-in and installing it will take only two to three minutes, and you'll only have to go through this process once.

Car manufacturers can also play an important role in selling used cars, using their branded corporate identity to provide credible guarantees. For instance, the highly advertised Pre-owned Ford Web site (www. fordpreowned.com), as shown in the figure on page 313, emphasizes haggle-free pricing and a range of policies aimed to build customer trust. Here is a list of those policies:

- "All vehicles offered on this site are three model years old or newer and have less than 36,000 miles.

- "Every vehicle has passed a rigorous 100-point inspection and is factory certified by Ford Motor Company.

- "Each car and light truck is backed with a minimum 12-month/12,000-mile limited warranty coverage and 24-hour Roadside Assistance.

- "If for any reason you are dissatisfied with the vehicle after the test drive, you are not obligated to purchase it.

- "Even after you take possession, you have three days or 300 miles to return the vehicle if you are not satisfied!"

Competition with Ford's pre-owned car purchase policy should cause other auto manufacturers to make similar provisions.

If by some chance you are a car expert, have a friend who is one, or can hire the services of one, you might want to shop at Web sites that offer the broadest possible selection of used cars. Such sites should conveniently present their inventory so that you can easily find the cars you might want and compare their features online. For example, Classifieds2000 (www.classifieds2000.com), as seen in the figure below, boasts over 250,000 vehicle listings. Your local newspaper probably has an online version of its car classified ads. Also check the newsgroups, particularly rec.autos.marketplace, and do general newsgroup searches at AltaVista (www.altavista.com) and Dejanews (www.dejanews.com). Include in your query the phrase "for sale" and the type of vehicle you are looking for.

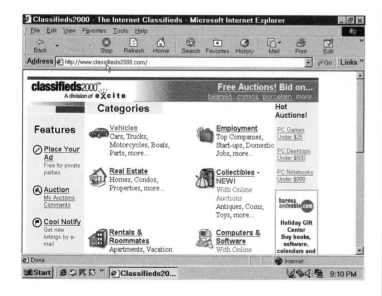

The Web site Classifieds2000 (www.classifieds2000.com) claims to have over 250,000 ads for cars.

If the process for buying a used car that we've described in this chapter suits your style, you may find yourself disappointed with the selection available today. Even with over half a million cars listed on the Internet, those vehicles are unevenly distributed, with many in some areas of the country and few in others. You may not find the car that you want within a reasonable distance from you. You may also discover that very few of the used car dealers in your area are included in the Internet's used car listings at all. Hence, for now, you might conclude that you can use the Internet's resources for research, but you'll have to find the actual car by traditional means, with print classifieds and/or in a dealer's lot.

Expect this situation to change soon. The car-selling Web sites are expanding their listings rapidly. Within a year or two, these Web sites will be reaching millions of potential car buyers and will also probably include listings from most of the dealers in your area.

In any case, look for used-car sites that offer solid guarantees and arrangements that build your trust. When it comes to used cars, trust is more important than either selection or price. A low-priced lemon is no bargain.

Also, look for sites that have active online forums and chats where you can openly share your questions and doubts, and get feedback from people who have owned this type of car. You may even find someone who has done business with a dealer you are considering purchasing from, so this cooperation and sharing from the online community can help you in important ways.

TALK TO MY AGENT: THE HUMAN ONE, NOT THE BOT

For many people, negotiation is the worst part of the car-buying process. We live in a society where, aside from yard sales and flea markets, a price is a price is a price. As consumers, whether we're buying a book, a software program, or a head of lettuce, the price is marked and that's what we pay, no questions asked. So when we go to buy a car, we are at a disadvantage. We have little experience in price negotiation, while, in contrast, the car salesperson does it every day. Yet we hear tales of individuals, whether family, friends, or friends of friends, who made great deals, not just on used cars, but on new ones as well. And "come-on" ads about "special, limited-time offers" and "end-of-year clearance sales" make us feel like opportunities are lurking everywhere. So, off we go to make our car purchase—armed with great information we got online, including the exact dealer cost from the manufacturer—but we are still likely to come away feeling we didn't make the best deal we could.

If feeling "ripped off" sums up how you feel each time you buy a car, then consider using a buyer's agent. This agent's role is to work for you in negotiating a better deal than you possibly could from any dealer. These buyer's agents typically work for a flat fee of around $400, and purportedly the average savings they deliver over what you would have been able to negotiate by yourself is about $1,000.

For details on an automobile buyer's agent's role, check the National Association of Buyers' Agents' Web

A COMPLETE WASTE OF TIME

The 3 Worst Things You Can Do When Buying a Used Car:

1. Buy from someone you don't trust (for whatever reason).

2. Buy without inspecting and test-driving the vehicle.

3. Pay the asking price.

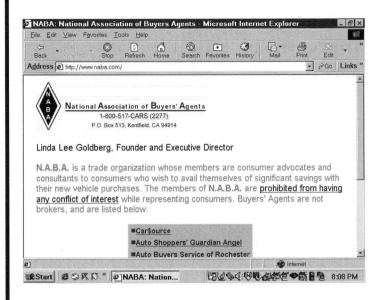

If you hate the negotiation part of car buying, consider hiring a buyer's agent from the National Association of Buyers' Agents (www.naba.com).

site at www.naba.com, as shown in the figure above. At this Web site, you'll find information on a handful of their members.

If you contact any of these companies or others who perform similar buyers' agent services, be sure to confirm that they abide by the basic tenets of the National Association of Buyers' Agents. You'll want to be sure that they are really representing you, and that they don't get rebates, commissions, kickbacks, fees, or any other form of compensation from dealers, manufacturers, or auto loan lenders. If they abide by the National Association's rules, then a buyers' agent can serve as your advocate and consultant: an experienced insider with the special knowledge needed to get you the car you want at a price that you could never get on your own.

For related kinds of buyer agent services, check the subjectively rated list of buyer services at Autohelper (www.autohelper.com/buying_services.html) This site also includes some of the do-it-all sites that connect you with a dealer (like Autobytel and DealerNet), but the site also has some listings that perform various buyer-related services on your behalf for a fee.

TECHNOLOGY MAKES THINGS POSSIBLE; CONSUMERS MAKE THINGS HAPPEN

The first rule of online shopping is to expect change. If you don't like the way an online company does business, speak up; then find others who feel the same and speak up together. Use e-mail, chat, forums, and newsgroups. If you find that you need an online service and don't yet see it, make that known to the online community at large. Other online community members will point you to a site that offers this service, or if enough interest surfaces, someone will start doing it.

When you shop online for a car, you are saving yourself time and money. You'll also be choosing a vehicle that is far more likely to meet your needs than one you might have found by traditional methods. At the same time, you are playing a role in changing how people do business with one another and transforming the entire automotive industry.

As you and hundreds of thousands of other people turn to the Internet for help in buying a car, these collective actions force car manufacturers and dealers to

Take a break from serious research and check out the Web sites of ridiculously expensive sports cars. Make a virtual purchase and enjoy a virtual vacation, driving your Alfa Romeo along the Monte Carlo.

make better use of the Web to serve you. As the traffic volume to car-sales sites increases, the amount of money to be made through them will increase dramatically. Actively competing with one another, these sites will offer more useful information and tools, and do whatever they can to grab and hold your attention. At the same time, the car dealers and manufacturers will have to change their procedures, policies, and offerings to take advantage of new opportunities and to be able to move as fast as their competition. Internet-based auto sales will cause customers to shop in wider geographic areas, and auto dealers will begin to compete with other dealers whom they used to consider outside their territory. Used car dealers won't be able to depend on their local reputation, but rather will need to bolster their credibility by participating in certification programs and offering strong guarantees.

With the increasing popularity of online car buying, the new car dealer's role will also change. As technology and innovation make it easier for consumers to select cars and work out online all the purchase details (including configuring all the options, settling on prices, and obtaining online financing), the new car dealership will become more of a "pickup spot" and a source for future auto service. At the same time, the dealer probably will not need to keep as many different new car models and color combinations in inventory when the available online tools make it easier for you, the customer, to imagine and examine—perhaps with Web-based three-dimensional effects—the very vehicle you want.

Getting Time On Your Side

	The Old Way	The Lazy Way
Checking the car listings	2 hours	30 minutes for 100 times the listings
Driving to the dealer to find the bargain has already been sold	2 hours	0 hours
Doing consumer research	3 hours	3 hours to access 10 times the information
Getting brochures	3 hours	15 minutes
Waiting for salespeople	2 hours	0 hours
Talking to salespeople	2 hours	0 hours
Selecting options	2 hours	10 minutes

ten

Home Sweet Home:
The Virtual Way
to Shop for Real Estate

Real estate is a complicated matching game. An unlimited number of unique properties (age, size, number of rooms, neighborhood, etc.) are to be matched with unique families. This matching arrangement is different from shopping for new books or music, where thousands or even millions of identical copies of each item may be available, and you just have to decide which title you want. It's also very different from buying a new car, where you can decide which model you want, put together a unique combination of options and colors, and have one made for you. Yes, you can build your own house, but the design, the materials, and the options do not define the property. The lot it sits on, the immediate surroundings, the neighbors, the community with its roads, traffic, schools, taxes, and crime rate, all make an enormous difference in your satisfaction and in the property's value.

You aren't going to go through the whole real estate shopping process lying in bed with our laptop. You will want to see the property and its neighborhood setting in person, not just online, before you make a decision. And you or your representative needs to be physically present to go through the legalities of closing. But whether you are looking for a roommate, an apartment, or a house, the Web is a way to:

- get the information you need to educate yourself about the process and the range of choices.

- try to narrow your search to a particular neighborhood or a set of likely houses/apartments.

- get you in touch with the people you need to help you.

- locate and get in touch with the resources you need for a myriad of related activities, from mortgages and insurance to home inspectors and movers.

The Internet gives you more information and a wider range of choices than you've ever had before. If you've bought homes in the past, you'll be delighted at how easily the Web will allow you to go through the traditional steps of picking a neighborhood, a real estate professional, a house, and a mortgage. But don't let your familiarity with the traditional process blind you to the new opportunities that the Internet has opened. The Internet is having a major impact on the real estate industry by opening new business models that give both buyer/renter and seller/landlord far more choices at lower cost. Keep in mind that the rules of the game are

A COMPLETE WASTE OF TIME

The 3 Worst Things to Do When Shopping for a House:

1. Search by price, without regard for neighborhood and crime rate.

2. Believe everything you hear from people who get paid for selling to you.

3. Sign documents without a lawyer's advice.

changing even while you are playing. Innovative companies are pioneering new territory. You ought to check out what they have to offer (in particular, buyers agents, a wide range of for-a-fee services, and easier access to homes and apartments for sale and rent by the owner). The Internet lets you do more of the legwork yourself; and if you take advantage of the new business models, you can save considerably on transaction fees and commissions while still getting the professional help you want and need.

GETTING STARTED—BUY OR RENT OR FIND A ROOMMATE

One of the first steps in shopping for real estate is to determine what you can afford, which may not be immediately apparent to you. Your desires may well exceed the limitations of your income. So use the Web to check the prices of available properties in the areas where you want/need to live, and to learn about bank lending rules and interest rates, and about all the other costs beyond the simple price: agent fees, deposits, taxes, closing costs, moving costs, etc. You may decide to rent a house rather than buy one, or to rent an apartment, or to look for roommates to share the cost of rental.

At this preliminary stage, the Internet's "do-it-all" real estate sites can be very valuable. Such sites have assembled a wide variety of information and tools to help you better understand what you want and how realistic your expectations are, and to help you get a feel for the overall process of buying or renting. In addition,

YOU'LL THANK YOURSELF LATER

When you search at a real estate site and you find a house that looks interesting, try to find that same house listed at other sites as well. Some sites will provide more info than others on the same property. Some might even have pictures.

they provide listings of available properties and links to realtors and other businesses that can help you. However, be skeptical of the listings and business referrals. Because they are national services, the listings they have in your area today are likely to be sparse. There's a lot more property available, and a lot more of it listed online than you will find at these national sites. Don't be dazzled by fancy calculators and decision-support tools. They often mask incomplete and sparsely populated databases. If you can browse and search the whole set of listings and can also navigate through the same information calculator-style, that's great. If not, beware. The results you get may be misleading, and perhaps might be pointing you, not toward the best selection out of the range of all that's possible, but rather toward only those that have submitted information here or paid to be included.

And the businesses (mortgage companies, movers, etc.) that these real estate sites refer you to will, for the most part, have paid fees for inclusion. So when you use an online tool to calculate the likely cost of a mortgage and see a list of rates and terms from particular lenders, remember that you are only seeing part of the picture. You have more choices than these sites would lead you to believe, including the option of dealing with real estate professionals who provide à la carte services for fixed fees, rather than working on a percentage.

Don't get me wrong. This is good stuff. You need this kind of help to get oriented. Just consider these sites as

starting points, not the complete real estate supermarkets that they present themselves to be.

- Microsoft's HomeAdvisor (homeadvisor.msn.com):
  This site offers an overview of what you need to
  know to buy a house, with lots of calculators
  intended to help you make decisions.

- HomeShark (www.homeshark.com): This site has
  resources for buyers, owners, renters, and realtors,
  and also people looking for mortgages. It also
  includes "for sale by owner" offerings. (See the
  figure below.)

- Home Buyer's Fair (www.homefair.com): This site
  offers listings of homes and apartments, info for
  home buyers and people relocating, and tools/
  calculators.

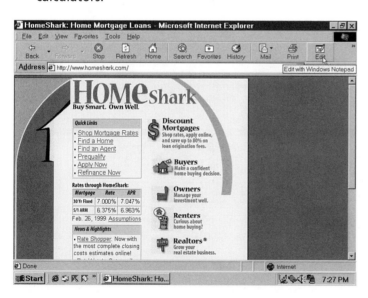

*The HomeShark site (www.homeshark.com) has resources
for anyone investigating a real estate transaction.*

- CyberHomes (cyberhomes.com): This site is a real estate search service with interactive, street-level mapping.

- Yahoo Real Estate (realestate.yahoo.com): In addition to classified listings of houses and apartments, this site provides city maps, profiles, and school reports, plus financial tools, mortgage rates, real estate news, and categorized lists of related links.

Let's take a closer look at one of these sites to get a better idea of what to expect and what to watch out for.

Microsoft's HomeAdvisor is organized around the usual steps involved in buying a house: getting started, neighborhoods, homes for sale, financing, and offer and closing. (See the figure below.) "Getting Started" guides you through the basic decisions. You should go through

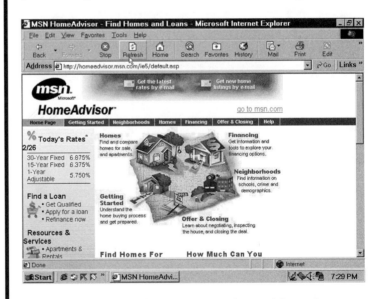

Microsoft's HomeAdvisor is organized around the traditional steps associated with buying and selling a house.

all these calculator exercises, and probably more than once. The different steps are interrelated; for instance, what you learn from the second or third step might affect what you'd want to enter as your preferences in the first. (Please note, however, that this site is a Microsoft site. If you use a Netscape browser, your back button probably won't work, and other features may not work. It sometimes crashes my system.)

- Are you ready to buy or should you rent?

- What's your price range?

- Do you qualify for the loan you want?

- How can an agent help you? HomeAdvisor's advice here is like television sound bites, and to help you find an agent, it just connects you to one of Microsoft's "sidewalk" sites (e.g., boston.sidewalk.msn.com).

The results in HomeAdvisor's "Neighborhoods" section don't match my experience and perceptions of neighborhoods around Boston, and the language used to characterize them strikes me as offensive and not particularly helpful: "Established Empty Nesters," "Upscale Blue-Collar Families," "Elite Ex-Urban Families," "Sophisticated Urban Fringe Couples," etc. The demographic information comes from Claritas, a company that gathers consumer spending and lifestyle data and correlates it with zip codes. Claritas markets its data to companies that are interested in identifying the optimum places to locate stores or those wanting to do targeted advertising campaigns. This marketing data approach

YOU'LL THANK YOURSELF LATER

If you believe in the ancient Chinese theory of site location, before you pick a house or a lot on which to build a house, check The Feng Shui Directory and Magazine (www. fengshuidirectory.com) and other related resources listed at www.ired.com/ dir/fengshui.htm.

does not at all seem appropriate in a home-buying context, where gross averages across an entire zip code are not particularly useful. A true housing neighborhood may be defined by a few blocks, and the territory of a zip code could include dozens of very diverse neighborhoods. In your home search, you are likely to find this kind of quite statistical pigeonholing more harmful than helpful.

The HomeAdvisor's "Home Finder" features are complex and time-consuming to use, not allowing you to browse or search, insisting that you fill out forms, which seems to mask how sparse their listings are. As their listings grow, so will the usefulness of this tool. For now, even with the broadest of criteria, I could find no listings at all in the zip code where I live (the West Roxbury area of Boston). In fact, HomeAdvisor found zero homes within five miles of where I live.

"Find a Loan" takes you through a lengthy set of questions, but then only provides you with loan information from three national mortgage companies. The questions here, and in the other sections, are very helpful at making you aware of what criteria are important, and where you may fit in the general scheme of things. But don't stop your search here. You are likely to get a better deal with a local bank that understands the neighborhood.

If you are new to real estate shopping, check all the sites listed above in this section. There's some overlap because they partner with some of the same companies, and because they are all trying to capture your full attention for anything and everything to do with real

QUICK ⬤ PAINLESS

Want to see where these houses and apartments are? Want driving directions? Go to MapQuest (www.mapquest.com). Then click on "maps" or "driving directions" and enter the address. Print out the results. It's free.

estate. But the insights you can gain by going through all their exercises and reading their articles are well worth the time. Just don't expect too much of any one or all of them. They can be very helpful in pointing out the kinds of things you need to know. Then you can go elsewhere to get the listings and other resources you need.

Also, keep in mind that finding a mortgage is an important part of shopping for a house. You should get preapproved before engaging the help of real estate professionals. You can do that online at mortgage sites linked to by the do-it-all sites. You should also check Priceline (www.priceline.com), Mortgage Auction (www. mortgageauction.com), and E-Loan (www.eloan.com) and mortgage lenders mentioned in Chapter 8, which deals with shopping for money.

SHOPPING THE TRADITIONAL WAY, WITH CLASSIFIEDS

Back in ancient times, before the dawn of the Web, your first step in finding a house, an apartment, or a roommate would probably have been to check the classified ads. That tradition is continued today at numerous online classified ad sites. Many of these sites simply move ad copy verbatim from printed newspapers to electronic form. Others follow old newspaper categories and format because users are already familiar with them, or just out of habit and inertia. Some even keep the cryptic newspaper-style abbreviations, despite the fact that on the Web, space is not limited the way it is in print. Nevertheless, these sites can be very useful. The nation-wide sites typically have tens of thousands of listings, and

YOU'LL THANK YOURSELF LATER

At major real estate sites, you can spend a lot of time filling out a detailed and complex form only to find that that particular site has no listings matching your needs and preferences. It's best to start very broad both with regard to location and to what you would like. Then if you are fortunate and there are many listings, get more specific.

If you haven't found exactly what you want in the real estate sites, go to AltaVista (www.altavista.com) and search for "home* for sale". Also search for +"home* for sale" +"by owner."

they provide sort and search capabilities so you can limit your search to the geography you want and then quickly pluck out those listings that match your requirements.

- Classifieds2000 (www.classifieds2000.com)
- Home Hunter (www.homehunter.com)
- Classified Warehouse (www.classifiedwarehouse.com)
- Property2000 (www.property2000.com): This site, shown in the figure below, is a nationwide site dedicated to real estate.

The problem is that these classified listings are likely to be unevenly distributed, with rich resources from one urban area where they have partnered with major newspapers, and very little in another. To get more

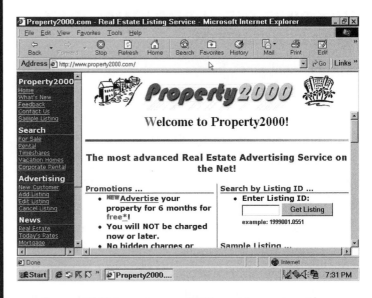

Property2000 (www.property2000.com) is a nationwide site dedicated to real estate.

listings in your geographic area, check the real estate and classified Web sites that focus on it.

To find those, first check the Web sites of the local newspapers, then check the Yahoo directory which has a section devoted to classifieds (http://classifieds.yahoo.com/). For example, in the Boston area:

- Boston.com (realestate.boston.com): This site is the online version of the *Boston Globe*.

- Boston Apartments (www.bostonapartments.com): This site serves Massachusetts and New Hampshire and features lots of apartments for rent and some houses for sale.

- Town Online (www.townonline.com): This site features classifed ads for Eastern Massachusetts, plus related real estate resources. (See the figure below.)

The Town Online (www.townonline.com) site features classified ads for eastern Massachusetts.

While nationwide real estate sites offers only a couple hundred listings, Boston.com features several thousand listings.

While the nationwide sites list a couple hundred homes for sale in the Boston area, Boston.com lists a few thousand, as shown in the figure above. These are all homes that were advertised within the last 7–14 days in the print newspaper, but all in the same brief cryptic form that is typical of newspaper classifieds. That form provides limited information and makes searching awkward.

ROOMMATE MATCHING SERVICES

The Internet features a few roommate services with listings nationwide or even worldwide. Even if you don't want to check these listings, you might want to look at their advice and links to related services.

▨ Roommate BBS 1.2 (www.gromco.com/roommate): This well-populated site has nationwide listings.

- The Roommate Assistant (www.roommateassistant. com): This site offers helpful advice, as well as nationwide listings.

- RoommateLocator.com (www.roommatelocator. com): This site, shown in the figure below, features worldwide listings, but today deals mainly with the United States.

For roommates, it makes more sense to check local sites rather than nationwide. Local sites typically provide a range of services—not just classified listings—and may charge fees for them. The services might include screening, advice, and opportunities to meet potential roommates at face-to-face events. Most urban areas in the United States should have at least a few. The problem is

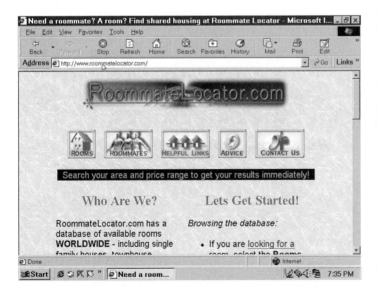

The RoommateLocator.com site (www.roommatelocator.com) features worldwide listings but deals predominantly with listings in the United States.

YOU'LL THANK YOURSELF LATER

For even more listings, check the newsgroups. At Dejanews (www. dejanews.com), search for phrases like "real estate," "apartment," "roommate wanted," or "for sale by owner." Also, click on Browse Groups and then on Regional to find newsgroups dedicated to your state or region.

that these are not easy to find. Look for links from general commercial sites that serve your geographic area, such as local newspaper sites. Here are a few of the more prominent ones:

- Roommate Finders (www.roommatefinders.com): Serving Manhattan, this site currently charges a $250 agency fee. They also have a "turkey file" of roommates blacklisted because of previous behavior.

- Roommate Express (www.e-roommate.com): This site serves just the West Coast.

- Roommate Matchers (www.roommatematchers. com): Serving the greater Los Angeles area, this site currently charges $49 membership fee.

- Roommate Access (www.roommateaccess.com): This site covers Los Angeles, Orange Country (Calif.), Chicago, New York, and Boston.

- The Real Estate Cafe (www.realestatecafe.com): Located in Cambridge, Mass., this site holds face-to-face gatherings for would-be roommates to meet. (See the figure on page 337.)

- Roommate Connection (www.dwellingsma.com/roommateco): This roommate site serves the Boston area only and currently charges a $75 fee.

- Matching Roommates (www.matchingroommates.com): This site is also a matching service for the greater Boston area.

The Real Estate Cafe (www.realestatecafe.com) holds face-to-face gatherings for would-be roommates.

RENTALS

While large national sites portray themselves as one-stop-shopping places, when it comes to real estate, bigger is not necessarily better. The odds of your finding just what you want at such a site are quite small. Keep in mind that those listings are spread across the whole country. For instance, AllApartments (www.allapartments.com) boasts over 5 million apartments listed, but I couldn't find any there for West Roxbury (the section of Boston where I live) and only 18 for all of Boston. That's typical of results at the other nationwide sites. But try them anyway; you'll get a quick feel for the variables and for what's possible. In addition, you'll see advice and related useful links. Other renters sites, in addition to AllApartments, include:

QUICK ⬤ *PAINLESS*

Looking for off-campus housing or roommates? A Break 4 Students (www.abreak4students.com) has listings of rentals near universities and is geared for the needs of students.

- Rent.net Online Rental Guide (www.rent.net): This site includes a "shopping cart" for you to earmark the rental selections that you might be interested in following up.

- Apartments.com (www.apartments.com): This site has separate listings for short-term housing.

- Apartments Nationwide (www.apartmentsnationwide. com): This site offers listings from members in 175 United States cities, with over 3 million apartments, as shown in the figure below. (Please note that there are no listings at all in some states, like Massachusetts.)

- Apartment Blue Book Online (www.abbonline. com/home): This site focuses on rental communities.

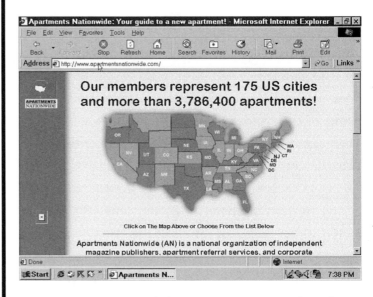

Apartments Nationwide (www.apartmentsnationwide.com) offers listings from members in 175 United States cities.

The Mining Company's real estate section (realestate. miningco.com) can provide you with rental listings for your area.

As with those for roommates, you are likely to see far greater selection in the rental sites dedicated to your local area. Try these sites, for example:

- Realty Trek (www.realtytrek.com): This site serves Boston and New York.

- Apartment Access (www.apartmentaccess.com): Serving greater Boston, Apartment Access lets you rent directly from the landlord, avoiding the typical broker's fee of one month's rent.

- Metro-Rent Online (www.metrorent.com): This site focuses on rental housing and roommates in the area from San Francisco to San Jose, Calif.

For a collection of other such sites, go to The Mining Company (realestate.miningco.com) and click on

IF YOU'RE SO INCLINED

Want to venture into the wilds of Internet newsgroups? The "regional" listing at Dejanews (www.dejanews.com) is a bit misleading, encouraging you to just click on a state. If you are interested in New England, enter ne.housing in the Dejanews search window. For the San Francisco Bay Area, enter ba.market.housing in Dejanews' search window.

Apartments for Rent or on your metropolitan area, as shown in the figure on page 339.

HOMEWORK THAT REALLY PAYS— USING THE WEB TO BUY A HOME

If you have decided to buy a home, you want to find the right one, with the minimum of hassle and wasted time. You want to negotiate a good price and close the deal. You also want guidance to make sure you have touched all the bases and taken care of all the related matters— and have done it well—in this very complex transaction, involving laws and regulations that you are probably unfamiliar with.

You can expect to go through two stages: First, you need to educate yourself about potential neighborhoods, the range of choices, the process, and particular houses. The Web can provide lots of information and advice so you can avoid the hard-sell tactics, the time-consuming contact, and the persuasive skills of a realtor, until you are ready. When you are ready, you can then contact a traditional realtor, or a buyer's agent, or a company that offers a menu of real estate services for a fee. Then they can guide you the rest of the way, and perhaps even help you with the negotiation and related matters.

This isn't a macho exercise. You don't have to show off how much you think you know about buying a house. Let's face it—most people rarely buy houses, and mistakes can prove costly. Unless you've worked in the business, you aren't likely to be an expert. That means just about everyone needs some help and hand-holding from people who really know.

Even if, armed with everything you can learn on the Web, you decide to buy directly from a homeowner, you'd still be well advised to get some paid professional help along the way.

Both the Web research and the personal professional help are particularly important if:

- You are selling one house while buying another and need to schedule those two events and synchronize the financial complexities of both transactions.

- You are relocating to another city with which you are unfamiliar.

Often you have to deal with both those circumstances at the same time.

With the right research on the Web, you can make good use of your time during your brief and expensive trips to the new city. By narrowing your choices before you arrive, you can cut down the number of houses you have to visit personally, and greatly reduce the time to purchase.

And while we won't deal directly with selling your home, you can use many of these same sites and services to help you with that as well.

Basically, if you use the Web effectively, you can expect more from the traditional players, like realtors. Knowing that you are ready, well informed, and motivated, real estate professionals can and should take you more seriously and give you more attention and help. Whether you are a buyer or a seller, if the first realtor you pick doesn't treat you that way, then go to another.

QUICK ⬤ PAINLESS

If you are relocating, check Virtual Relocation.com (www.virtualrelocation. com), which bills itself as a "moving and relocation mega-site." It has gathered in one place all the resources you are likely to need.

RESEARCH AND THEN MORE RESEARCH

Although there are brand name realtors, there are no brand name houses. Hence there are no reference books listing all the choices. Each property is unique. Even condominiums in the same building are on different floors or have different views, and cookie-cutter houses in a development have different physical locations. And over time, owners make improvements and cause damage and wear, so the older the property, the more unique it is likely to be. At the same time, the actual purchase of a house is just one step in a whole complex network of related activities——from getting a mortgage and insurance to moving, furnishing, and then making changes to the property to suit your tastes.

So while you would like to get as much information as you can about a particular property, you also need to familiarize yourself with a wide range of subjects. And for all these subjects there are dozens, if not hundreds, of Web sites that can help you.

After you've checked the do-it-all sites listed above, check some of these advice sites:

Advice for Buyers and Sellers

- Time Warner's Pathfinder (www.pathfinder.com/money/home): This site offers advice on shopping for homes from *Money* magazine.

- OurBroker's Consumer Real Estate Center (www.ourbroker.com): This site offers information and advice for consumers.

- BuyMyself, from *International Real Estate Digest* (www.ired.com/buymyself): This site offers advice for buyers and sellers.

- Internet Realty Network (www.gorealty.com): This site offers information on buying, renting, and selling.

- Real Estate in the United States, at The Mining Company (http://realestate.miningco.com/): This site is aimed primarily at realtors and home sellers rather than home buyers. It includes a bulletin board to post questions, and "For Sale by Owner" chat; click on specific cities under Net Links to find local resources.

- HomePath (www.homepath.com): HomePath offers articles and calculators to help buy and finance a house.

- Better Homes and Gardens Real Estate Service (bhg-real-estate.com): This site offers advice from the well-known magazine. (See the figure on the top of page 344.)

- AARP Housing (www.aarp.org/programs/housing): This site offers housing advice for seniors. (See the figure on the bottom of page 344.)

- Real Estate Resources, from the *International Real Estate Digest* (www.ired.com/dir/): This site links to consumer resources of all kinds.

- Dwellings (www.dwellings.com): Dwellings focuses on the Boston area.

IF YOU'RE SO INCLINED

Are you really interested in that house? Want to know who the neighbors are and maybe give one or more call? Go to AnyWho (www.anywho.com) and enter the street name and the zip code. In the query result, you'll get the names, addresses, and phone numbers of everyone on that street.

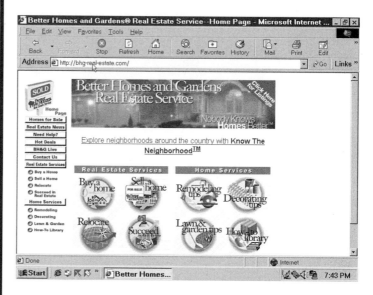

Better Homes and Gardens *magazine offers real estate advice online at this site (bhg-real-estate.com).*

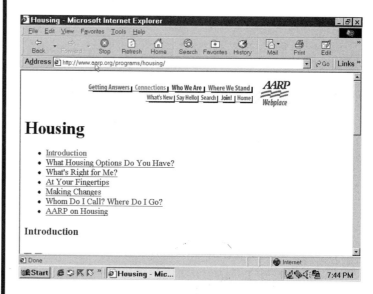

The AARP Housing site (www.aarp.org/programs/housing) offers housing advice for seniors.

If you want to do in-depth research on a neighborhood or specific property, first check the "Home Values" section at Yahoo Real Estate (realestate.yahoo.com/realestate/homevalues). There you can search by location to find all homes that have sold on a particular street since 1987, or the sales history of a specific address. You can also search by price to find all homes sold within a certain price range in one city. You can also sign up (for free) to get automatic e-mail notification when a house sells in a particular neighborhood. Yahoo draws this information from a database of 20 million U.S. home purchase price records, updated weekly, with info typically available six weeks after the close of sale.

Other resources for in-depth research include:

- Acxiom/Dataquick (products.dataquick.com/consumer): This site provides custom reports for sale: for example, "Home Sales Report," which determines a property's current market value; "Neighborhood Demographic Report"; "Local Crime Report"; and "Home Sale Price Trends" by zip code.

- Experian's Online Real Estate Property Reports (www.experian.com/cgi-bin/reis.cgi): This site offers custom reports for sale, such as "Property Profile Report," "Recent Home Sales Report," and others.

- American Society of Home Inspectors (www.ashi.com): This site, as shown in the figure on page 346, includes a membership list and information for home buyers and owners.

IF YOU'RE SO
INCLINED

Did you buy a fixer-upper? Or do you want to turn a house that's almost what you want into your dream house? For remodeling, repairing, gardening, landscaping, and furnishing, go to LookSmart (www.looksmart.com). Then click on Home & Family, and House & Garden. Follow those links, and you'll find enough ideas and resources to keep you busy for the rest of your life.

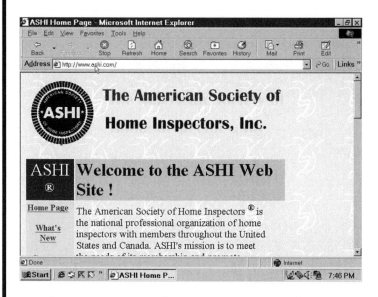

The American Society of Home Inspectors (www.ashi.com) includes a membership list and home buyer and owner advice.

- AMS Home Finder Resource (www.amshomefinder. com): This home-finding site offers relocation information, including community profiles for about 13,000 cities and towns in the United States.

- CASA (Characteristics and Sales Analysis) (www. cswcasa.com): Based on a large filtered property records database and market-specific analysis (similar to what a home appraiser uses), this site provides estimates of the current market value of single family homes. Banks use this service, and individuals can as well for $25 per estimate.

Other sites provide resources intended for people building their own home or buying new or for sale by owner, both of which present their own unique challenges and opportunities.

Building Your Own Home and Buying New

If you decide to explore the realm of newly built houses or perhaps even have one built to order, beware of builders that offer to do everything for you—arranging for mortgage money, doing the appraisal, and even setting you up with property insurance. They could get profit from each of those operations at your expense. Proceed with caution and do your own research into those matters.

- NewHome Search Systems (www.newhomesearch. com): This site is dedicated to new homes, with over 100,000 builder listings. It offers resources for consumers, builders, and agents/brokers.

- American Builders Network (www.americanbuilders. com): This directory also lists all of their qualified home builders. (See the figure below.)

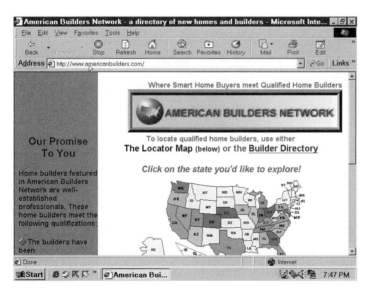

The American Builders Network (www.americanbuilders. com) Web site lists all their qualified home builders.

IF YOU'RE SO INCLINED

Looking for a unique vacation home, perhaps outside the United States? At AltaVista (www. altavista.com), click on Usenet, and search for "real estate." Then add other query terms to focus your search. You'll find intriguing listings of property for sale in such unexpected newsgroups as rec.travel.africa and rec.nude.

Builders and Construction, from the International Real Estate Digest (www.ired.com/bld): This site links to dozens of related Web sites.

ArchitectsOnline (www.architectsonline.com): ArchitectsOnline is a New England-based resource for and about architects, interior designers, and landscape architects.

New Home Network (www.newhomenetwork.com): With a variety of resources to make it easier to buy a new home, this site provides listings, floor plans, advice on how to get prequalified for a mortgage, and tips on what to look for in a condominium.

Homes for Sale By Owner

If you are interested in buying a house directly from the owner or selling a house yourself, first check the article by Pat Rioux, "What's New in Discount Listing Services for FOR SALE BY OWNERS," at the International Real Estate Digest site (www.ired.com/buymyself/rioux/fsbo), and check the related state-by-state directory of resources (www.ired.com/dir/fsbo.htm).

Also check the following sites:

Owners.com (www.owners.com): This site offers listings, information, and advice related to "for sale by owner" situations. (See the figure on page 349.)

FSBO.com (www.fsbo.com): This site includes an easy-to-use database of real estate "for sale by owner," plus helpful hints for selling or buying real

Owners.com (www.owners.com) offers guidance for individuals attempting to sell their homes on their own.

estate. Listings include houses, condominiums, commercial real estate, and vacant land.

- The Mining Company (realestate.miningco.com): To get to the Mining Company's real estate section, click on For Sale by Owner for useful links.

- Builders and Construction, from the International Real Estate Digest (www.ired.com/bld/): This site links to dozens of building- and construction-related Web sites.

- ArchitectsOnline (www.architectsonline.com): This New England-based resource is for and about architects, interior designers, and landscape architects.

Looking for luxury? Even if you can't afford it, check out The duPont Registry of Luxury Homes (www.dupontregistry.com) and Who's Who in Luxury Real Estate (www.luxury-realestate.com).

The Lazy Way

If you aren't in a hurry and you have a particular dream image of a house in mind, make your own Web page (as described at the end of Chapter 3). Describe your dream house in detail, and ask people to e-mail you if they know of a house like that for sale.

If you don't see what you want there, then check within these more generic sites that have most anything one would need regarding Real Estate.

- International Real Estate Digest (www.ired.com): This site is a reviewed directory of 25,000 real estate Web sites, with related articles and advice.

- Yahoo (dir.yahoo.com/Business_and_Economy/ Real_Estate): This directory links you to resources for buying, selling, and renting, both regional and national.

- LookSmart (www.looksmart.com): Click on Home & Family, then on Real Estate to access the real estate section of this directory.

This is where you are likely to find links to Web sites dedicated to the geographic area where you want to move.

REALTORS AND BUYERS AGENTS— WHEN YOU ARE READY FOR THE REAL THING

When you have done enough research and have a clear idea of what home you might want to buy and what you are going to have to do to get it, then it's time to turn to a local Realtor or buyers' agent.

Traditional Listing Agents

Many sites, including the do-it-all ones, provide search tools for finding realtors. I'd recommend using the International Real Estate Digest (www.ired.com). This site doesn't list every Realtor in the country, but it does provide quality ratings on those it does list and indicates the range of their services. And it includes just about everyone that has a Web site. These Realtors are the ones you can check out online and learn about before spending the time and effort to call or visit them. They are likely to provide, online, complete descriptions, costs, photos, and floor plans of the houses they list. Some may even offer online video tours of some homes.

Other realtor sites to keep in mind include these four specific areas in the list that follows.

National Sites

- new.REALTOR.com (new.realtor.com): This is the site of the National Association of Realtors. Here, you can find a home, a Realtor, or a neighborhood. (See the figure below.)

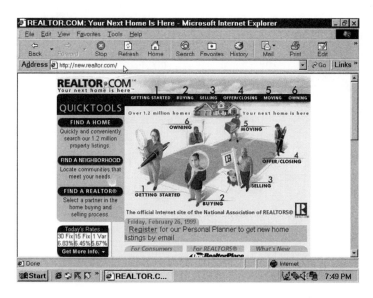

The National Association of Realtors has its Web site at new.REALTOR.com.

- Realty Referral Network (mmink.cts.com/mmink/dossiers/rrn.html): This site helps you find a Realtor in 5,000 cities and towns in the United States.

National Chains

- Century 21 (www.century21.com)

- ERA (www.era.com)

- Coldwell (www.coldwellbanker.com)

- Prudential (www.prudential.com/realestate) (See the figure below.)

- RE/MAX International (www.remax.com)

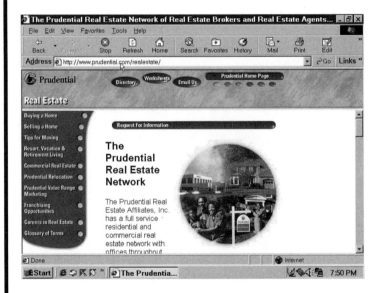

Prudential offers a Web site (www.prudential.com/realestate) for its real estate activity.

Selected Regional and Local Sites

- The Corcoran Group (www.corcoran.com): This site is a resource finder for luxury residences in Manhattan.

- MLS Online (www.mls.ca): This site, a service of the Canadian Real Estate Association, offers information on real estate throughout Canada.

- John L. Scott Real Estate, Seattle, Wash. (www.johnlscott.com): This Realtor has offices in Washington, Oregon, and Montana.

- Weichert Realtors (www.weichert.com): This site covers Connecticut, New Jersey, New York, Pennsylvania, Maryland, Delaware, Virginia, and Washington, D.C.

Buyers Agents

Legalities vary from state to state, but most Realtors are "listing agents" who represent the seller, while buyer's agents represents the buyer. Ask your Realtor/agent to clarify his or her role and responsibilities.

Buyer's agents, like traditional Realtors, have access to the Multiple Listing Service (MLS) to help you find homes in your target geography.

Do you pay more for a buyer's agent? Perhaps, but perhaps not. For instance, some for sale by owner sites don't offer any commission at all. In that case, the buyer working with an agent may end up paying the fee to the agent. But with a professional on your side, you are more likely to actually get the property you want and to

negotiate a lower price and other terms favorable to you. Then again, if negotiation is all you want, you could consider someone who specializes in that on a fee-for-service basis.

In the typical case, the price of the house has a commission of about 5–7 percent built in, which is split 50–50 between either the listing agent and the Realtor, or between the listing agent and the buyers' agent. The listing agent is the one who gets the information from the seller for inclusion in the Multiple Listing Service, puts the "for sale" sign in the front yard, and acts as the seller's coach through the whole process.

Some agents purport to represent both the buyer and the seller—an obvious conflict of interest. Make sure you understand your agent's role and if the agent will receive any payments from the seller or other players in the process (such as a recommended mortgage lender).

Also, keep in mind that if you deal with a large brokerage company, you might run into an instance of "competing buyers," where the buyers' agent's company might represent more than one individual interested in buying the same property.

To find buyer's agents in your area and to learn more about the role of a buyers' agent, check:

- National Association of Exclusive Buyer Agents (www.naeba.org) (See the figure on page 355.)
- True Agents, from the International Real Estate Digest (www.ired.com/dir/trueagnt.htm): This listing is a much larger list than the one from the National Association, based on a broader definition of the role.

You can obtain a list of many buyers' agents at the National Association of Exclusive Buyer Agents (www.naeba.org).

NEW BUSINESS MODELS: CHOOSE FROM A "MENU OF SERVICES"

Considering the way the Web is changing the real estate sales business, one would expect a greater variety of sales-related services to be available from new kinds of businesses at costs far less than the standard 6 percent sales commission. That is happening, and happening fast.

Basically, the Internet enables both the buyer and seller to do much more of the work themselves, and new businesses are experimenting with ways to provide buyers and sellers better services at far less than the traditional cost.

Today's fee-for-services companies charge less if the seller or the buyer takes more responsibility. The

IF YOU'RE SO
INCLINED

A new Internet standard (XML) for marking up the text of Web pages should make it easy for buyers to search through real estate listings from any online source around the country. One search and you'll see them all, instead of having to search through one site after another. The standard and the technology are in place, but it will take a few years for this to be implemented. For details on this, see www.4thworldtele.com/public/rs/rsarticle.html.

resources available on the Internet make it much easier for you to do just that. The services and their cost may vary widely. And there are also new services—beyond what traditional real estate professionals normally do—to make it easier for you to cope with the myriad of activities related to home buying and owning. Picking from a menu, you choose and pay for only what you need. Read the promotional material carefully. Make sure you know what you will pay, what you should get for it, and what your role will be. The savings could be considerable—perhaps as much as $5,000–$10,000 for an average house in a major metropolitan area—but only if you play the active role that is expected of you.

Note that the new fixed-fee seller services make it far easier for homeowners to sell their own property. You don't have to be a pioneer do-it-yourselfer anymore. There are companies that can help you in the ways that you want to be helped, at far less cost than a full-service realtor.

Today there is no professional organization or central site from which you can readily search for all fee-for-services companies. For starters, check your state in the United States real estate list at the International Real Estate Digest (www.ired.com/usa), as shown in the figure on page 357. Then check your state in the list of buyer's agents www.ired.com/dir/trueagnt.htm. As examples of what's possible, consider the following sites, which serve local communities. These options include buyers services for a fee and seller services for a fee.

356

SHOP ONLINE The Lazy Way

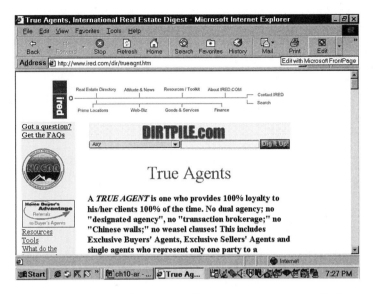

To begin your real estate search, start at www.ired.com.dir/ trueagnt.htm, the International Real Estate Digest's Web site.

Buyer's Services for a Fee

- The Real Estate Cafe (www.realestatecafe.com): This site offers a "menu of services" for real estate consumers, including products, services, and courses related to buying, selling, renting, relocating, and finding roommates. Located in Cambridge, Mass., it's a good example of using the Internet to help consumers save money, online or in person.

- Soma Living (www.somaliving.com): Teaming with many vendors, this site provides a wide variety of services related to home buying, including moving, home maintenance, home systems (like plumbing and electric wiring), design (like architecture, furniture, and interior decorating), and renovation. It serves San Francisco.

Seller Services for a Fee

- List for Less (www.listforless.com): This site provides information and services to help folks sell their homes themselves, including links to over 500 Web sites offering discount or fee-based property listing services. The discounted fee includes placement in the Multiple Listing Service in Massachusetts.

Getting Time On Your Side

	The Old Way	The Lazy Way
Identifying likely properties	1 day (on-site at a realtor's office)	2 hours
Doing basic research on the city, neighborhood, etc.	1 day	2 hours
Locating a realtor or buyer's agent in the area	Probably depend on referral from new employer	1 hour
Getting preapproved online for a mortgage	1 hour filling out forms and answering questions at a bank; waiting days or weeks for a decision	30 minutes filling out forms, then waiting less than 24 hours for a decision
Finding and engaging other real estate professionals (e.g., home inspectors)	Probably won't do it because of lack of information and time	2 hours
Narrowing the list of likely properties to half a dozen to visit	Can't do it because of lack of info. Instead you'll set up a couple dozen time-consuming home tours	2 hours

More Lazy Stuff

How to Get Someone Else to Do It

Remember that the Internet is a community of people who help and share with one another. The old pioneer culture of the newsgroups and e-mail distribution lists is perpetuated in the auction sites like eBay and in chat rooms and forums all over the Web. eBay expresses these principles very well in its Community Guidelines: "eBay is a community where we encourage open and honest communication between all of our members. Our Community Guidelines are based upon five basic values:

- "We believe people are basically good.
- "We believe everyone has something to contribute.
- "We believe that an honest, open environment can bring out the best in people.
- "We recognize and respect everyone as a unique individual.
- "We encourage you to treat others the way that you want to be treated."

Basically, if you pitch in and help others, you should have no problem finding help when you need it.

If you are trying to remember a site mentioned here and can't find it in the index, don't despair; let me help you. Just go to the shopping directory that I put together at my Web site (www.samizdat.com/shopping.html). There you'll find a list of every store and resource mentioned in this book, organized in the same order in which the book is organized, all with hyperlinks, so you don't even need to type in the addresses—I did it for you.

If you don't have time to keep up with all the new and interesting shopping sites coming online, I'll be doing my best to keep that directory page up-to-date. So keep coming back and checking. Also, if you find sites you believe should be included in this directory, please send me e-mail to tell me about those sites (seltzer@samizdat.com). If they are on target, I'll add them very quickly. That's how you can help me, as well as everyone else. Also, I plan to use my constantly updated online directory at my Web site as the starting point for future editions of this book.

For advice on how to create and maintain your own little Web site, check my book, *The Social Web*, which is available for free on the Web at www.samizdat.com/#social. You could use the techniques discussed there to build your own shopping directory page or to create Web pages where you share advice with those who have interests similar to yours, or where you list the rare things you are looking for and would like to buy so people who are trying to sell such things can find you.

If you'd like to learn more about how to get the most out of search engines, and AltaVista in particular, check my online tutorial starting at www.samizdat.com/script/title.htm. Also check the related articles at my Web site at www.samizdat.com/#altavista.

If you would like some hands-on experience in using chat, or if you would like to talk with me directly online about matters relating to business on the Web, please feel free to join my weekly chat sessions. If I don't have an answer to your question, perhaps one of the other participants will.

Transcripts of previous sessions are available at www.samizdat.com/#chat. You'll also see at that site notices about future topics of discussion and any changes in the schedule. The sessions usually take place on Thursdays from noon to 1 p.m. EST at www.web-net.org. To join the session, just click on Richard Seltzer's Chat, then fill out the ID form. You don't need any special software—just your browser.

If you are interested in trends in online shopping, Internet business in general, and what's happening with electronic books, check my free newsletter, *Internet-on-a-Disk*, at www.samizdat.com/#ioad. And if you have thoughts on similar matters, send me e-mail, for possible inclusion in the Letters to the Editor.

In any case, feel free to send me e-mail. If time allows, I'll do what I can to help you (seltzer@samizdat.com).

If You Really Want More, Read These

For basics on how to find your way around the Internet, check *Surf the Net the Lazy Way* by Shelley O'Hara, published by Macmillan.

For a quick introduction to Internet business (so you can see what's happening from the storekeeper's perspective), try *Essential Business Tactics for the Net* by Larry Chase, published by Wiley.

If you are curious about the tradition of community on the Internet, read *The Virtual Community* by Howard Rheingold, published by HarperCollins.

For guidance on how to get the most out of the AltaVista search engine, check my book, *The AltaVista Search Revolution*, published by Osborne/McGraw-Hill, or check the free resources at my Web site (www.samizdat.com/#altavista).

If you want advice on how to set up your own Web site for free and how to get people to find you, check my book, *The Social Web*, which you can get from my Web site or from Amazon.com.

If you are tempted to open your own low-cost online store, be sure to read the excellent article, "The 10 Secrets of Selling Online," by Paul Graham at store.yahoo.com/vw/secrets.html.

For an excellent tutorial on collectibles and what to consider when buying them online, check the articles by Lee Bernstein at the eBay site, starting at http://pages.ebay.com/aw/catindex-collectibles-hist.html.

If you are interested in online investing, be sure to read The Gomez Advisors Investor's On-Ramp, a series of files beginning at www.quote.com/gomez/content/step1.htm that cover opening an account, researching a stock, entering your order, and reviewing your account.

If you want to buy a house and/or sell your present one, read the article by Pat Rioux, "What's New in Discount Listing Services for FOR SALE BY OWNERS" (www.ired.com/buymyself/rioux/fsbo) and check related articles at the state-by-state directory of resources (www.ired.com/dir/fsbo.htm).

If you are curious about the crazy and rapidly changing world of high-tech business—why computers and related products keep getting less and less expensive, and why the companies that make them come and go so fast—then you'd probably enjoy *Crossing the Chasm* and *Inside the Tornado* by Geoffrey Moore, published by HarperBusiness.

If You Don't Know What It Means, Look Here

Agent, robot, bot, crawler   Programs which mimic the actions of human users, automatically fetching information over the Web and sometimes performing other Web-related functions.

Browser   The software running on your computer that enables you to navigate around the Web by pointing and clicking.

Chat   "Real-time" dialogue that occurs on the Internet between several people who are online simultaneously in the same chat area. In that chat area, you will be able to see what other participants type and they see what you type, live, as it's happening in real-time.

Directories   Categorized lists of Web sites, based on information collected by hand—either by people hired to look at sites for possible inclusion, or by accepting submissions of brief descriptions from Web site owners.

E-mail distribution lists   Online, e-mail-based discussions. You "subscribe" to receive and send e-mail messages in a given subject area. These e-mail distribution lists are sent by and to other online participants who also subscribe.

Forums Online bulletin boards, where you can post messages and others can later post responses, and responses to those responses. Over the course of days, weeks, months, and years, threads of discussion grow.

Internet Millions of computers around the world connected so they become tools for communication and shopping, instead of just "computing machines."

Link or hyperlink Word(s) in the text of a Web page that have a Web address (URL) associated with them, so that clicking on the word(s) is the equivalent of typing in that address and takes you right to the new page.

Newsgroups Also known as "Usenet newsgroups," these groups allow you to post and read messages in a given subject area without having to "subscribe."

Search engines Web sites that allow you to search in a few seconds through the full contents of millions of Web pages. Search engines collect their information about the Internet by sending out robot programs to find all the pages that they can and add the full content of those pages (not just brief descriptions of entire sites) to their indices.

URL Universal Resource Locator, a Web address, which typically begins with www (for World Wide Web) followed by the domain name (usually the name of the company) followed by .com (if the site is a commercial enterprise in the United States).

Web Short for World Wide Web, the software that makes it possible for you to go from one document on the Internet to another, without having to learn a complex address or having to log in at each separate site.

Web page A "page" on the Web is a separate document, no matter how small or large. It could be just a picture or a paragraph or two, or it could be an entire book.

Do you need to know the meaning of an Internet-related word and you don't see it here? Then look it up at www.whatis.com.

D

It's Time for Your Reward

Once you've done this

Bought your first dozen items online.

Visited your first dozen online stores.

Participated in an online discussion group (newsgroup, chat, e-mail distribution, etc.).

Bought a dozen books online.

...reward yourself with this

For a change of pace, turn off the computer and drive to the mall.

Go to online coupon sites, like www.supercoups.com, www.coolsavings.com, www.coupondirectory.com, and www.supermarkets.com. Print out the ones you want, drive to a nearby store, and use them there.

Use the money you've saved from shopping online to throw a real world party for the friends you've met online.

Take a break and read a book, instead of buying another one. Or, better still, go chat with an author at Barnes and Noble (www.barnesandnoble.com) in their "Authors Online" area.

Once you've done this

Checked half a dozen house-finding sites and used half a dozen mortgage calculators, trying to find a house you'd like and a way to pay for it.

Used online budget tools to try to curb your expenses, and used online investment companies to try to make the most of your meager savings.

Shopped for insurance or retirement plans online.

Checked half a dozen car sites and not yet found one that you can both love and afford (so you have the tastes of a princess and the bank account of a secretary).

...reward yourself with this

Let loose your imagination and dream for a while. Check out the homes you could never afford at The duPont Registry of Luxury Homes (www.dupontregistry.com), and Who's Who in Luxury Real Estate (www.luxuryrealestate.com).

Go to the Personal Finance section at The Mining Company (pfinance.miningco.com), click on "Windfall Wealth," and read about the headaches winners face. You'll feel better about your current uncomplicated life style, and you'll also be better prepared when you hit it big.

Go to the Mining Company's Personal Finance section (pfinance.miningo.com) and click on Financial Funny Bones. At this location, you'll find links to five sites packed with money-related jokes.

Save up for a trip to Europe and rent that dream car during your vacation. Check 1001 European Rentals (www.1001rentals.com) to see exotic autos that are available for short-term lease.

Once you've done this	...reward yourself with this
Taken half a dozen test drives, but still can't make up your mind on a new car.	Find a car rental place that offers cars of the kind you are interested in. Rent one for a getaway weekend, and let the entire family go for a trial ride.
Placed your first online grocery order.	Hop in the car and head to the supermarket. Bring a lounge chair and relax on the grass near the parking lot. It's time to gloat while everyone around you is scrambling to do their "real world" shopping.
Taken your first two online-purchased trips.	Go to 1travel.com (www.1travel.com/postcard/card.htm) and enjoy a few cartoons about the hassles of travel; maybe e-mail them to your friends.
Booked a dream vacation online.	Go to Travel Preview (www.travelpreview.com) and send digital postcards for free. The recipient gets e-mail telling him or her to check a specific URL where the photo you chose, together with your personal message, are located. To be wickedly lazy, send the postcards before you leave on your trip—take care of your social obligations quickly and easily, and then you can forget everyone but yourself while you're gone.

Where to Find What You're Looking For

New York Stock Exchange, 278–79
New York Times, 277
Nissan, 297
Northern Light, 55, 56–57
Northwest Airlines, 214
Norton AntiVirus, 175
NVST.com's Private Equity Network, 281

OfficeMax, 156
Office supplies, 156
Online Investor, 277
Online trading. *See* Investing; Trading, online
On Now, 85
Onsale.com, 76, 182
Opt-in e-mail, 43–44
O'Reilly Associates, 147–48
Organic foods, 225
Osborne Books, 146
OurBroker's Consumer Real Estate Center, 342
Owners.com, 348

Pace Buyer's Guides, 309
Pacific Exchange, 279
Paine Webber, 284
PalmPilot, 170–71
Palm-sized computers, 170–71
Pastas, 227–28
PC Computing, 144
PC Connection, 160–61
PC Magazine, 143, 175
PC Week, 144
PC World, 144–45
Peapod, 235–36
Pennsylvania Travel, 211
Pentium III chip, 39–40
PersonaLogic, 291–95
Philadelphia Stock Exchange, 279
Pictures, saving, 14
PointCast, 278
Politics and Prose Bookstore, 108
Porsche, 297
Portals, 20–28, 48, 50–53
Postcards, digital, 220
Powells, 104
Preview Travel, 189, 194–96

Priceline, 212–13, 267, 331
Pricescan, 113, 152–53
Price Watch, 153
Printing, 7, 15
Privacy concerns, 37–45
Property2000, 332
Prudential, 352
Public Eye, 34–35

Quality comparisons, 65–66
Quantum Books, 108
Que, 147
Quick & Reilly, 283
Quicken.com, 255–57, 266, 274, 276
Quicken InsureMarket, 272
QuickenMortgage, 266
QuickQuote, 272
Quote.com, 280

Rail Services, 198, 200
Real estate, 323–58
   classifieds, 331–34
   mortgages, 265–66, 272, 331
   rentals, 337–40
   roommate services, 334–36
   vacation homes, 340, 348
Real Estate Cafe, 336, 357
RealNetworks, 128–30
Realty Referral Network, 352
Realty Trek, 339
Rebate Company, 50
Recipes, 228, 249–50
Reel, 132
Registration forms, online, 32, 40–41
RE/MAX International, 352
Rent.net Online Rental Guide, 338
Retirement planning, 272–74
Rewards programs, travel, 40, 45, 187–88, 200–1, 215–16
Robots, 62–64, 66–69, 71
Rolls Royce, 300
Roommate Access, 336
Roommate Assistant, The, 335
Roommate BBS 1.2, 334
Roommate Connection, 336
Roommate Express, 336
Roommate Finders, 336
RoommateLocator.com, 335

Roommate services, 334–36
Rough Guides, 200

Saab, 297
SABRE, 191
Salomon Smith Barney, 284
Saturn, 297, 298–99
Schoenhof's, 106, 108
Screenwriter's Utopia, 133
Scripts, 133–34
Scripts Now, 133
Seafood, 225
Search engines, 23–24, 48–50
   syntax, 48, 59
Search Engine Watch, 62
Searches
   comparison, 62–64
   using bots, 62–64, 66–69, 71
Second Spin, 128
SecureTax.com, 271
Securities and Exchange Commission (SEC), 276, 280–81
Security concerns, 31–36
Security First Network Bank, 263
SendWine, 231
Senior Vacation and Home Exchange, 216
Shareware, 173–74, 176–77
Shipment methods, 30–31
Shipping charges, 30, 112–13
ShopLink, 238
ShopperConnection.com, 28
Shopping 2000, 28
Shopping bots, 62–64, 66–69, 71
Shopping carts, 29–30
Shopping.com, 28, 104
Shore to Door Seafood, 225
Sidewalk City Guides, 66, 190–91
SiebertNet, 283
Ski Travel Online, 216
Sky Publishing, 108
Smart Money, 277
Snap, 28
Snowbound Herbals, 229, 231
Social Security Online, 274
Softcrawler, 176

Now you can do these tasks, too!

The Lazy Way

Starting to think there are a few more of life's little tasks that you've been putting off? Don't worry—we've got you covered. Take a look at all of *The Lazy Way* books available. Just imagine—you can do almost anything *The Lazy Way!*

Handle Your Money The Lazy Way
By Sarah Young Fisher and Carol Turkington
0-02-862632-X

Build Your Financial Future The Lazy Way
By Terry Meany
0-02-862648-6

Cut Your Spending The Lazy Way
By Leslie Haggin
0-02-863002-5

Have Fun with Your Kids The Lazy Way
By Marilee Lebon
0-02-863166-8

Keep Your Kids Busy The Lazy Way
By Barbara Nielsen and Patrick Wallace
0-02-863013-0

Feed Your Kids Right The Lazy Way
By Virginia Van Vynckt
0-02-863001-7

*All Lazy Way books are just $12.95!

additional titles on the back!

Learn French The Lazy Way
By Christophe Desmaison
0-02-863011-4

Learn German The Lazy Way
By Amy Kardel
0-02-863165-X

Learn Italian The Lazy Way
By Gabrielle Euvino
0-02-863014-9

Learn Spanish The Lazy Way
By Steven R. Hawson
0-02-862650-8

Shed Some Pounds The Lazy Way
By Annette Cain and Becky Cortopassi-Carlson
0-02-862999-X

Get in Shape The Lazy Way
By Annette Cain
0-02-863010-6

Clean Your House The Lazy Way
By Barbara H. Durham
0-02-862649-4

Care for Your Home The Lazy Way
By Terry Meany
0-02-862646-X

Redecorate Your Home The Lazy Way
By Rebecca Jerdee
0-02-863163-3

Stop Aging The Lazy Way
By Judy Myers, Ph.D.
0-02-862793-8

Learn to Sew The Lazy Way
By Lydia Wills
0-02-863167-6

Train Your Dog The Lazy Way
By Andrea Arden
0-87605180-8

Organize Your Stuff The Lazy Way
By Toni Ahlgren
0-02-863000-9

Manage Your Time The Lazy Way
By Toni Ahlgren
0-02-863169-2

Take Care of Your Car The Lazy Way
By Michael Kennedy and Carol Turkington
0-02-862647-8

Get a Better Job The Lazy Way
By Susan Ireland
0-02-863399-7

Cook Your Meals The Lazy Way
By Sharon Bowers
0-02-862644-3

Cooking Vegetarian The Lazy Way
By Barbara Grunes
0-02-863158-7

Master the Grill The Lazy Way
By Pamela Rice Hahn and Keith Giddeon
0-02-863157-9